Social Justice Perspectives on English Language Learners

ISSUES IN BLACK EDUCATION

Series Editor, Abul Pitre, San Francisco State University

In this series a wide range of scholars, educators, and activists are called upon to speak to the issues of educating Black students. The series is designed to not only highlight issues that that may negatively impact the education of Black students but also to provide possibilities for improving the quality of education for Black students.

Books in the Series

Ashraf Esmail, Abul Pitre, Alice Duhon-Ross, Judith Blakely, and Brandon Hamann (2023). *Social Justice Perspectives on English Language Learners*. Hamilton Books.

Social Justice Perspectives on English Language Learners

Edited by

Ashraf Esmail
Abul Pitre
Alice Duhon-Ross
Judith Blakely
Brandon Hamann

HAMILTON BOOKS
AN IMPRINT OF
ROWMAN & LITTLEFIELD
Lanham • Boulder • New York • London

Published by Hamilton Books
An imprint of The Rowman & Littlefield Publishing Group, Inc.
4501 Forbes Boulevard, Suite 200, Lanham, Maryland 20706
www.rowman.com

86-90 Paul Street, London EC2A 4NE, United Kingdom

British Library Cataloguing in Publication Information Available

Library of Congress Cataloging-in-Publication Data

Names: Esmail, Ashraf, editor. | Pitre, Abul, editor. | Duhon-Ross, Alice, editor. | Blakely, Judith, editor. | Hamann, Brandon, editor.
Title: Social justice perspectives on English language learners / edited by Ashraf Esmail, Abul Pitre, Alice Duhon-Ross, Judith Blakely, Brandon Hamann.
Description: Lanham : Hamilton Books, [2023] | Series: Issues in black education | Includes bibliographical references and index. | Summary: "This book is written from a practitioner's perspective and is designed for practitioners. Social change is guiding theme throughout each of the chapters. The book focused on elements such as cultural relevance, multiculturalism, learner centered, authentic assessment, and diversity. Each chapter will be based on theory with a focus on practice"—Provided by publisher.
Identifiers: LCCN 2023003388 (print) | LCCN 2023003389 (ebook) | ISBN 9780761873082 (cloth) | ISBN 9780761873099 (epub)
Subjects: LCSH: English language—Study and teaching—Foreign speakers. | English language—Study and teaching—Social aspects. | Social justice and education. | LCGFT: Essays.
Classification: LCC PE1128.A2 S5936 2023 (print) | LCC PE1128.A2 (ebook) | DDC 428.0071—dc23/eng/20230320
LC record available at https://lccn.loc.gov/2023003388
LC ebook record available at https://lccn.loc.gov/2023003389

To all educators in the United States and around the world who devote their time and energy in working with our diverse student population

Contents

List of Figures

List of Tables

Foreword

Jancarlos Wagner-Romero

This book is evidence of scholars coming together for a common purpose to drive equity forward through scholarship and lived experiences. For far too often, issues affecting English Language Learners have been left to the wayside—or have been tabled—so much so that they go unspoken about or unresolved in the education spectrum. From a lack of language access to a lack of promoting multilingualism in schools and higher education spaces, English Language Learners continue to be a population of students that policymakers and education leaders consider the least when engaging in critical dialogue and decision-making processes. I can attest to this and speak from very personal experiences as a former English Language Learner, myself, and as a current education policymaker, serving as an elected school board member and vice president of the New Orleans Public School Board.

Social Justice Perspectives on English Language Learners brings together scholars from across the country who have dedicated their careers, and even their lives, to lifting up the voices of those who might be unable to speak for themselves or who simply need someone to share their stories. This book comes at a pivotal time in American history when, amid a global pandemic, how we *do* education has been at the forefront of national discussions. Some might argue that COVID-19 has needed intentional reflection on how educators move forward with best practices, how they better engage families and communities, and how the social institution that we know to be "education" can be one that is more innovative, inclusive, and a catalyst for driving large-scaled equity in our communities.

Social Justice Perspectives on English Language Learners is a catalyst for driving equity. The authors that have engaged in this book immerse readers into the lived experiences of limited English proficient students and communities, require that readers reflect on and understand the positionality they bring to social spaces, and encourage us to take lessons learned by some of our most marginalized populations and use them as driving forces for shifting how we *do* education for English Language Learners.

The editors of *Social Justice Perspectives on English Language Learners* intentionally brought together champions to share the stories of what is working in some communities, what might need some improvement in others, and how we, as a society, can do better to promote social justice for our English Language Learners, their families, and even those teachers who are continuing to work on the front lines to carry our students through what can often times be an intimidating education system. Each chapter of this book can be a transformational piece to a larger puzzle for those of us engaging in work that is intended to improve the quality of life of those we serve—whether in a classroom or larger community.

Dr. Jancarlos Wagner-Romero is an assistant professor of global and multicultural education at the University of Wisconsin–La Crosse.

Preface

Judi Blakely and Alice Duhon-Ross

The recent increase in immigration patterns in the United States has meant an increase in the number of children whose first language is not English entering American schools. Some reports show that as many as one in four students come from families where the language spoken in the home is not English. Therefore, it is imperative that all teachers have access to credible information that will aid them understand the English language learner, develop effective strategies to teach English language learners, create effective learning environments and use assessments to meet the needs of English language learners as well as garner community resources to support for English language learners. Adopting social justice as a lens through which to centralize the needs of Emergent Bilingual Learners is an avenue through which to narrow the achievement gap supported by current policy and practice. Social justice refers to the reconstruction of a given space to ensure equity, recognition, and inclusion (Bell, 2016).

Social Justice Perspectives on English Language Learners shares a practitioner's perspective and is designed for teachers and practitioners. Social change will be a guiding theme throughout each of the chapters. Using a scholarly voice with a focus on elements such as cultural relevance, multiculturalism, learner centered, authentic assessment, and diversity, each chapter will be based on theory with a focus on practice. The focal points of this edition are:

- Multilingual English Language Learners: A social change perspective
- Equitably assessing emergent bilinguals
- Translanguaging as a tool for social justice
- Towards a globalized and translingual perspective on emerging bilinguals
- Rethinking assessment of English learners: The role of connection

ORGANIZATION OF THE BOOK

Chapter 1 supplies an attempt to address some of the deficiencies that exist in the way mediation is currently being addressed. Chapter 2 covers how educational equity for young people includes their role in assessments and performance, especially with regards to standardized assessments. Chapter 3 addresses how the purpose of focusing on STEM subjects is because success in these subjects can translate to success in other subject areas. The focus of Chapter 4 is about how to engage in culturally sustaining pedagogy seeks to affirm the cultural and linguistic gifts of each student in a classroom. Chapter 5 aims to illuminate the voices of African English learners as this population still is understudied, and invisible in terms of literature (Allen et al., 2012). Chapter 6 shares a definition of social justice in education, describe our context and our efforts to promote culturally responsive pedagogy, recount Indigenous language suppression and loss, share how American Indians qualify as ELLs, and discuss the barriers to be identifying and supporting these students. Chapter 7 exams the process as well as key examples of asset-driven instruction, coordinators, administrators, professional learning communities (PLCs), and teacher education professionals can engage in transformative collaborative practice to build on student assets and improve outcomes for emergent bilingual learners. Chapter 8 combine core practice scholarship with a language-centered lens on culturally sustaining pedagogy scholarship to create a set of four core instructional practices tailored to address the learning needs of MLL students in general education classes. Chapter 9 attempts to reignite a vision for bilingual education perspective for African American students via Antiracist Black Language Pedagogy. This scholarship offers critical discourse interrogating US language education through a lens of Anti-Black Linguistic Racism and provides implications for practice for educators who serve African American students. Chapter 10 explores translanguaging, a strategic approach for instruction that supplies space for students to draw from all their resources in both English and their other language(s) to best learn and demonstrate their knowledge and skills without being limited to the English language alone. Chapter 11 aims to supply more holistic strategies for serving ELLs by illustrating how one school's bilingual program works from a social justice standpoint to foster the personal and academic growth of its students. Chapter 12 examines that there are indeed universal principles and practices that all teachers of emerging bilinguals should know, and at the same time, all teachers need to be prepared to contextualize those global ideas with explicit attention to local spaces and identities. Chapter 13 covers the importance of the use of terms for students that clearly and fairly show the characteristic(s) important to our investigations or policy recommendations.

Chapter 14 provides insights into the ways that translanguaging—the notion and practice that center on emergent bilinguals' (EBs') language practices as fluid, heteroglossic, and holistic—can serve as a tool for social justice by prioritizing students' whole linguistic repertoires when engaging with curricular materials in the classroom. Chapter 15 outlines how a Spanish teacher supported her English Language Learners in a charter school operationalizing neoliberal market approaches within its academics and school policies. It will set the stage by describing the school before detailing the neoliberal policies pushed forth by the school administrators and then implemented by novice teachers. Chapter 16 documents the work of one institution, a public, 4-year, research university (from here on referred to as High Plains University), and its community college, Hispanic Serving Institution (HSI) partners over the past 20 years as they engaged in equity-oriented, cross-institutional collaborations in their predominantly rural state. Chapter 17 examines how when Latinx students instructed by a Latinx teacher show higher academic achievement. Chapter 18 examines a study focusing on teacher attitudes and beliefs are a major influence on the learning of students. Chapter 19 focuses on two studies: (1) a two-semester long fieldwork with ENLACE students enrolled in in-person classes pre–COVID-19 pandemic, and (2) the other study involves five students (three high school and two middle school students) enrolled in online learning during the pandemic. Chapter 20 supplies an overview of English language instructional pedagogies in the nation, exploring the underlying goals of each, and critically examining the equity issues that exist in one specific additive model of ELL education—dual language education. Chapter 21 shows how using cultural and political vignettes (CPVs) in the professional development of teachers of ELLs to explore social justice perspectives can have positive impacts on teachers, as well as on their students.

Dr. Judi Blakely, Walden University
Dr. Alice Duhon-Ross, Walden University

Acknowledgments

The editors would like to thank all the contributors to this volume for their interest and arduous work on this important topic: English Language Learners.

Chapter 1

Linguistic Mediation Strategies for Promoting Equity and Social Change in the Bilingual Education Classroom

Miguel Fernández Álvarez and
Amanda L. G. Montes

Linguistic mediation was conceived by Trovato (2016) as a didactic tool intended to promote and strengthen the acquisition of certain skills. These skills make up the so-called intercultural approach, which recently occupies the first places in the methodologies and didactic approaches of foreign and second language teaching due to the promotion of multilingual and multicultural contexts, with the aim of integrating all languages and cultures under equal conditions. The language activities proposed by the *Common European Framework of Reference* (CEFR) (Council of Europe, 2001) are action-oriented, which means that they must be conducted both in formal contexts, such as the classroom, and in social settings not related to the educational field. To put these activities into practice, it is necessary that the interlocutors have certain skills and use strategies to activate the linguistic and communicative processes.

In an increasingly global, multicultural, and multilingual world, mediation is a fundamental part of daily life. In the context of language learning, mediation develops a combination of receptive, productive, and interactive skills, as well as secondary skills that include the ability to agree and acknowledge cultural differences, which are essential life skills. Linguistic mediation strategies and activities are essential aspects that need to be fostered to promote equity and social change in the classroom. They can serve various functions in the classroom setting, and they can have a beneficial effect not only on the building of relationships between students, but also on facilitating the learning process. Thus, taking into consideration the implementation of linguistic mediation into the bilingual education classroom, the lack of teacher training and the need of research in this area, this book chapter is an attempt to address some of the deficiencies that exist in the way mediation is currently being addressed.

EQUITY AND SOCIAL CHANGE IN BILINGUAL PROGRAMS

While emergent bilingual students are as adept to succeed as their peers, many of them face unique challenges, including distinct social emotional needs. Furthermore, emergent bilingual students are often navigating new cultural landscapes and social norms with inappropriate or little to no support. Educators can play a vital role in facilitating the formation of new social support networks for these students; those committed to social change are constantly reevaluating their practice to meet the needs of students. Those needs are not static; thus, educators must constantly commit themselves to the endeavour of introspection, of always learning about the very real details that encompass who their students are at any given time, and of the goal of embracing what works for each of those individual learners. It is a constant exercise in practicing empathy and humility, with the willingness to learn new things that will add or transform existing knowledge and assumptions.

Inspired by extensive research on culturally responsive/relevant teaching, Paris (2012) has offered an invigorated perspective on these approaches, proposing the term culturally *sustaining* pedagogy, which points to what he calls the "best research and practice in the resource pedagogy tradition and as a term that supports the value of our multiethnic and multilingual present and future. Culturally sustaining pedagogy seeks to perpetuate and foster—to sustain—linguistic, literate, and cultural pluralism as part of the democratic project of schooling" (p. 93). Within this framework, educators who commit to using linguistic mediation for fostering these truly democratic spaces, will find that in implementing it effectively, it can be a powerful tool for promoting equity and social change. Moreover, Kohler (2015) points to the need for teachers who possess intercultural communicative competence, which calls for teachers who involve themselves in the cultures of their students, not just from the outside, but by immersing themselves in their ways of living, to better understand their experiences as well as allowing themselves to also undergo the liberatory process of transformation.

According to Montes et al. (2018), teachers must come with an awareness of their impact on students' sense of worth, as their attitudes can be easily detected, particularly when teachers come from ethnic and linguistic backgrounds different than those of their students. Moreover, Montes et al. (2018) point to the deficit perspectives that teachers may hold of their students as a key factor in culturally and linguistically diverse students' potential disengagement in the classroom and with teachers alike. This points to the vital need for teachers' commitment to the development of their own intercultural communicative competence, which is further elaborated by Dasli (2011) through the notions that support effective classroom uses of linguistic mediation, which include cultural awareness, cross-cultural mediation, and critical intercultural language pedagogy.

As part of the process of working towards these notions for creating culturally responsive spaces, educators and students must practice cultural humility, engage in critical self-reflection, work together towards a common goal that has been found through open dialogue, and be able to detect the starting point of all involved. In recognizing the wide range of diversity within bilingual education settings, it is imperative that educators not emulate the oppressive practices students may be bombarded with in all other facets of their lives. Resolute educators create spaces where students feel safe to learn and grow, and where dialogue is critical to this growth. In actively working towards the goal of cultivating spaces that are culturally sustaining, teachers must commit themselves to the pursuit of social justice, which can be achieved through intercultural communicative competence applied through mediation tasks (discussed in the section on linguistic mediation as a cultural and linguistic bridge).

THE INTERCONNECTION BETWEEN SOCIAL INTERACTION, ACADEMIC PERFORMANCE, AND LANGUAGE PROFICIENCY IN THE MULTICULTURAL CLASSROOM

The necessity for creating classroom environments that make room for what Kramsch (1993) called a "third place," speaks to the need for spaces that allow for students that exist *within* cultures; that of their heritage or home culture and of the culture associated with the language(s) they are learning. One of the most widely recognized theories of learning, sociocultural yheory, coined by Lev Vygotsky,[1] acknowledges the differences in individuals within and across cultures. With this dynamic relationship, learners are thought to be shaped by the society in which they live, thus shaping learners' "intrapsychological" development. Within the Vygotskian view of cognitive development, it is the socially constructed activities in which learners take part, with the guidance of a more experienced learner, which are in turn internalized, leading to newly acquired knowledge and gains in language acquisition. Intercultural language learning speaks to the interrelatedness of culture and learning and centers this relationship at the core of the learning process (Liddicoat et al., 2003). Consistent with theoretical perspectives grounded in sociocultural theory (Vygotsky, 1997), usage-based language learning (Cadierno & Eskildsen, 2015), and conversational analysis (Sacks, 1992), Lee and Jeong (2020) expound on these underpinnings in saying that social learning is crucial for children learning a new language. They propose that as part of a dynamic developmental process, L2 acquisition—a second language that is not native but is studied to be used later—can be facilitated through interaction in cultural and social contexts that assist learners towards individual gains in language development.

It cannot be said enough that the application of classroom practice that is grounded in these well-supported theoretical foundations is best implemented through a culturally sustaining lens, in that teachers must be strategic and thoughtful about the uses of social interaction within classroom settings. They must also consider the ways in which they promote social interaction among their students outside of the classroom. This social interaction can be helped through training teachers to effectively implement the tools proposed in section 3.

LINGUISTIC MEDIATION AS A CULTURAL AND LINGUISTIC BRIDGE

According to Blini (2009, pp. 45–60), linguistic mediation can be described as an activity that is necessary when two individuals or two language communities come into contact bearing specific and peculiar cultural and idiosyncratic traits. As a result of such contact, misunderstandings, misconceptions and, eventually, conflicts may arise that threaten to hinder communication and prevent agreement or understanding. These conflict situations find their basis not only in linguistic but also in cultural differences. This is where the work of mediation comes in, which is conceived as "a process that attempts to resolve a conflict situation by opening channels of communication that were blocked" (Pérez Vázquez, 2010, p. 48).

Although the concept of linguistic mediation was already included in the *Common European Framework of Reference* in 2001, it focused mainly on aspects related to interpreting and translating, which is reflected in these words (Council of Europe, 2001, p. 14):

In both the receptive and productive modes, the written and/or oral activities of mediation make communication possible between persons who are unable, for whatever reason, to communicate with each other directly. Translation or interpretation, a para- phrase, summary, or record, provides for a third-party a (re)formulation of a source text to which this third party does not have direct access. Mediating language activities—(re)processing an existing text—occupy an important place in the normal linguistic functioning of our societies.

In contrast to the linguistic activities of reception, production, and interaction, mediation activities did not receive more attention because tables of descriptors for each level had not been developed. In the *Companion Volume*, the Council of Europe (2020) presents a broader vision of mediation that goes beyond the translation and interpretation of a text (Fernández Álvarez & García Hernández, 2021). It is a type of interaction that takes place when people are unable to communicate effectively, when speakers do not have a common language, or when speakers speak the same language but one of them has a much broader, technical, or specific knowledge about what is being talked about.

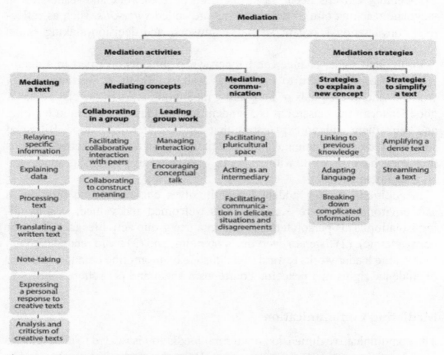

Fig. 1.1. Linguistic mediation activities and strategies, according to the *Companion Volume.* **Council of Europe, 2020, p. 90**

According to the *Companion Volume*, mediation activities are divided into three groups, as shown in Figure 1, which also holds several mediation strategies that are very useful in the teaching-learning process.

Mediating Concepts

According to the *CEFR Companion Volume* (Council of Europe, 2020), mediation tasks and strategies are particularly relevant for teaching in the context of small group and collaborative tasks. Tasks can be organized in such a way that learners must share different inputs, explain their information, and work together to achieve a goal. We propose that by exploring their principles and uses, and the relevant ways they can be effectively implemented in the bilingual classroom, educators will be equipped with a new tool to ease communication, language learning, and conflict resolution in any multilingual/multicultural setting.

Conceptual mediation focuses on both group work and leadership within a group. This approach to language teaching focuses on traits of transversality, which help to promote and merge other kinds of useful skills that 21st-century citizens need. Tasks focusing on teamwork and leadership in language teaching aim to develop what are called *soft skills*, such as reflective, conversational, organizational, teamwork, and decision-making skills, to mention some.

Equity and social change can happen when students take part in a democratic process and learn to function as leaders (Biddle & Berliner, 2002), which is one of the goals of integrating meditation tasks in the classroom. A good leader in the classroom is a student who guides classmates in learning and helps them with an explanation that can be better understood. Bilingual students face this challenge multiple times throughout the school day as they may have to work with students who have diverse backgrounds and language demands.

In addition, a good student leader involves classmates and provides a safe environment where everyone feels welcomed and valued, thus avoiding isolation. This person tends to (1) organize group activities (academic or nonacademic), (2) listen to everyone's opinions, and (3) try to reconcile them. Finally, the leader works toward social justice by promoting demands in favor of students' rights in a peaceful, courteous manner and per school rules.

Mediating Communication

The communicative dimension of cultural mediation is related to all linguistic aspects of intercultural communication. Thus, the mediation process serves to make oral interventions explicit and to avoid misunderstandings and overcome communication blockages. Within the communicative dimension, the figure of the mediator is like that of the negotiation interpreter: this person acts as a communication bridge between two or more interlocutors. In fact, the mediator's role is not only to translate messages and information faithfully, but also to clarify any implicit aspect of communication, especially in the field of intercultural pragmatics. However, the first element with which the mediator comes into contact is verbal communication, i.e., the reception, processing and later interlinguistic delivery of a message. Therefore, the relevance of the communicative dimension in any act of mediation cannot be underestimated, as words decide the full process of communication and interaction.

In multicultural contexts, there are some aspects that make the need for mediation different and more relevant than in others. First, there are students belonging to different sociocultural and ethnic groups sharing the same social space. There is usually a majority group whose values and cultural codes are the dominant ones, and several minority groups that are different. As a resource, intercultural mediation can be helpful in preventing and resolving certain conflicts that arise in multicultural contexts. It can help communication between culturally diverse people and groups, as it contributes to cultural understanding and better mutual knowledge of cultural codes. This limits the emergence of conflicts based on misunderstandings due to lack of knowledge of each other's values. In addition, mediation reduces the weight of stereotypes and prejudices, which are one of the main obstacles to cultural agreement, and promotes attitudes of openness, social commitment, and a positive attitude in dealing with conflicts.

CONCLUSION

As we have seen, while linguistic mediation has been claimed to have a positive effect in the classroom, little research has been done in this area. In her work, Stathopoulou (2015, pp. 214–215) states that "it is true that mediation can serve various functions in the classroom setting, and it can have a beneficial effect not only on the building of relationships between students, but also on facilitating the learning process. Research in this area of interest is nearly non-existent." A few studies have proved their benefits (Nikula, 2007) and explained why bilingual students outperform students in nonbilingual contexts (Baetens-Beardsmore, 2008). However, there are no studies focused on the mediation activities and strategies employed by teachers and students in a bilingual context and "how their use can foster multicultural understanding, social interaction, academic performance and language proficiency" (Fernández Álvarez & García Hernández, 2021, p. 4).

It is crucial that in knowing about the positive effects of social interaction in language learning settings, that there be more work conducted to specifically decide the effectiveness of mediation in classroom settings. This will allow for educators, both teacher educators and teachers alike, to use mediation tools with the confidence that they will help gains in students' language acquisition, promote inclusive and culturally sustaining classroom environments, and allow students the autonomy needed for them to feel empowered.

NOTE

1. For a more comprehensive overview of sociocultural theory see P. Miller (2011), *Theories of developmental psychology*, 5th ed. (Worth Publishers).

REFERENCES

Baetens-Beardsmore, H. (2008). Multilingualism, cognition, and creativity. *International CLIL Research Journal, 1*, 4–19.

Biddle, B. J., & Berliner, D. C. (2002). Small class size and its effects. *Educational Leadership, 59*(5), 12–23.

Blini, L. (2009). La Mediación lingüística en España e Italia: difusión de un concepto problemático. *ENTRECULTURAS, 1*, 45–60.

Cadierno, T., & Eskildsen, S. (2015). *Usage-based perspectives on second language learning.* De Gruyter Mouton. https://doi.org/10.1515/9783110378528

Council of Europe. (2020). *Common European framework of reference for languages: Learning, teaching, assessment. Companion volume with new descriptors.* Council of Europe.

Council of Europe. (2001). *Common European framework of reference for language learning, teaching and assessment.* Cambridge University Press.

Fernández Álvarez, M., & García Hernández, S. (2021). Teachers' perceptions of linguistic mediation in the curriculum for advanced English in Madrid secondary schools. *Language Teaching Research.* Online First.

Kohler, M. (2015). *Teachers as mediators in the foreign language classroom.* Multilingual Matters.

Kramsch, C. (1993). *Context and culture in language teaching.* Oxford University Press.

Liddicoat, A. J., Scarino, A., Papdemetre, L., & Khler, M. (2003). *Report on intercultural language learning.* Canberra. Department of Education, Science and Training.

Montes, A. L. G., Valenciano, C. K., & Fernandez, M. (2018). Training bilingual educators at a pbi. *Multicultural Learning and Teaching*, *13*(1), 637–644. http://dx.doi.org/10.1515/mlt-2017–0006

Nikula, T. (2007). The IRF pattern and space for interaction: Comparing CLIL and EFL classrooms. In C. Dalton-Puffer & U. Smit (Eds.), *Empirical perspectives on CLIL classroom discourse* (pp. 170–204). Peter Lang.

Paris, D. (2012). Culturally sustaining pedagogy: A needed change in stance, terminology, and practice. *Educational Researcher*, *41*(3), 93–97. https://doi.org/10.3102/0013189X12441244.

Pérez Vázquez, E. (2006). Mediación lingüística y cultural en el ámbito de los movimientos migratorios. In G. Bazzocchi & P. Capanaga (Eds.), *Mediación lingüística de lenguas afines: Español/italiano* (pp. 347–362). Gedit.

Sacks, H. (1992). *Lectures in conversation*. Basil Blackwell.

Stathopoulou, M. (2015). *Cross-language mediation in foreign language teaching and testing*. Multilingual Matters.

Trovato, G. (2016). *Mediación lingüística y enseñanza de español/LE*. Arco Libros.

Vygotsky, L. S. (1997). *The collected works of L. S. Vygotsky, Vol. 4: The history of the development of higher mental functions*. Plenum Press.

Chapter 2

Rethinking Assessment of English Learners and the Role of Connection

Kyongson Park

As the changing demographics of America once again shift, with the beneficial addition of many different immigrants, refugees, and first-generation Americans, the public education system needs to coherently address the needs and goals of culturally and linguistically diverse (CLD) students. A large part of addressing educational equity for these young people includes their role in assessments and performance, especially with regards to standardized assessments. Although some improvements have been made in the last two decades regarding so called "high stakes testing," there still exists a gap between how English learners (EL) typically perform compared with the achievement seen in their non-EL peers. Although some may mistakenly think that standardization of items and administration create equity among students, the reality is far from that fallacy (Gottlieb, 2016).

The actual situation for EL and non-EL students alike can be illustrated in the allegorical tale, "The Woodcrafter's City" by Rick Traw (2002). In this story, John the Woodcrafter learns woodworking through an individualized process where his teachers placed their faith in him, as they knew his personality and abilities, and with their gentle "nudges" (scaffolding), he became a master artisan. When the educational culture changes, however, the expert-priests standardize both the instruction and the assessment model—students must pound nails effectively before all else. Students who previously whittled wood could no longer create, merely whittle as a drill; numerical figures drove instruction, in place of authentic assessment; learners saw no

11

connection to the real world, as "they never made anything of use" (p. 201); and teachers left the field out of despair.

The fictional story would be entertaining if it weren't so accurate. When educators and administrators reflect on the needs of EL students, and the subsequent assessment of their knowledge, they must account for many different factors not necessarily considered in the mainstream, non-EL population. Gottlieb (2016) argues that an examination of CLD students is useful in revealing "how language, culture, and prior experiences help shape [their] identities" (p. 13). Teachers who have unconsciously adopted the dominant culture's schooling structure often think that good teaching is just good teaching for everyone, regardless of the situation; while Au (2016) points out that this is simply not the case. One must consider the cultural and linguistic repertoires that students bring with them and simultaneously connect those experiences to the learning process, while validating them as on par with the dominant culture that they will organically learn as well. Assessments that are designed without these personal histories and differences kept in mind may as well just be asking students to hammer nails in isolation, devoid from any meaningful building project. In culturally responsive pedagogy, teachers should provide ELs both competitive and cooperative worldviews and a deep connection between home and school. Based on this background, CLD students can feel comfortable just like at home during a part of school day and eventually gain capacity to read, write and communicate at school (Au, 2016; Ladson-Billings, 1994).

Even though certain basic mini lessons on phonics or spelling may appear to be done in isolation, everything a teacher instructs to their students should be connected to a meaningful activity and their cultural "funds of knowledge" (Moll, 1994). English Learners come to school already knowing much about the world and various subjects. The issue arises when they can't express all that they know due to limited English proficiency. This gap between what they know and what they can convey is problematic to say the least: students with even little gaps in vocabulary knowledge go on to have large problems in comprehension and further problems in school itself (Silverman et al., 2016). Therefore, students need to be explicitly taught all tiers of vocabulary, with special attention to the academic language found in tiers 2 and 3. For emergent bilinguals or newcomers ELs, tier 1 vocab should be focused, though. To do otherwise restricts them from showing what they know on assessments, whether they are standardized or simply not fashioned with them in mind.

Because English learners face these many challenges, assessments need to be constructed differently and be planned within a different pedagogy than in years past. To facilitate effective teaching and learning while preparing them for the rigors of future testing, assessments need to be authentic in design and purpose. According to Herrera et al. (2020), authentic assessments differ from traditional assessments in that they are developed from instruction, group work, and other class interactions that value the student's participation in the process; are both reliable and valid; have measured meaning for both teacher and learner; and are connected to real-world problems and the student's language community.

Correctly planned and implemented authentic assessments can "avoid a number of linguistic biases inherent in traditional tests" (Herrera et al., 2020, p. 23). Oftentimes, the nuances of English are overlooked by native speaking teachers and items on assessments may include idioms, regional practices, or academic vocabulary that are unfamiliar to EL students. By reforming the idea of what constitutes an assessment (and often without overemphasis on grades), an educator can finally determine what a CLD youth knows and how to then tailor instruction to that student's level of development. As aforementioned, the student already comes to school with many strengths, such as "language, prior experiences, interests, and funds of knowledge" (Herrera et al., 2020, p. 23), and these cannot be built upon if biases and unfamiliar codes keep them hidden from the light.

When planning for the authentic assessment of English learners, Gottlieb (2016) states that one should consider three things: why you are using them, what information you are looking to obtain, and how that information can inform teaching and learning. In keeping with the larger concept of tailoring instruction to each EL student's level of ability, an educator needs to know the student's background beyond simple demographics, know their interests, and have them perform in many different domains. Gottlieb argues that authentic assessments need not be apart from instruction, but rather embedded in it. In this way, these assessments are more likely to be formative, helping develop skills in the process. Yet, both formative and summative assessments play a role in facilitating learning.

Of the three classifications of assessments that Herrera et al. (2020) identify, two are directly related to what the classroom teacher can control. These are named assessments *for* learning and assessments *as* learning. The first are types of assessments, usually formative, that can be used at once to properly scaffold, adjust, and plan the next steps of instruction. The other type of assessment, assessment *as* learning, places more of a focus on how a student can self-assess and peer-assess to foster more knowledge. In fact, self-assessment and peer assessment are inextricably linked. Students learn to assume the role of teacher and to be objective through peer assessment and they then transfer that introspection to self-assessment, while being supported by classmate and teacher alike (Black et al., 2004).

Black and colleagues (2004) promote the idea of the "traffic light" assessment tool, in which students self-identify their level of understanding from good, or partial, to little comprehension. This can be done as preassessment to inform instruction (*for* learning) or during assessment (*as* learning). The process can also be used on summative assessments in a formative manner: students can peer-assess end-unit work, self-code their understanding, and discuss their misunderstandings with their partners, as a means of forming methods of metacognitive learning.

Another component of instruction and assessment that needs to be considered is the development of high ordered thinking (HOT) skills among the English learners in the classroom. In a rush to develop basic skills like grammar and spelling, teachers may often neglect to engage EL students in critical thinking skills, due to perceptions about their low English proficiency. To properly support their academic development alongside their language acquisition, these skills need to be attended to (WIDA, 2020).

High ordered thinking skills can be structured into a variety of ways, most of which are things being doing in non-EL settings all the time. In developing the proper pedagogy for teaching writing to low proficiency EL students, based on a structured HOT model, Singh et al. (2018) identified various components teachers used to guide them in teaching these skills. They include allowing students to expand on main ideas and topics using graphic organizers and thinking maps; having students compare perspectives among their peers; asking student to discuss and write about cause-and-effect relationships; questioning students with varying degrees of answer type, from short, closed answers to expansive open-ended ones; and practicing how to draw inferences from context. In effect, teaching all types of metacognitive strategies while facilitating collaborative group work—work focused on the social interaction of language—is something that all teachers of EL students should be doing to increase high ordered thinking skills. These skills are what are needed to be successful in both academia and in life; unfortunately, they are not always gauged on the high stakes tests that purport to be evaluating one's academic knowledge.

If English learners are expected to meet the same high standards as native English speakers, how come the standardized tests used to measure them are not created with them in mind? And what can be done to prepare students for these types of assessments?

To answer these questions, it is the opinion of this author that teaching to the test (especially a test whose exact content is not known) is a misuse of time. Additionally, teaching test-taking strategies, although not as wasteful, is not as meaningful as teaching the skills behind these strategies, which connect to the real world of the student. Teachers cannot disregard the research that says these connections are vital (Moll, 1994; Helman, 2016) merely because educators fear inferior performance on a mass-produced test.

Given the abundant research, one would hope that policymakers and society at large would recognize the need for a change in high stakes testing culture. Certainly, some things have changed since the days of No Child Left Behind and a mandate for 100% proficiency rate. As compared to NCLB, and ESEA Flexibility after it, there are some definite improvements in the current Every Student Succeeds Act (ESSA), mainly through the elimination of unnecessary components of the previous laws. The new reauthorization gets rid of Annual Yearly Progress mandates, the effectively unachievable 100% proficiency goal, and "super subgroups" (Wright, 2016). It is also possible to include EL students who have been reclassified as fluent to be included in testing data as emergent bilinguals for up to 3 years; García and DeNicolo (2016) urge all educational personnel to take advantage of this allowance.

However, some of the changes seem to be of a cosmetic nature, if seen with a skeptical eye. According to the overview of Michigan's Consolidated State Plan for ESSA, the purpose and role of accountability in this new reauthorization is to support districts, "rather than simply labeling and sanction[ing] them" (ESSA, 2017, p. 6). Still, schools still can fall into one of three "support" categories: comprehensive, targeted, and additional targeted. If a school does not make progress within four years, the state can take over the school, fire the principal, convert it to charter, or effect some other drastic intervention (Wright, 2016). As usual, one would suspect that schools with less resources and a student body with lower socio-economic status and more faces of color would face more challenges in properly intervening to avoid takeover. More English learners attend schools fitting this description than not.

ESSA legislation aside, EL students must still take standardized tests that dually test them in content and English proficiency, at the risk of barring them from answering about content they know but cannot access on the test. One might ask what the best way forward is, if it is not teaching to the test. The answer is complex; however, there are a few things certain to close the equity gap. Within the classroom, educators must ensure that they are maintaining high standards; allowing EL students to engage in meaningful speech; learning comprehension strategies, e.g., context clues; developing high order thinking skills; and acquiring all three tiers of vocabulary concurrently. These research-based practices will gain the students some support when it comes time to take an inequitable high stakes test, but it will likely not fully prepare them.

Yet, that cannot be the concern, at least not right now. As educators agitate for less arbitrary testing and more authentic testing within a universal design, they must first adjust that which is in the scope of their control: the classroom. Teachers must build relationships with students and build on those ties. Teachers must rethink what an assessment is and embrace its power to drive teaching and learning when it is the correct and appropriate assessment

(Broad, 2001). They must equip their EL students with everything they would have given their non-EL students and more.

This mode of rethinking is more important than preparing for standardized tests but even more difficult to reach. Rethinking of this scale extends beyond assessment into the groundwork of pedagogy. The teachers who have internalized the dominant culture's educational system, especially if White and monolingual, need more education in understanding the social context in which their English learner students are living and learning (Ajayi, 2011). Moreover, they need to "challenge their cultural assumptions, and in the process, expand and transform their own sociocultural consciousness and knowledge of ethnic groups' way of learning and being" (Flores et al., 2008, cited in Ajayi, 2011). Only by changing the system in which we assess, while changing how and why we assess, can we bring equity to all students and strive towards creating an educated society that lives and breathes social justice.

REFERENCES

Au, K. (2016). Culturally responsive instruction: Application to multiethnic, multilingual classrooms. In L. Helman (Ed.), *Literacy development with English learners: Research-based instruction in grades K–6* (2nd ed., pp. 20–42). Guilford Press.

Ajayi, L. (2011). How ESL teachers' sociocultural identities mediate their teacher role identities in a diverse urban school setting. *Urban Review, 43*(5), 654–680. doi: 10.1007/s11256-010-0161-y.

Black, P., Harrison, C., Lee, C., Marshall, B., & Wiliam, D. (2004). Working inside the black box: Assessment for learning in the classroom. *Phi Delta Kappan, 86*(1), 9–21. doi: 10.1177/003172170408600105.

Broad, B. (2001). The power of tests: A critical perspective on the uses of language tests. *Journal of Writing Assessment, 3*(1), 55–60.

García, G., & DeNicolo, C. (2016). Improving the language and literacy assessment of emergent bilinguals. In L. Helman (Ed.), *Literacy development with English learners: Research-based instruction in grades K-6* (2nd ed., pp. 78–108). Guilford Press.

Gottlieb, M. (2016). *Assessing English language learners: Bridges to educational equity* (2nd ed.). Corwin.

Helman, L. (2016). Factors influencing second-language literacy development. In L. Helman (Ed.), *Literacy development with English learners: Research-based instruction in grades K–6* (2nd ed., pp. 1–19). Guilford Press.

Herrera, S., Cabral, R., & Murry, K. (2020). *Assessment of culturally and linguistically diverse students* (3rd ed.). Pearson.

Michigan Department of Education. (2017). *Michigan's approach to Every Student Succeeds Act: Overview of Michigan's consolidated state plan.*

Moll, L. C. (1994). Literacy research in community and classrooms: A sociocultural approach. In R. B. Ruddell, M. R. Ruddell, & H. Singer (Eds.), *Theoretical models and processes of reading* (4th ed., pp. 179–207). International Reading Association.

Silverman, R., Barber, A., Doyle, C., & Templeton, S. (2016). Vocabulary instruction for English learners across the elementary grades. In L. Helman (Ed.), *Literacy development with English learners: Research-based instruction in grades K–6* (2nd ed., pp. 232–257). Guilford Press.

Singh, C., Singh, R., Singh, T., Mostafa, N., & Mohtar, T. (2018). Developing a higher order thinking skills module for weak ESL learners. *English Language Teaching, 11*(7), 86–100. doi: 10.5539/etl. v11n7p86.

Traw, R. The woodcrafter's city. *Language Arts, 79*(3), 200–202.

Wright, W. (2016, July 8). *Every Student Succeeds Act (ESSA) and English Language Learners (ELLs)* [Video]. YouTube.

Chapter 3

SySTEMic Issues

Exploring the Effects of Colonialism on English Language Learners' Academic Outcomes

Uchenna Emenaha

Often, language policies put in place post-colonialization are covert attempts to maintain the status quo that creates socioeconomic disadvantages for Indigenous people. The language of the oppressing nation becomes the language of social status, government, and economic stability (Broom, 2004; Oliver & Oliver, 2017). The role of the colonizers' language often plays such a large societal role that Indigenous people just abandon the language after decolonization; instead, proficiency in the language becomes vital for their survival. Colonial language can become so embedded within the society that Indigenous people often struggle to find a place of significance for their native language. Indigenous people are at a disadvantage socially, politically, and economically if they are not able to master a language and cultural norms that are quite different from their own. Dual or multiple language use becomes a matter of necessity in some cases, thus, creating a need for a multilingual educational system.

Multilingualism describes language use ranging from communities where several languages have been spoken for hundreds of years to the more modern use of language through immigration and migration of different people groups (Snow & Kang, 2006; UNESCO, 2003). As communities around the world become more diverse, preservation of Indigenous languages is presently noted as one of the most urgent needs in the world today (UNESCO, 2003). Many countries that were affected by colonialism experience a subjugation of their Indigenous languages, which leads to reduced usage of their language and cultural identity issues.

This divide between Indigenous languages and the language of the colonizer is exemplified by the language of instruction or the language used by school-aged children for the purpose of learning and teaching. In countries that have experienced colonization, particularly by European nations, we see that the language of learning is different from that of the student's Indigenous or "Mother-Tongue." In a position paper by UNESCO (2003), Mother-Tongue is defined as "the language(s) that one has learnt first; the language(s) one identifies with or is identified as a native speaker of by others; the language(s) one knows best and the language(s) one uses most, 'Mother-Tongue' may also be referred to as 'primary' or 'first language.'" Research shows that when students' home language differs from that of the language of instruction, they will often experience educational disadvantages (UNESCO, 2003; Broom, 2004; Skutnabb-Kangas, 2009). These disadvantages can also hinder upward social and economic mobility of Indigenous peoples.

WHY STEM MATTERS

Some of the negative implications that are noted when students' home language differs from the language used during instruction can be seen more drastically when examining the outcomes of science, engineering, technology, and math (STEM) subjects. The purpose of focusing on STEM subjects is because success in these subjects can translate to success in other subject areas. For example, science writing can help to sharpen students' literacy and reading skills. Also, the process of sharing scientific findings enhances students' oral and written communication skills. Academic success in math can support reasoning and critical thinking skills. Students' understanding of modern technology that contribute to social issues, such as global warming, deforestation, or other human effects on the environment, can be used to develop social consciousness and civic engagement in students. Therefore, STEM serves as an encompassing medium for analysis in teaching and learning across multiple learning indexes. For these reasons, STEM subjects can be a pivotal point in supporting students' overall academic development and providing context on ways to address equity and inequality for second language learners.

The academic disparities in the success of STEM students among second language learners are an international issue. Due to the global trajectory that careers in STEM have had in recent years (LaCosse et al., 2020), there is a shift in the workforce, which increasingly relies on STEM technologies, creating a need for a more multilingual workforce (LaCosse et al., 2020).

However, if students are underperforming due to gaps in language skills, the challenges that second language learners face indeed require a closer look.

RELEVANCE OF SINGAPORE AND SOUTH AFRICA

The language of learning is decided by government policy, predicated by what the country has recognized as their official language. The effects of immigration, colonization, and the move towards a global economy have made it difficult for many of the world's nations to adhere to a one language ideology (Shin, 2013, p. 97). Many countries now have more than one official language (UNESCO, 2003). To analyze the effects of European colonization, the Indigenous languages of South Africa and Singapore will be used as the focal points.

South Africa and Singapore are both nations that have adopted multiple official languages in post-colonial rule from Great Britain. In addition to both nations being under former colonial rule, both countries received their independence around the same time, Singapore in 1965 and South Africa in 1961. Yet the educational outcomes from the two nations are vastly different. One contributing factor to these disparities can be attributed to the language policies within the educational systems of each nation.

The methodology used to analyze the differences between these two nations' education systems draws from the historical contexts of multilingual research rather than empirical evidence. Through an understanding of multilingual education, it can be observed that languages have been used to support and/or deconstruct learning experiences for students in nations that were formally under colonial rule.

South Africa

According to international data sources, South Africa ranks among the bottom five nations in science and math scores (Juan et al., 2020). South Africa's multilingual education system provides a wonderful opportunity to understand how colonization can impact the study of language of the Indigenous people. The nation's official languages in order of Mother-Tongue dominance are Zulu, Xhosa, Afrikaans, English, Northern Sotho, Tswana, Sotho, Tsonga, Swati, Venda, and Ndebele (South African History Online, 2019; Sinclair, 2018). Although, less than one fourth of the population claims English or Afrikaans as their Indigenous language, the two are viewed as the language of prestige and affluence (South African History Online, 2019).

Apartheid laws called for all students to be taught in their Indigenous language during the primary grades. However, when students move up to secondary school, they are faced with the challenges set in place by the laws of Apartheid. From the start of secondary school, all pupils are taught in a full immersion English only education system. This full immersion into a language that students had little academic exposure to has shown to be a recipe for huge failures for Black South African students. The problem with this language transition is that students had not learned to read and write in English. Black South African students' learning environment resulted in lower success rates compared to their White South African counterparts. White South African students often afford the privilege of learning their subjects in English throughout their primary school (Broom, 2004).

Additionally, in the very first year of being exposed to English in an academic setting, students are given mandatory assessments to measure their cognitive ability. A study that measured the literacy and reading skills of 845 South African students showed a statistically significant difference between the reading skills of students at the end of grade three who had been taught in English compared to those taught in their Indigenous languages (Broom, 2004).

Additionally, many South African teachers are not given adequate training or the necessary resources to adhere to these new policies. For instance, a high number of teachers were not proficient enough in English to use the English only resources (Gumede, 2017). The government has invested very few resources to support teachers in the transition to teach English at earlier grades. In 2010, a report release found that only 33% of teachers were able to pass math skills test at the same level as their students (Chaka, 2015).

Today, South Africa's educational system is ranked as one of the lowest in the world. A closer look shows that this gap pertains mostly to Black South Africans while White South Africans fare much better because of the challenges imposed by laws and unfair learning environment for Black students. Students whose home language is an African language go from learning only in their Mother-Tongue to a complete immersion in a new language during grade three, which leads to the Mathew Effect. The Mathew Effect occurs when initial failure due to a poor reading ability creates reduction in students' academic efficacy and interest in learning (Broom, 2004). Poorer ability in reading in English causes students to fall further, contributing to the current national scores of South Africa in science and math.

Singapore

Singapore became free from the British colonial rule in 1964. After its emancipation as a newly independent country, the small island faced many early challenges. The new nation was in a state of high unemployment with most of the employment concentrated among its youth. At this time, the youth comprised 50% of the nation's population (Dixon, 2005).

After receiving its independence, the Singaporean government's first order of business was to declare four official languages: Malay, Mandarin, Tamil, and English. Of the population of Chinese heritage, 77% spoke Mandarin, 14% spoke Malay, and 70% of the Indian population spoke Tamil (Dixon, 2005). English was seen as a neutral language.

After colonization, English was designated as the language of learning and teaching. In many instances, this would have put students at a disadvantage, but, today, Singaporeans lead the world in math and science scores (Coughlan, 2016). How can this be possible? It can be observed that national identity in Singapore is one that is more inclusive of the various ethnic groups in Singapore. National laws mandated education for all regardless of gender or socioeconomic status. Bilingual education also became mandatory for every school-aged pupil in Singapore shortly after the end of its colonial rule (Dixon, 2005).

The end of colonialism was marked by a push towards equitable learning for all students as the nation worked towards establishing itself globally as a new nation. The government created the Curriculum Development Institute, designed to increase teacher autonomy in the class. There was a shift from the top-down approach to teaching to an approach that recognized teachers as experts within their filed. Unfortunately, quite the opposite is true of South Africa's curriculum reform.

The Singaporean government created the Thinking Schools Learning Nation (TSLN) with the sole purpose of supporting students in reaching their full potential (Norruddin, 2018). Government sponsored think tanks also work to develop polices to make education more equal and equitable for all learners. At the end of primary school, students either continue to vocational or academic training based on standardized test scores. These high-stakes exams include math, science, and proficiency tests that are given to students in their Indigenous language. The message is the clear understanding of one's indigenous language is essential to students' academic success.

Although, English was designated by the government as the language of learning, students are also assigned to one of the three main ethnic groups. Once a student receives their ethnic designation, they are required demonstrate understanding of their ingenious language (Dixon, 2005). The success of Singapore can be linked to its commitment of developing ethnic identity in students of the public-school system. Their academic success was tied to their understanding of their home language. Singapore's mandatory language education supported the learning and development of students' ethnic identity. Students did not have to abandon their Indigenous language because

their educational language policies implemented pedagogical practices that
supported diversity in education.

ETHNIC IDENTITY DEVELOPMENT

The dedication to preserving students' Indigenous language was paramount
in supporting students' academic growth and development. Singapore recognized and nurtured the cultural background of its Indigenous students. Both
South Africa and Singapore received their freedom from colonial rulers less
than five years apart from one another. Yet Singapore is a world leader in
education while South Africa's education system unfortunately ranks as one
of lowest in the world.

What makes Singaporean language education unique is the ethnic identity
support provided to its students. Multilingual researchers have proposed a
solution of giving credence to ethnic identity development to reduce language
disparities (Martínez-Roldán & Malavé, 2004). Ethnic identity is often used
interchangeably with racial identity, but an individual's ethnicity is more
than just his or her heritage. Ethnicity is the culture, beliefs, and values of
one's heritage (Phinney, 1996). Ethnic identity development can take many
forms. One way to develop ethnic identity is by having plurality of multi-
linguistic learning in schools. In a case study conducted among elementary
aged students, an increase in ethnic identity was shown in students who were
allowed to complete literacy activities through a narrative story telling in
their Indigenous languages (Bell et al., 2004). Students reported having a
higher-level of ethnic identity paired with success in the literacy classroom.
This study and others show that students' concepts of who they are and what
value they bring to the learning space is paramount to their success.

When students' culture and ethnic identities are subjugated to language
discrimination, it can handicap their success and be demoralizing. The recognition and appreciation of students' culture will affect how the students see
themselves in relationship to literacy and learning (Perry, 2008). Deterioration
of ethnic identity has occurred through the removal of Indigenous language
and culture from the school curriculum. Developing curriculum and teaching
practices that recognize students' ethnic identities is one way to counter years
of degenerative messages that have been associated with students' Indigenous
languages.

CULTURAL COMPETENCY

Cultural competency is not just understating one's own culture, but it is the learning and development of appreciation for at least one other culture beside one's own culture (Ladson-Billings, 1995). The use of culturally competent teaching is not an expensive endeavor. Singapore incorporated cultural competencies by simply creating a space for students to use their Indigenous language in the school setting. These same efforts can be duplicated in places like South Africa by providing opportunities past primary school for students to learn, read, and write in their Indigenous language.

Linguistic researchers have presented overwhelming evidence that students who have a good grasp of learning and reading in their Mother-Tongue perform better when learning a second language (Bell et al., 2004; Ottmann et al., 2007; Perry, 2008). However, parents of Black South Africans push for instruction to be provided in English because of the impact of socioeconomic challenges on these communities because of the Apartheid (Skutnabb-Kangas, 2009). When students' identities and ethnicities are not valued in the learning space, it can lead to feelings of inadequacy and limit the student's ability to be academically successful.

DUAL LANGUAGE SUPPORT

The current state of multilingual education is by no means ideal, which is why educators should adopt an attitude of critical hope. Critical hope is the belief that systems of oppression can be dismantled to improve conditions of marginalized people. Critical hope is an essential element needed to support efforts being made to reform South Africa's education system (Zembylas, 2014, p. 13). It might be unrealistic for students to solely learn their home language as this would be debilitating by limiting their opportunity to take part in the multilingual STEM workforce. However, to support students in nations where the dominant language differs from their home language, efforts must be made to increase the use and value of their home languages in teaching and learning. One way to accomplish this is with dual language programs.

Dual language learning settings work to teach both language and content at the same time (de Jong, 2011). Dual language programs provide an additive learning environment for students because the goal is not to only master one language (i.e., English), but to obtain fluency in two languages (Warhol & Mayer, 2012). Dual language programs provide opportunity to support all students' ethnic identities as one language is perceived as the dominant language.

Another benefit of supporting literacy skills in both one Indigenous language and English is that these skills are transferable. As such, as students increase in language skills in their home language, these skills can be also used to develop academic fluency in English as well. When teachers in South Africa were allowed to switch between English and Xhosa, evidence shows that students were better able to communicate their responses in their science classes as compared to those who had only received instruction in English (Probyn, 2006). Dual language programs provide a unique cultural appreciation that improves the cultural competency of teachers and curriculum.

Although the focus of this chapter has been to provide context of the effects of colonialism on language policy that affect the science and math success of students in South Africa and Singapore, other nations with similarities can draw from the lessons observed in both nations. Academic achievement in the STEM field is important on an international level as the world becomes more reliant on technology and more interconnected in business and trade. This realization is why it is important to prioritize and fix the academic gaps that exist when Indigenous language is not supported in the educational system.

Language is a powerful social construct that can bring people together; however, it has been used as a tool to reduce Indigenous speakers to lower language status. Educators seeking ways to empower students will find success when they begin to draw from the cultural identities of students in the classroom. What we can learn from the comparison of these two nations is that support of one's ethnic identity is important to create the student's success in literacy, which can in turn support other academic content. Supporting students' ethnic identities is essential to increase their feeling of belongingness and provide them the freedom needed to thrive and reach their full potential.

REFERENCES

Bell, D., Anderson, K., Fortin, T., Ottmann, J., Rose, S., Simard, L., & Spencer, K. (2004). *Sharing our success: Ten case studies in Aboriginal schooling.* Society for the Advancement of Excellence in Education (SAEE).

Broom, Y. (2004). Reading English in multilingual South African primary schools. *International Journal of Bilingual Education and Bilingualism, 7*(6), 506–528. https://doi.org/10.1080/13670050408667828

Chaka, C. (2015). An investigation into the English reading comprehension of grade 10 English first additional language learners at a senior secondary school. *Reading & Writing, 6*(1), 62–68. http://dx.doi.org/10.4102/rw. v6i1.62

Coughlan, S. (2016, December 6). Pisa tests: Singapore top in global education rankings. BBC News. https://www.bbc.com/news/education-38212070

de Jong, E. J. (2011). *Foundations for multilingualism in education.* Caslon.

Dixon, L. Q. (2005). Bilingual education policy in Singapore: An analysis of its socio-historical roots and current academic outcomes. *International Journal of Bilingual Education and Bilingualism, 8*(1), 25–47. https://doi.org/10.1080/jBEB.v8.i1.pg25

Gumede, M. (2017, July 31). Teacher training in spotlight. *Times Live.* https://www.timeslive.co.za/news/south-africa/2017-07-31-teacher-training-in-spotlight/

Juan, A., Reddy, V., & Arends, F. (2020). South Africa. In D. L. Kelly, V. A. S. Centurino, M. O. Martin, & I. V. S. Mullis (Eds.), *TIMSS 2019 encyclopedia: Education policy and curriculum in mathematics and science.* TIMSS & PIRLS International Study Center.

LaCosse, J., Canning, E. A., Bowman, N. A., Murphy, M. C., & Logel, C. (2020). A social-belonging intervention improves STEM outcomes for students who speak English as a second language. *Science Advances, 6*(40), eabb6543. https://doi.org/10.1126/sciadv.abb6543

Ladson-Billings, G. (1995). But that's just good teaching! The case for culturally relevant pedagogy. *Theory Into Practice, 34*(3), 159–165. https://doi.org/10.1080/00405849509543675

Martínez-Roldán, C. M., & Malavé, G. (2004). Language ideologies mediating literacy and identity in bilingual contexts. *Journal of Early Childhood Literacy, 4*(2), 155–180.

Norruddin, N. (2018, May 7). *Thinking schools, learning nation.* eResources. http://eresources.nlb.gov.sg/infopedia/articles/SIP_2018-06-04_154236.html

Oliver, E., & Oliver, W. H. (2017). The colonization of South Africa: A unique case. *Theological Studies, 73*(3), 1–8. https://doi.org/10.4102/hts.v73i3.4498

Ottmann, J., Abel, J., Flynn, D.; & Bird, S. (2007). *A survey of the literature on Aboriginal language learning and teaching.* Alberta Education.

Perry, K. (2008). Primary school literacy in Southern Africa: African perspectives. *Comparative Education, 44*(1), 57–73. https://doi.org/10.1080/03050060701809433

Phinney, J. S. (1996). Understanding ethnic diversity: The role of ethnic identity. *American Behavioral Scientist, 40*(2), 143–152. https://doi.org/10.1177/0002764296040002005

Probyn, M. (2006). Language and learning science in South Africa. *Language and Education, 20*(5), 391–414. https://doi.org/10.2167/le554.0

Shin, S. J. (2013). Bilingualism and Identity. In *Bilingualism in schools and society* (pp. 97–118). Routledge.

Sinclar, J. (2018). "Starving and suffocating": Evaluation policies and practices during the first 10 years of the U.S. Bilingual Education Act. *International Journal of Bilingual Education* and *Bilingualism, 6*(21), 710–728.

Skutnabb-Kangas, T. (2009, January 19–21). The stakes: Linguistic diversity, linguistic human rights, and mother tongue—based multilingual education—or linguistic genocide, crimes against humanity and an even faster destruction of biodiversity and our planet [Keynote Presentation]. Bamako International Forum on Multilingualism, Bamako, Mali.

Snow, C. E., & Kang, J. Y. (2006). Becoming bilingual, biliterate, and bicultural. In A. Renninger & I. Sigel (Eds.), *Handbook of child psychology: Volume 4—Child psychology in practice* (pp. 75–102). John Wiley & Sons.

South African History Online. (2019, July 23). *A history of apartheid in South Africa.* SA History. www.sahistory.org.za/article/history-apartheid-south-africa

UNESCO. (2003). *Education in a multilingual world* [Position paper]. UNESDOC Digital Library. http://unesdoc.unesco.org/images/0012/001297/129728e.pdf

Warhol, L., & Mayer, A. (2012). Misinterpreting school reform: The dissolution of a dual-immersion bilingual program in an urban New England elementary school. *Bilingual Research Journal, 35*(2), 145–163. https://doi.org/10.1080/15235882.2012.703636

Zembylas, M. (2014). Affective, political, and ethical sensibilities in pedagogies of critical hope: Exploring the notion of "critical emotional praxis." In V. Bozalek, B. Leibowitz, R. Carolissen, & M. Boler (Eds.), *Discerning critical hope in educational practices* (pp. 11–25). Routledge.

Chapter 4

The Power of a Story

Catalyzing Social Change
Through Photovoice Projects

María L. Gabriel and Kevin Roxas

"I'm so proud for being a Muslim and Libyan; an Arab girl."—Farah, high schooler

The focus of this chapter is to engage and invite readers to live the work of honoring multiculturalism and diversity by addressing the needs of English Language Learners (ELLs) based in culturally sustaining pedagogy (Paris, 2012). Culturally sustaining pedagogy seeks to affirm the cultural and linguistic gifts of each student in a classroom. In alignment with this theory, the authors seek to honor students' home language, heritage, and cultural ways of knowing and doing by sharing aspects of a year-long research project where the creation of Photovoice poster projects highlighted family and student cultural gifts and strengths as described in their own words and captured through their own photography.

The project was held with students and families of students learning English and the teachers who collaborated with them. Participants in the project uncovered and directed the researchers' attention to social issues through participation in the creation of individual Photovoice posters. Several participants grew to become social change agents, and a few of their stories are presented in this chapter as brief, but critical counter-stories.

The chapter begins with an overview of literature that guides the research project: culturally sustaining pedagogy and critical counter-stories. Second, Photovoice, a qualitative community-based participatory action research method used as a form of culturally sustaining pedagogy with ELLs and their families, is described. Third, the findings from the study are shared from a practitioner's voice that gives credence and voice to the firsthand experiences and stories of ELLs. Three stories of participants' experiences are described using critical counter-storytelling that highlights the "unique voice of color" (Delgado & Stefancic, 2001, p. 9) of the immigrant participants in the study. The chapter continues with a discussion of the findings and concludes with suggestions based on the research for current practitioners to support ELLs in educational settings utilizing culturally sustaining pedagogy.

LITERATURE REVIEW

The chapter begins with a brief discussion of literature of the theoretical framework underlying the research project: (1) culturally sustaining pedagogy and (2) critical counter-stories.

Culturally Sustaining Pedagogy

Culturally relevant pedagogy (Ladson-Billings, 1995, 2009) rests on a tripod of: (1) cultural competence, (2) academic achievement, and (3) sociopolitical/ critical consciousness. All three of these components are necessary to increase access to learning. One major function of culturally responsive teaching includes incorporating multiple aspects of students' cultural experiences as part of their learning (Gay, 2010; Ladson-Billings, 1995, 2009; Trumbull & Pacheco, 2005). In this approach to teaching, children learn about themselves and the world around them within the context of culture, but they also begin to learn how culture impacts teaching and learning.

Building from these earlier theoretical frameworks and framings for including student's culture in teaching and learning, Django Paris (2012) developed a new term, "culturally sustaining practices," to highlight the need for educators to focus their work on the affirmation and engagement of a student's home language as well as on the importance of their cultural norms. Paris writes:

> The term culturally sustaining requires that our pedagogies be more than respon-
> sive of or relevant to the cultural experiences and practices of young people—it
> requires that they support young people in sustaining the cultural and linguis-
> tic competence of their communities while simultaneously offering access to
> dominant cultural competence. Culturally sustaining pedagogy, then, has as its
> explicit goal supporting multilingualism and multiculturalism in practice and
> perspective for students and teachers. That is, culturally sustaining pedagogy

seeks to perpetuate and foster—to sustain—linguistic, literate, and cultural pluralism as part of the democratic project of schooling. (Paris, 2012, p. 95)

Photovoice was the chosen method for the research project because as a
process it seeks to engage participants as co-researchers, teachers, and agents
of social change (Blackman & Fairey, 2007; Wang, 1999; Wilson, Dasho,
Martin, Wallerstein, Wang, & Minkler, 2007). The authors did not want the
participants to feel viewed only as study participants, but to consider themselves as co-researchers who were acknowledged and affirmed by educators
within their school community. Additionally, the authors wanted to employ a
culturally sustaining approach through the project by intentionally focusing
the work on the use of participants' home language, on supporting participants as they identified their own cultural norms and values and increasing
opportunities for students and families to share their multicultural histories
and heritage with their school and local communities.

The authors seek to build on a larger field of educational research on the
role schools can play in improving academic engagement and achievement
for immigrant youth, ways to improve school-family-community partnerships, and a better understanding of the process of identity formation for
immigrant youth (Cooper, Riehl, & Hasan, 2010; Guerra & Nelson, 2013;
Suarez-Orozco, Onaga, & Lardemelle, 2010). The culturally sustaining pedagogy embedded in this project is innovative in its design and timely given the
anti-immigrant sentiment that is alive and well throughout the USA given the
recent "travel bans" instituted by former President Trump that banned people
from Iran, Libya, North Korea, Syria, and Yemen (and others) from entering
the U.S. (BBC News, 2018).

The Photovoice posters created through this project highlight students
and their stories from each of these countries and offer a critical counternarrative to the majoritarian narrative that was painted of Muslims in the U.S.
between 2015 and 2020 through national politics and rhetoric. This politically
charged climate was reported by Costello (2016) who wrote that "more than
two-thirds of the teachers reported that students—mainly immigrants, children of immigrants, and Muslims—have expressed concerns or fears about
what might happen to them or their families after the election" (p. 4).

Critical Counter-stories

Critical race theory (CRT) offers important tools for academics and researchers to employ to interrogate systemic racism through examinations of the
permanence of racism in the U.S. (Bell, 1992); color blindness, neutrality, and
liberalism; interest convergence (Bell, 1980); interdisciplinary perspectives
and intersectionality (Crenshaw, 1991); and the sharing of experiences of

people of color, each as a call to end racial oppression (Alemán, 2009; DeCuir & Dixson, 2004; Delgado & Stefancic, 2001; Matsuda, Lawrence, Delgado, & Crenshaw, 1993). This chapter highlights one important tenet of CRT, the notion of "a unique voice of color" (Delgado & Stefancic, 2001), surfaced through critical counter-story.

Based upon the work of critical race theorists, researchers, and other community-based practitioners collaborating with people who have been marginalized in schools and other community settings (Yosso, 2006), this research examines the creation of counter-stories that these Photovoice posters bring to the existing research on personal agency of participating students, parents, and caregivers and the value of their linguistic and cultural norms and ways of being. "Counter-storytelling is a means of exposing and critiquing normalized dialogues that perpetuate racial stereotypes. The use of counter-stories allows for challenging privilege discourses, the discourses of the majority, therefore serving as a means for giving voice to marginalized groups" (DeCuir & Dixson, 2004, p. 27).

The presentation of data exists within the framework of "composite counter-stories" which includes: (1) empirical research data from archival data and focus groups, (2) literature on the topic, (3) judicial records, and (4) author's professional and firsthand experiences (Solórzano & Yosso, 2002). Using these four critical components as a foundation, a brief form of critical counter-story is presented in the findings of this chapter; three separate counter-stories as demonstrated by the participants. The following section provides more detail about the collaborative research project to create further context for the reader.

METHODOLOGY

The qualitative study described in this chapter was conducted during the 2012–2013 academic school year in a preschool to grade 12 (PK–12) school district in the Mountain West region of the U.S. District officials reported a growing population of approximately 358 identified immigrant students located in each of the fifty schools in the urban school district. The immigrant students and families enrolled in the district were from countries around the world and spoke over 70 distinct languages. Many of these students were from Spanish-speaking countries, but important to this study, there was a breadth of diversity among the students. Despite the growing enrollment of immigrant students, little data existed on their multicultural backgrounds, particularly regarding their academic, social, cultural, and linguistic needs and experiences.

The student participants in this research project were identified as immigrant youth based on school data collection and were enrolled in the district's English Language Acquisition (ELA) classes due to their district-identified status as ELLs. The authors also refer to ELLs as multilingual learners throughout the chapter to affirm the multilingual capacity of the incredible youth who participated in the study.

The photovoice method utilized in the study seeks to engage participants as co-researchers, teachers, and agents of social change (Blackman & Fairey, 2007; Delgado, 2012; Wang, 1999; Wilson, Dasho, Martin, Wallerstein, Wang, & Minkler, 2007). The method also inherently helps build empathy and understanding of the real lives of multilingual learners as told through their own pictures and stories written in text in their home language. People who have never encountered a Mexican, Syrian, Yemen, or Libyan child may be surprised to know of their individual story shared through photos and text that Photovoice offers.

FINDINGS: SHARING THE STORIES

Findings from the study are shared here from a practitioner's voice that gives credence and voice to the firsthand experiences and families stories of ELLs. Both authors of this chapter have experience working in schools in teaching, academic support, and administrative leadership roles. Their positionality as parents of school-age children, scholars, and teacher educators inspired their continued support of students in practicing how to tell their own personal story utilizing Photovoice as a method; to acknowledge and create a school-based space to honor multicultural backgrounds, heritage, language, and uplift their voices. The three critical counter-stories in this section of the chapter include stories of the power of culturally sustaining pedagogy in public schools that further built personal agency for participants in the project.

Farah: Personal Agency in Ethnic and Religious Identity

At the conclusion of the Photovoice poster creation workshops, each poster was carefully hung in a warehouse turned coffee house in the community. Over a month's time, all 160 posters were hung throughout the building to celebrate the work of the participants and for participants to have opportunities to share their stories. At the end of the month, an exhibit to honor the co-researchers turned artists and storyteller was held. As a high schooler, Farah states in her own words in a video recorded at the exhibit,

> At the beginning . . . I did not think that my culture and my race was so special until I made it [the poster], and it made me feel so special to my family and close to them, too.

Due to her willingness to be on camera during the exhibit, the lead researchers invited her to co-present at a Diversity Summit at the local university in the fall. When Farah arrived at the event, she was wearing a hijab. One of the researchers noticed an upbeat more confident young woman during the presentation. In a follow-up conversation, Farah shared that she was embarrassed of her religion before the Photovoice project due to the anti-immigrant and anti-Muslim rhetoric she was hearing in the community. However, due to her work and thinking in creating her own project, she shared that she now felt stronger in "owning" her religion and that practicing her religion more openly felt empowering. Given the anti-immigrant sentiments in the USA, particularly against Muslim community members, Farah's story is an important one among a collection of unique individual immigrant student's perspectives and experiences, particularly related to religious persecution in the USA.

Madeline: Personal Agency and Social Change

Madeline was a 10th grader who participated in the project in one of the high schools the research team worked with. Madeline seemed originally reticent to share her thinking and her photos during in-class work sessions. Members of the research team could see that she had taken photos for her individual project and had written text and narrative to provide context for each photo. However, when it was time to share her photos with class, she was hesitant. On the day students were scheduled to share their photos with their peers in class, the research team could hear one of the teachers checking in with Madeline and encouraging her to share her photos with her classmates and underscoring the importance of her photos. The teacher explained how the power and beauty of Madeline's story was one that connected with so many of her peers in class. During the open group sharing of photos, Madeline walked to the front of the classroom and began to show her photos via the digital projector. Madeline's teacher provided encouragement to her as she began her presentation.

As Madeline showed her slides and began to explain why she had chosen her photos, the entire classroom fell silent, and students and their teachers paid close attention. Madeline talked about all the difficulties her family had faced in Haiti and about the death of her mother. She talked about how her aunts and sisters wanted to be able to take care of her but could not because they did not have the financial resources. Madeline explained how they faced the difficult decision of taking her to an orphanage and how this series of unfortunate events eventually led her to being adopted by her "beautiful adoptive family." She spoke (and wrote in her poster) of being excited at the move and getting to know her new family but also about her profound sadness of leaving her biological family and friends. She went on to say how much her family and friends loved her in Haiti, but they wanted her to have the chance to "go to the U.S. because they wanted me to have a better life."

As Madeline finished her presentation students in the class were quiet at first, but then began to share, one by one, how Madeline's story touched them because they all had some variation of that story they wanted to share in terms of loss, difficulty in leaving loved ones and family in their home country, and trying to find their way as immigrant and refugee students new to the U.S. Madeline, through her photos and sharing, had opened new ways that students in the class could share their own immigrant experiences with each other and feel comfortable in doing so. The poster she created for the project become another place where she could also share in public her experiences and her dreams of finishing college (and an advanced graduate degree) with the eventual goal of going "back to help my family, my people, and country." The Photovoice project and process then provided Madeline and other students in class opportunities to share about their own experiences, to connect with others in class who had had similar experiences, and to powerfully express in writing and in presentations their dreams for their experiences in schools and their goals in life once they finished school.

Rosalinda: Family Unit as Agency and Social Change

Each week the participants would share pictures of their community and family, and later began to share stories that went along with the photographs. They were quickly invited to practice the photography tips taught during sessions. A few weeks into the project, a mother, Rosalinda, brought in a picture of her daughter doing her homework in their kitchen. The mother explained that she preferred that her children did their homework in the kitchen and not in other rooms of the house, so that when they had questions, she was located nearby to respond and help them. She shared that their schedule as a family was busy and that she needed to start cooking dinner for the family when the children arrived home from school.

While she described her sense of disempowerment with not understanding the English language, she also shared that her personal agency and commitment to being present with her children was important to their success. This brief anecdote highlights a notion previous scholars have stated "many Latino parents constantly communicate the importance of education to their children through words and actions" (Guerra & Nelson, 2013, p. 436), and it debunks an ongoing myth that educators have stating that Latino parents do not value their children's education. It also demonstrates that honoring diverse cultural norms and ways of engaging in homework can be effective. The norm does not have to include having a personal quiet desk space in a bedroom away from others to be successful as is often told to families. This mother demonstrated her personal agency and a commitment to supporting her children while honoring her culture.

DISCUSSION

Two stories of students' experiences and one family member's experience are described through the impacts of theory meshing with practice and the powerful results of a collaborative co-research project on participants' lives. This partnership between a school district and local university researchers brought different resources to the school community. A culturally sustaining practice in classrooms and family engagement was formed and implemented within the time frame of one school year. Administrators, teachers, and other leaders at the school- and school district-level were willing to think creatively to consider the needs of students from an assets-based and culturally sustaining lens. Educators, in this case, were willing to acknowledge that they did not know everything they thought they knew. They sought help, support, and resources. Due to this public display of vulnerability by teachers and other school and district leaders, the 21 students and 6 family members who participated in the project were positively and fully engaged as their complete selves which, at times, led to social change. The three selected stories shared in this chapter demonstrate the importance of the personal agency of student and parent participants that could be leveraged further in classrooms and family engagement efforts.

IMPLICATIONS AND SUGGESTIONS

We conclude this chapter by sharing suggestions based on the research for current practitioners to support multilingual learners in educational settings using culturally sustaining pedagogy. In the case of immigrant family school involvement, counter-stories serve to challenge dominant perspectives of deficit-based (Valencia, 1997, 2010) parental approaches and perceived lack of interest in education and instead advance alternative strengths-based perspectives on family support for their child's education. Researchers have discussed the need to focus on the strengths of Latina/o parents and recognition of their funds of knowledge and noted the required shift away from deficit thinking or blaming students and families for what is perceived and labeled as their inherent deficits, to a focus on internal strengths of families (Gabriel, Martinez & Obiakor, 2016; Gabriel, Roxas, & Becker, 2017; Gorski, 2013; Valencia, 2010).

In order to catalyze social change, practitioners in educational settings can: (1) attend to the multicultural backgrounds of their students and families in their instructional practices, assignments, and tasks; (2) hold family engagement events that honor and engage family's culture in authentic ways; (3) hold student and family events in ongoing ways that invite connections and build informal networks where students and families can rely on each other for support; and (4) watch for and promote social change for disenfranchised students and families.

As the authors continue to present at national and international conferences on this research project, they work to actively engage educational researchers, school administrators, and practitioners in further discussions around the potential and ongoing employment of this continued collaborative work. They find that it is critical that practitioners insist on providing multiple, varied, and creative opportunities such as Photovoice projects for ELLs and their families so that spaces are created for students and parents to tell their powerful stories to challenge and change the world we live in, rather than reinforce the status quo.

Due to the continuing increase of immigrant, migrant, and refugee families seeking asylum and refuge in the U.S., it behooves educators to prepare themselves for ways to employ culturally sustaining pedagogy in the classroom. Utilizing the photovoice method while attending to multicultural backgrounds and language has proven to be a successful strategy for the co-researchers in this study. The opportunity to utilize home language and English demonstrates the support for within-group cultural practices and common across-group cultural practices, both of which are needed in a pluralistic society (Paris, 2012).

REFERENCES

Alemán, E., Jr. (2009). Through the prism of critical race theory: Niceness and Latina/o leadership in the politics of education. *Journal of Latinos and Education, 8*(4), 290–311. doi: 10.1080/15348430902973351

BBC News (2018, June 26). Trump travel ban—What does this ruling mean? https://www.bbc.com/news/world-us-canada-39044403

Bell, D. A. (1980). *Brown v. Board of Education* and the interest convergence dilemma. *Harvard Law Review, 93*(3), 518–534.

Bell, D. (1992). *Faces at the bottom of the well: Permanence of racism*. Basic Books.

Blackman, A., & Fairey, T. (2007). *The PhotoVoice manual: A guide to designing and running participatory photography projects.* PhotoVoice. https://photovoice.org/wp-content/uploads/2014/09/PV_Manual.pdf

Cooper, C. W., Riehl, C. J., & Hasan, L. (2010). Leading and learning with diverse families in schools: Critical epistemology amid communities of practice. *Journal of School Leadership, 20*(6), 758–788.

Costello, M. B. (2016). *The Trump effect: The impact of the presidential campaign on our nation's schools.* Southern Poverty Law Center. https://www.splcenter.org/sites/default/files/splc_the_trump_effect.pdf

Crenshaw, K. (1991, July). Mapping the margins: Intersectionality, identity politics, and violence against women of color. *Stanford Law Review, 43*(6), 1241–1299.

DeCuir, J. T., & Dixson, A. D. (2004, June/July). "So, when it comes out, they aren't that surprised that it is there": Using critical race theory as a tool of analysis of race and racism in education. *Educational Researcher, 33*(26), 26–31. doi:10.3102/0013189X033005026

Delgado, M. (2012). *Urban youth and photovoice: Visual ethnography in action.* Oxford University Press.

Delgado, R., & Stefancic, J. (2001). *Critical race theory: An introduction.* New York University Press.

Gabriel, M. L., Martinez, J., & Obiakor, F. (2015). Dismantling deficit thinking through teacher preparation. In F. Obiakor, A. Rieger, and A. Rotatori (Eds.), *Critical issues in preparing effective early child special education teachers for the 21st century classroom: Interdisciplinary perspectives* (pp. 25–36). Information Age Publishing.

Gabriel, M. L., Roxas, K. C., & Becker, K. (2017). Meeting, knowing, and affirming Spanish-speaking immigrant families through successful culturally responsive family engagement. *Journal of Family Diversity in Education, 2*(3), 1–18.

Gay, G. (2010). *Culturally responsive teaching: Theory, research, and practice* (2nd ed.). Teachers College Press.

Gorski, P. (2013). *Reaching and teaching students in poverty: Strategies for erasing the opportunity gap.* Teachers College Press.

Guerra, P. L., & Nelson, S. W. (2013). Latino parent involvement: Seeing what has always been there. *Journal of School Leadership, 23*(3), 424–455. https://www.researchgate.net/profile/Sarah_Nelson_Baray/publication/283225717_Latino_parent_involvement_Seeing_what_has_always_been_there/links/5646806608ae45188 0aa6016.pdf

Ladson-Billings, G. (1995). Toward a theory of culturally relevant pedagogy. *American Educational Research Journal, 32*(3), 465–491.

Ladson-Billings, G. (2009). *The dreamkeepers: Successful teachers of African American children.* John Wiley & Sons.

Matsuda, M. J., Lawrence, C. R., III, Delgado, R., & Crenshaw, K. W. (1993). *Words that wound: Critical race theory, assaultive speech, and the first amendment.* Westview Press.

Moll, L. C. (1992). Bilingual classroom studies and community analysis: Some recent trends. *Educational Researcher, 21*(2), 20–24.

Moll, L. C. (2010). Mobilizing culture, language, and educational practices. *Educational Researcher, 39*(6), 451–460. doi:10.3102/0013189X10380654

Paris, D. (2012). Culturally sustaining pedagogy: A needed change in stance, terminology, and practice. *Educational Researcher, 41*(3), 93–97.

Solórzano, D. G., & Yosso, T. J. (2001). Critical race and LatCrit theory and method: Counter-storytelling: Chicana and Chicano graduate school experiences. *Qualitative Studies in Education, 14*(4), 471–495.

Solórzano, D. G., & Yosso, T. J. (2002). A critical race counter story of race, racism, and affirmative action. *Equity and Excellence in Education, 35*(2), 155–168.

Solórzano, D. G., & Yosso, T. J. (2009). Critical race methodology: Counter-storytelling as an analytic framework for educational research. In E. Taylor, D. Gillborn, & G. Ladson-Billings (Eds.), *Foundations of critical race theory in education* (pp. 131–147). Routledge.

Suárez-Orozco, C., Onaga, M., & Lardemelle, C. D. (2010). Promoting academic engagement among immigrant adolescents through school-family-community collaboration. *Professional School Counseling, 14*(1), 15–26.

Trumbull, E., & Pacheco, M. (2005). *Leading with diversity: Cultural competencies for teacher preparation and professional development.* Brown University and Pacific Resources for Education and Learning. http://www.alliance.brown.edu/pubs/leading_diversity/lwd_entire.pdf

Valencia, R. R. (Ed.). (1997). *The evolution of deficit thinking: Educational thought and practice.* The Falmer Press.

Valencia, R. R. (2010). *Dismantling contemporary deficit thinking: Educational thought and practice.* Routledge.

Wang, C. (1999). Photovoice: A participatory action research strategy applied to women's health. *Journal of Women's Health, 8*(2), 185–192.

Wilson, N., Dasho, S., Martin, A. C., Wallerstein, N., Wang, C. C., & Minkler, M. (2007). Engaging young adolescents in social action through Photovoice: The youth empowerment strategies (YES!) project. *The Journal of Early Adolescence, 27*(2), 241–261. doi: 10.1177/0272431606294834.

Yosso, T. J. (2006). *Critical race counter stories along the Chicana/Chicano educational pipeline.* Taylor & Francis Group.

Chapter 5

(Re)Conceptualizing Strategies for Teaching African English Learners in U.S. Classrooms

Brenda Muzeta

INTRODUCTION

Coming to America

"My cultural heritage was never included as part of any curriculum."

Throughout its history, the United States has been known as a major destination for immigrants. Every single year thousands of immigrants from all over the world enter the U.S.—the land of opportunity—in pursuit of their American dream (Arthur, 2010). During the past 40 years, there has been a rapid increase in the numbers of Africans entering the U.S. from Africa. According to the US Census Bureau (2014) the population of Sub-Saharan Africans is expected to increase the most, with figures ranging from 83,000 in 2014 to just over 250,000 in 2060. The flows of African immigrants—a growing component of the U.S. population—have contributed to the racial and ethnic transformation of 21st century America resulting in diverse school populations (Kent, 2007).

African Students in US Public Schools

With this increase in numbers, comes the need to understand student schooling experiences in U.S. public schools. However, despite the rise in the numbers of Africans entering the U.S., research that focuses on the experiences of African high school students is sparse and limited. There is still extraordinarily little known about how African students experience school because most of the research on immigrant education has disproportionately focused on certain immigrant groups namely Asian, Latino, and West Indian immigrant communities (Okwako, 2011).

The Ultimate Response

In response, this chapter aims to illuminate the voices of African English learners as this population remains understudied, and invisible in terms of literature (Allen et al., 2012). Drawing on a phenomenological study on six African high school students, this chapter presents findings on how four of the six African ELLs navigated the U.S. education system in relation to their teachers and the curriculum.

TRANSITIONING TO US PUBLIC SCHOOLS

The Role of Schools

Schools are known as spaces where students become initially socialized into their new US.culture (Olsen, 1997). As Nygreen (2013) points out, "the school is not just a place where students learn academic curriculum and skills, it is also a place where they develop a sense of what kind of people they are, where they belong in the world . . ." (p. 9). For African English learners entering US public schools, the transition into US public high school is a two-fold process; social and academic. The school, therefore, plays an important function in how students adjust to their unfamiliar environment. The transition is not easy as they are grappling with various migration pressures as well cultural and linguistic barriers that can lead to challenges in mastering the school curriculum content and requirements (Tilleczek, 2008). Mastering the curriculum is not always easy as students are not always represented in the content.

The Eurocentric Curriculum

Public schools are unable to provide African immigrant students with culturally appropriate teaching methods, curriculum and materials despite significant data confirming that these cultural accommodations make a significant difference in the lives and education experiences of young African immigrants (Traore & Lukens, 2006). Despite the significant increase of

African-born immigrants in the United States of America, their presence remains invisible in the education system, and little has been done to facilitate their integration via the implementation of necessary curricular adjustments (Harushimana & Awokoya, 2011). Teachers do not understand the unique needs and learning styles of children of African descent. Consequently, they have low expectations of them and fail to connect schooling to their cultural experiences (Traore & Lukens, 2006).

Misrepresentation and Lack of Reference

The current US school curriculum is focused on the European perspective and places emphasis on their history and culture (Lea & Sims, 2008). Upon examination of the curriculum, Harushimana and Awokoya (2011), found that the Eurocentric curriculum model alienated African students. Furthermore, the misrepresentation or lack of reference to African cultures in the curriculum is in direct opposition to culturally responsive pedagogy. The African perspective in the multicultural education debate is critical in ensuring the representation of African immigrant students in the US educational system (Harushimana & Awokoya, 2011).

One of the biggest challenges in integrating African culture into the curriculum is a lack of knowledge and expertise on the part of pre-service teachers (Akoma, 2007). Pre-service teachers are not equipped with the necessary skills, expertise, or knowledge to work with students of African backgrounds. There is a need for teachers to be culturally competent (Akoma, 2007) to effectively instruct African students.

NEWCOMER AFRICAN HIGH SCHOOL STUDENTS

Participant Selection

This chapter will revisit conversations [with four of the six African high school students] that emerged during a one-year phenomenological study. Participants in the study were selected using a homogeneous purposive sample technique, from the population of African high school students attending US public schools in Western Pioneer Valley, on the east coast of the United States. This was a homogeneous population regarding ethnicity and migration background. The selection criteria required participants to have arrived in the U.S. at least 5 years prior to the study. Participants included students, grades 9 to 12, ages 14 to 18. The specific sample consisted of six African students: five females and one male student. The countries represented in the sample

included Kenya, Nigeria, Malawi, and Guinea. This chapter will focus specifically on the experiences of Nylidi, Eleena, Aisha, and Kayride.

FINDINGS

Two Major Findings

In what follows, I detail two major findings of the study. The first finding
details the role of the teacher in the transitional processes of the newly arrived
African ELL students. The second finding focuses on the student experiences
of navigating the new curriculum. The first finding revealed that, overall,
participants reported finding their teachers supportive. Regarding the curriculum, participants generally felt ignored and excluded from the curriculum.

MEETING THE TEACHERS

Fatou's Experience

During the early days in the U.S., participants overall, found their new teachers to be helpful. At age 14, Fatou a female student from Guinea, was excited
to finally reunite with her family after a 12-year separation. For Fatou, coming to America was not only about reuniting with her family, but it was also
about something that she had dreamed of for so many years: Fatou was looking forward to enjoying the new educational opportunities that lay ahead. She
described her anticipation: "I was excited that I am finally getting to go to
school, and I hear that there was a great education in the U.S. So, I was like,
'I am gonna get a good education and I am gonna go to college' . . . 'cause I
wanted to go to college . . . my dream was finally coming true."

For many immigrants coming to the U.S., education is the key to future
security and a good life. There have been many narratives about immigrants
and the American Dream (Moore, 2013). Fatou saw her education in the U.S.
as a passport to her American Dream—a rare chance to take advantage of
the educational opportunities in the U.S. Her new school was an urban high
school in a big metropolitan city in the northeast of the U.S. The size of the
school and the diversity overwhelmed her. In addition, she did not have the
best first impression of her new school: "The school was very big. There were
a lot of Africans, African Americans, and Latinos. There were not very many
Whites. The school had a bad reputation, and some groups were violent. I was
scared that someone is just gonna fight me . . ."

Fatou felt unsafe and feared that someone [one of the students] would bully
her or harm her by starting a fight. This fear did not help in her transition

process. At the height of her helplessness, things turned around for Fatou when one of the teachers reached out to her. He had noticed that Fatou was new to the school and decided to speak to her. Fatou narrated this initial interaction: "He said in French, 'Je suis votre ami. 'Est-ce que vous parlez anglais?' [I am your friend. Do you speak English?] I said, 'yes,' so I was just like, 'Oookay.' So, he took me to his office, and he was like, 'How are you? How are things going? If you need help let me know.'"

Fatou later narrated how the teacher looked out for her the days that followed. He would ensure that Fatou was in the right class and saw to it that she was participating. He was helpful with her homework as Fatou narrated: "If I had writing homework, he would call me in his office and he would make sure that I sit in his office and work on my writing. He was very kind . . . if they had a field trip, he made sure that I was participating, so he was kind. . . . That was my best time in high school."

The above narrative illustrates the transitional challenges that Fatou encountered during her earlier days, but most importantly, the role that teachers can play in aiding newcomer students to navigate their new environment.

Aisha, Eleena, and Kayride's Experience

Like Fatou, other participants also stated they had teachers who had helped them in their earlier days. When asked how she found her new teachers, Aisha stated:

> I found the teachers pretty helpful. I mean, like a lot of times they would say, "Oh you can stay after school" and also in terms of . . . in general, I think they also wanted to talk to you 'cause it was like, after every assignment I would get back, there would be like some form of comment about, "Oh, you should see me, so I can explain" . . . so I think that they wanted to have every student interact with them, which I wasn't necessarily used to.

Another participant, Eleena, reported that there were on one hand, teachers that were supportive, but on the other hand there were also teachers that showed little or no support. When asked about her perspective towards the teachers, Eleena stated: "They were approachable. I think it varied from teacher to teacher because I did prefer some teachers to others. And there were some teachers that I just did not have a good time with, sitting in their classes. So . . . yeah."

The above narrative illustrates the challenges that the participants endured. While participants in general found their new teachers to be accessible, there were instances when the participants did not feel comfortable with certain teachers. Overall, participants found the teachers to be helpful, especially in those critical earlier days. Kayride a female student from Nigeria recalls the assistance she received from her teacher during her first day of school:

> I remember like, my first class . . . and I remember leaving the class thinking, "this is going to be challenging. I am gonna have to step up." But after that, I just let the teacher know and then . . . after that things just like, kinda like flowed smoothly because the teacher was always there. It wasn't like . . . in terms of transitioning academically it wasn't difficult. Yah . . .

Navigating a new environment was challenging as is evident from the above narratives. Teachers, overall, played a critical role in helping the newcomer students make sense of their new setting. As soon as Kayride received the necessary assistance from her teacher, she found the transition to be less stressful.

NAVIGATING THE CURRICULUM

The second finding revealed that participants, overall, felt excluded from the curriculum—that there was little focus on curriculum that spoke to their personal backgrounds. Nylidi, a 16-year-old female student from Malawi had learned in her world civilization class that they would be studying different regions of the world including Africa. She was extremely excited at the opportunity to finally share a little about her beloved continent. Unfortunately, students had little time to complete the project as Nylidi recalls: "It was a short class, and it was really compressed up . . . it was all squished into the last week and a half of school and I remember thinking that it's not enough time because we spent four weeks on Greece and Rome. I remember being frustrated. But we had a whole project to complete in only a short time. It was not fair."

Other participants also echoed similar sentiments about feeling lost and excluded from the curriculum. During the first day at her new school, Kayride narrated how she was introduced to a topic she knew nothing about:

> I remember like, my first class . . . I think my first class was U.S. history. And the teacher had us label all the 50 states like in America. That was like the first day of class, first assignment. And I was like, "I don't even know where Massachusetts, is on this map" 'cause, I just didn't know anything and I . . . um (laughs) and I remember leaving the class thinking, this is going to be challenging. I am gonna have to step up.

A Curriculum of Inclusiveness

While in general, participants reported feeling excluded from the curriculum, there were however, a few teachers that made the effort to integrate aspects of the African experience into their students' work. Eleena's experience in her art class was quite different from other participants. Her art teacher was very particular about ensuring that Eleena includes her cultural background in her artwork. Eleena felt that her teacher recognized and acknowledged her heritage, and she was excited about that, as she narrated:

> My Art teacher, he was American. He was a man, bald head, really funny, super sweet, very talented. Yeah. Yes, I really liked Art in 9th and 10th grade. My 10th grade Art teacher, really . . . He really liked Africa . . . He was a sculptor. So, he really liked African art and Nigerian art and patterns and . . . yeah, he did show some interest in my culture . . . and he would ask me to incorporate that into my art and I would be like, "Oh, that's great." I was always there after school to get assistance. We had painting projects and he'd be like "use these patterns, think of the patterns from back home." It was nice.

The encouragement that the art teacher provided, resulted in the sharing, and exchanging of cultural experiences. As a new student from Africa, Eleena was excited to have a teacher who expressed interest in her culture and consequently, a mutual friendship based on cultural interest was born. Eleena's experience, however, was more of the exception.

Kayride's Experience

Unlike Eleena who had an enjoyable learning experience with her art teacher, other participants like Kayride reported that they did not feel that teachers were particularly interested in their background history, and that the curriculum did not consider their lived experiences:

> African history, if taught at all, was confined to some diluted cultural event during Black History month. My cultural heritage was never included as part of any curriculum. The closest we got to having our cultural backgrounds acknowledged and integrated into the classroom was during annual cultural events which I could term as "just a formality": No, I don't think that there was any teacher that necessarily wanted to know about my background. Um, we like had an international students' club where like they would be like, "Oh, share your cultural history" but I think it was just one of those things where it was like, "we have this more of a formality."

CONCLUSION

This chapter explored the experiences of African English learners in US public schools—illuminating their voices and learning via their personal narratives the challenges they encountered in navigating the US education system, vis-à-vis their teachers and the curriculum. Additionally, the chapter highlighted the student narratives as well as the tremendous role that teachers play in students' transitional processes. It is important that teachers pay attention to these student narratives. These narratives have implications for both teacher education programs, as well as basic classroom practices.

As the US classroom becomes diverse, teacher education programs such as the one I am a part of, are confronted with an urgent need to train teachers on best practices in working with the increasingly diverse student population in US schools today. African students coming to the U.S. have contributed to that diversity. It is worth noting that while the student body grows increasingly diverse, the demographic of the teacher workforce remains white. This disparity in diversity has resulted in grave challenges for the US education system. Teachers and students come from two vastly distinct cultural and socioeconomic backgrounds. As a result, the US education system is faced with broader issues of policy and preparing teachers to work with a more diverse population. These challenges call for the re-examination of teacher education programs as well as the re-evaluation of pedagogical practices in the classroom. At a macro level, there is a pressing need for teachers to be trained to understand the background histories and experiences of the students they serve, and to implement a more inclusive curriculum.

REFERENCES

Akoma, E. (2008). *African centered curriculum and teacher efficacy: Contributors to African American student achievement.* [Thesis]. Georgia State University. https://scholarworks.gsu.edu/epse_theses/1

Allen, K. M., Jackson. I., & Knight, M. G. (2012). Complicating culturally relevant pedagogy: Unpacking west African immigrants' cultural identities. *International Journal of Multicultural Education, 14*(2), 1–28.

Arthur, J. (2010). *African Diaspora identities: Negotiating culture in transmigration.* Lexington Books.

Harushimana, I., & Awokoya, J. (2011). African-born immigrants in U.S. schools: An intercultural perspective on schooling and diversity. *Journal of Praxis in Multicultural Education, 6*(1), 6.

Kent, M. M. (2007). *Immigration and America's Black population.* Population Reference Bureau.

Lea, V., & Sims, J. (2008) *Undoing Whiteness in the classroom: Critical Educultural Teaching approaches for social justice activism.* Peter Lang Publishing.

Nygreen, K. (2013). *These kids: Identity, agency, and social justice at a last chance high school.* University of Chicago Press.

Okwako, B. A. (2011). *Engendering subjectivities: Narratives of African immigrant girls in public high schools* [Dissertation]. University of Michigan. ˙

Olsen, L. (1997). *Made in America: Immigrant students in our public schools.* New Press.

Traoré, R., & Lukens, R. J. (2006). *This isn't the America I thought I'd find: African students in the urban U.S. high school.* University Press of America.

Tilleczek, K. C. (2008). *Why do students drop out of high school? Narrative studies and social critiques.* E. Mellen Press.

U.S. Census Bureau. (2014, October 1). African-born population in U.S. roughly doubled every decade since 1970, Census Bureau reports. United States Census Bureau. http://www.census.gov/newsroom/press-releases/2014/cb14-184.html

Chapter 6

Looking at the Past to
See the Future

Montana's Underserved Native
American English Language Learners

Jioanna Carjuzaa and Holly Hunts

The number of English Language Learners (ELLs) in classrooms across the United States surged 28.1% between 2000–2001 and 2016–2017 and reached an all-time high of 10.1% in the fall of 2017 (Mitchell, 2020). It is estimated that by 2025 one out of every four students in the nation's K–12 public school classrooms will be an ELL (National Education Association [NEA], 2020). During the same time frame we have witnessed an increase in the number of ELLs, the pressure placed on district, state, and national accountability has been compounded by the heightened focus on high stakes standardized test scores as indices of academic achievement (National Center for Education Statistics [NCES], 2018). Yet, the Native American ELL student population in Montana remains underidentified and inadequately served (Carjuzaa & Ruff, 2016; Education Commission of the States, 2013; Stockwell & McCracken, 2018).

All students deserve access to an education that challenges, inspires, and prepares them for life's demands, and a future career or higher education (U.S. Department of Justice & U.S. Department of Education, n.d.). Unfortunately, according *to The Condition of Education 2020* report by the National Center for Education Statistics (NCES), Native students in the nation's K–12 schools continue to struggle as evidenced by reading and math scores which remain two to three grade levels lower than those of White students, high dropout rates, and low college enrollments (NCES, 2020). Nonetheless, in Montana, we are focused on closing this longstanding achievement trend between Native and non-Native students by looking at the language practices and education policies of the past and critically assessing the present instructional shortcomings to implement systemic changes to improve learning outcomes for American Indian/Alaska Native (AI/AN) students (Brayboy & Lomawaima, 2018; Montana Office of Public Instruction [OPI], 2018; Northwest Regional Education Laboratory; 2020).

In this chapter we share a definition of social justice in education, describe our context and our efforts to promote culturally responsive pedagogy, recount Indigenous language suppression and loss, share how Indigenous people qualify as ELLs, and discuss the barriers to identifying and supporting these students. Most importantly, we highlight how by participating in restorative acts of social justice to right the wrongs of the past, we can provide American Indian ELLs with the opportunity to gain experience in their heritage languages in tandem with improving their academic literacy skills in English.

SOCIAL JUSTICE IN EDUCATION

During the COVID-19 global pandemic health and economic crises and the Black Lives Matter political and social movement, social justice work has been embraced as a core value to create change. There is a plethora of social justice definitions. The comprehensive definition laid out by Nieto (2006) and Nieto and Bode (2007) describes social justice in education as both a political and democratic project, political because it entails power and privilege and democratic because it is about promoting inclusiveness and equity. Nieto (2006) defines social justice ". . . as both a philosophy and actions that embody treating all people with fairness, respect, dignity, and generosity" (p. 2).

Nieto and Bode's (2007) theory of social justice includes four components. First, it addresses and ends the myths, misconceptions, and stereotypes that result in systemic inequality and discrimination based on cultural differences. Secondly, they point out how important it is to assure all students have the necessary material resources (books, curricula, money) as well as emotional resources (positive connections, conflict resolution, high expectations) to meet their needs and prepare them for the future.

A third component of a social justice perspective asks educators to refute the deficit perspective and help students uncover their unique gifts and talents including those associated with their languages, cultural heritages, and life experiences. A fourth essential component according to Nieto and Bode (2007) focuses on creating a learning environment that promotes critical thinking skills and supports student efforts to engage in social change in preparation to play an active role in civic engagement.

In Montana we have adopted a statewide improvement plan to address the four social justice components outlined here by mandating Indian Education for All (IEFA), supporting Indigenous language revitalization efforts, and embracing culturally responsive pedagogy to address components one and two. To tackle components three and four, we need to accurately identify AI/AN ELLs and provide them with the necessary literacy instruction to be academically successful. Since tension and distrust have qualified the relationship members of American Indian tribes have experienced in their dealings with the US government and this misgiving has carried over to the education of Native students, we have looked at the past educational practices to envision a more promising future (Jaime & Rush; 2012; Lomawaima & McCarty, 2006; McCarty & Lee, 2014; Reyhner & Hurtado, 2008).

OUR CONTEXT

Montana is a sparsely populated state in the Western U.S. whose total number of inhabitants only surpassed the million mark in 2012 (Montana Census and Economic Information Center [MCEIC], 2021). Today, 12 tribal groups constituting 8 sovereign nations call Montana home: Assiniboine, Blackfeet, Chippewa, Cree, Crow, Gros Ventre, Kootenai, Little Shell, Northern Cheyenne, Pend d'Oreille, Salish, and Sioux. According to the 2020 Census, Native Americans make up approximately 8% of the state's population (U.S. Census, 2020) and during the 2017–2018 academic year, 14% of the K–12 students in Montana identified as AI/AN, which is more than 10 times the national average (OPI, 2018). Many of Montana's AI/AN are ELLs, but unfortunately, they remain underidentified. (Carjuzaa & Ruff, 2016).

Of the 826 public schools which comprise the 403 school districts in Montana, two-thirds, are small rural districts with fewer than one hundred students (OPI, 2020). According to the *Condition of Education 2020* report, approximately 95% of AI/AN students across the country are enrolled in public schools attended by other AI/AN students, as is the case in Montana where 44.6% of Native students attend schools physically located on a reservation (NCES, 2020; OPI, 2020).

MONTANA'S AMERICAN INDIAN ELLS

According to the Office of English Language Acquisition (OELA), Montana has the highest percentage of ELLs who are AI/AN (OELA, 2015). The smaller group of AI/AN ELLs whose first language is an Indigenous language and who are learning English as a second language are easier to identify as ELLs than AI/AN students who do not speak a heritage language but have not acquired the foundation in academic English literacy to thrive academically. These students whose inadequate academic English proficiency affects their opportunity to compete with their never-EL peers and obtain content mastery do not necessarily speak their tribal language, but they grow up in households and communities where Standard English is replaced as the daily mode of communication with an Indigenous language of impact (Carjuzaa & Ruff, 2016). This unique group of ELLs has their English acquisition framed by parents, grandparents or guardians who were products of the Native American boarding schools, are ELLs who did not acquire Standard English themselves, and currently speak and model a nonstandard or nonacademically proficient variety of English (Carjuzaa & Ruff, 2016; Hollbrook, 2011).

Despite both federal and state law specifically stating that children who are "Native American or Alaska Native, or a native resident of the outlying areas and who comes from an environment where a language other than English has had a significant impact on the individual's level of English language proficiency" (Education Commission of the States, 2013) are eligible to be identified as ELLs, we have found that Montana teachers hold stereotypical images of ELLs that do not include AI/AN students. "But we don't have any Mexican or Somali students here . . . no, Native students can't be ELLs. They speak English," are common retorts when educators are asked about their ELL student population (Personal communication with a state level administrator, November 17, 2015).

The number of ELLs has steadily increased over time in Montana, yet the reported number of American Indian ELLs has decreased according to the OPI. In 2014, the OPI reported that AI/AN students made-up 75.9% of all the 3,443 Montana ELLs in alignment with what the OELA reported for Montana (OPI, 2014). In contrast, in 2015 OPI reported a decline in the overall number of ELLs even though the National Education Association reported that Montana is one of just three states that experienced a more than 50 percent increase in ELL student enrollment over the past ten years (ESLteacherEDU.org, 2021). Then, two years later, the OPI reported that the AI/AN ELL percentage dropped to 69% even though that meant they still make up most ELLs in Montana, this reduction seemed suspect. In 2021, the OPI reported that the number of American Indian ELLs plummeted to just 56% of the 3,711 Montana ELLs (OPI, 2020).

While on the surface this may appear to show either a decrease in the number of AI/AN students and/or substantial improvements in AI/AN English proficiency, neither conclusion is accurate. From 2014 to 2019, the number of Indigenous children ages 5 to 18 increased by 1,806 students (19,703 to

21,509) which makes up 50% of the total growth of 3,775 children state-wide across the same period (MCEIC, 2021). Educators across the state are concerned that this reported decline does not accurately reflect the number of ELLs, but points to the challenges in identifying American Indian ELLs (Personal communication with school district Title III administrator, June 22, 2021).

STUDENT ACHIEVEMENT DATA

Sadly, the past decade has not seen an improvement in AI/AN student performance. When analyzing a series of Montana American Indian Student Achievement Data Reports from 2010–2020 a persistent gap in achievement between AI/AN students and their White counterparts has been reported (OPI, 2018). The state Criterion Referenced Test (CRT) results from 2006 to 2010 indicate that on average the percentage of White students with reading scores in the *proficient and advanced range* was 84% compared to 54% for AI/AN students (OPI, 2010). Since the creation of the National Education Assessment Program (NAEP) in 1994, the reading and math scores for fourth and eighth grade AI/AN students has been reported as the lowest in the nation, compared with students of other races/ethnicities. Unfortunately, Montana's data from 2006 to 2012 showed AI/AN students in 4th and 8th grades scored below the alarmingly low national average for AI/AN students in both math and reading (OPI, 2018). In 2015, with the passage of the Every Student Succeeds Act (ESSA, 2015), Montana changed from CRT tests to "Smarter Balanced" tests. From 2015 to 2020 there is a consistent 30% point difference in the percentage of children achieving *proficiency or better* in reading averaging 23.3% of AI/AN students compared to 55.2% of their White counterparts reaching that level.

INDIAN BOARDING SCHOOLS

In a state with a large AI/AN student population it is important that educators learn about the miseducation of these students since the intergenerational trauma experienced by countless Indigenous people today can be directly traced back to the Indian Boarding Schools which operated from 1860 to 1978 in the U.S. (Hopkins, 2020; McCarty & Lee, 2014). Students had their hair cut short; they were given English names; they were denied their spiritual practices; and they were forbidden to speak their languages. In these schools, students often suffered a myriad of physical, verbal, emotional, sexual, psychological, and cultural/identity abuse. These institutions were schools, but the students spent only three hours per day on rudimentary academics including reading, writing, and speaking in the English language and basic math. Although required to speak English, the students did not have access to an adequate model of academic standard English since their education consisted of introductory language lessons which focused on nothing higher than third grade irreducible reading skills (Crawley, 2020).

LANGUAGE OPPRESSION AND LOSS

There are accounts of various forms of humiliation and abuse Native students suffered for speaking their languages at the Indian boarding schools (NIEA, 2016). Interview excerpts from the 2008 compelling documentary by Rich-Heape Films, *Our Spirits Don't Speak English: Indian Boarding School*, highlight the stories of survivors whose native tongues were "metaphorically ripped out of their mouths" (Mahmood, 2014). Andrew Windy Boy, a Chippewa Cree elder, describes the indignity and punishment he endured for speaking his native language while attending two different boarding schools, Wahpeton in North Dakota, and Flandreau in South Dakota, during the late 1960s and early 1970s, in a heart-wrenching account of the soulful pain these experiences have left him with.

> They took me to the boarding school where I wasn't allowed to talk my native tongue or practice my native ways . . . numerous times they put on this big white cone; it says dunce . . . I didn't know what it meant. I didn't know English. . . . They put it on me, make me wear it all over. The kids would laugh at me . . . They punished me for talking what was my first language. I didn't know any other language. . . . When I talked . . . Cree would come out . . . whenever I talked, I'd get hit. . . . I got hit so much. I lost my tongue. I lost my native tongue. . . . The only one thing I remember is my Indian name. Se New Kihew means Old Man Eagle. The only Cree I know. They beat me; every day they beat me. . . . Someday somebody will hear me. I hope nobody has to go through this. We have to have our own language. Because what will we do when we talk to our spirits; . . . they don't understand English. (Rich-Heape Films, 2008)

Aaniiih elder, Na Gya Tha (Dr. Lenore A. Stiffarm) shares her story as a second-generation boarding school survivor and describes how the language was beaten out of her relatives. The contemptuous irony of this traumatic loss is captured in her description of her father's experience,

> My late father, *Ah Hock Nak* (The Rock), told me that he did not want me to learn the language because as a child the language was beaten out of him. He said, the white man is *Hok Ats* (crazy). When I was taken to the St. Paul's

Mission School in Hays, MT the language was beat out of me by the Catholic nuns—beating my fingers each time I spoke the language. I had no other way to talk with my younger brothers and sister who were crying. I tried to comfort them in the only language that I knew. . . . My brothers and sister were still crying so I tried to speak with them through sign language. The Catholic nuns beat me again. . . . Then, my late father would hold his hands up where his fingers were deformed because the Catholic nuns beat the language out of him. . . . He then stated, today, the crazy white man wants to pay me $100.00 to go into the schools to teach my grandchildren how to speak our language. The tobacco is still here on the table. I am not sure whether I should teach our language. What if the white man gets crazy again and beats the language out of my grandchildren? (Stiffarm & Stiffarm, 2017)

These compelling accounts detail the atrocities committed and point to the need for educational practices to support the healing of boarding school survivors and their descendants. At the end of the 15th century, more than 400 unique Indigenous languages were spoken. Today, only 250 are still in existence, and most are critically endangered including the 11 Indigenous languages spoken by Montana Natives (Carjuzaa, 2017; Littlebear, 2017). The effects of this unfortunate paradox, the stripping away of their Mother-Tongues which were replaced with substandard English, continues to plague students, their families, and their communities throughout Native American country today (August, Goldenberg, & Rueda, 2006; Best & Dunlap, 2012; McCarty, 2014; Oesch, 1996; Stockwell & McCracken, 2018).

Consequently, many Native American youth speak a nonstandard variety of English (Holbrook, 2011; Leap, 1993). Leap (1993) presents a convincing case for the fundamental influence of ancestral AI/AN languages and cultures on spoken and written expression on contemporary Indian English codes. In *American Indian English*, he documents the diversity of English in American Indian speech communities. According to Leap, two-thirds of today's Indigenous youth learn Indian English as their first language; however, in cases when a speaker is not fluent in his/her ancestral language, he/she is influenced by the grammar rules and discourse associated with ancestral language traditions. Speaking Indian English can impact educational success and employment opportunities (Leap, 1993).

INDIAN EDUCATION FOR ALL

To address the ramifications of this attempt at cultural genocide, the Montana State Constitution in 1972 was amended to include the unprecedented IEFA legislation to address the historical and contemporary oppressions of Indigenous peoples by transforming educational policy, curriculum, and pedagogy (Carjuzaa, Jetty, Munson, & Veltkamp, 2010; Juneau, 2006; Mont. Code. Ann.). In standard K–12 public school curricula in the U.S., Natives are often inaccurately portrayed, and their contributions are inadequately represented so the OPI created numerous resources and provided professional development to ensure cultural enrichment, academic engagement, and equitable pedagogy for all students. The praises of IEFA have reverberated around the globe. In fact, IEFA has served as a model for educators dedicated to embracing ideals of social justice and educational equity (Carjuzaa et al., 2010).

Since the integration of IEFA across the curriculum at all grade levels P-20, we have amassed anecdotal evidence that AI/AN students are building self-esteem and cultivating cultural pride, but scores on standardized tests used to meet the requirements of the ESSA report that many AI/AN ELLs remain in the novice category in reading and are in jeopardy of not reaching proficiency in challenging state academic achievement standards. American Indian ELLs need to have comprehensible input with scaffolding and support to broaden their vocabulary and improve their academic English skills.

US FEDERAL NATIVE AMERICAN LANGUAGE POLICY

In 1990, Congress passed the Native American Languages Act (NALA), which recognizes the unique status of AI/AN languages and cultures and is seen as the first federal policy protecting the usage of Indigenous languages as the medium of instruction. According to NALA, it is US federal policy to "preserve, protect, and promote the rights and freedom of Native Americans to use, practice, and develop Native American languages" (Native American Languages Act of 1990 [NALA], 25 U.S.C. 2903). The authors of NALA highlight the significant role instruction in native languages plays in language preservation and community pride, but also point out how it contributes to improved educational opportunity and increased student achievement. Providing AI/AN students with instruction in their heritage languages is critical since culture and language are so inextricably intertwined (Littlebear, 2014). In fact, research has shown that culturally based education, including the use of native languages, can have significant positive effects for students, including improved retention, graduation rates, college attendance rates, and standardized test scores (Demmert & Towner, 2003). Still, it has not been enough to improve reading comprehension and narrow the achievement gap.

ELL LABELING, BICS AND CALP

Since there have been concerted efforts to wipe out Indigenous peoples' languages, cultures, and identities and many AI/AN ELLs today are not speakers of their heritage languages, ELL labeling must be broached with comprehensive sensitivity and limitless humility. To suggest that the English AI/AN students speak is somehow deficient is offensive. It is also "crazy making" to boarding school survivors to suggest preserving Indigenous languages and mastering academic English are not at odds. Suggesting that AI/AN students low reading scores have dire consequences for academic and future success is often met with skepticism, misinterpretation, and resistance. Therefore, we need to look at re-messaging our "labeling" strategy. Reframing the discussion to point out how AI/AN students would benefit from literacy instruction so they can master school English while becoming bilingual/multilingual and biliterate/multiliterate in their heritage languages may be met with greater acceptance and assure parents, students, teachers, and other stakeholders that our quest to improve the academic English literacy skills of AI/AN ELLs is not at the expense of our Indigenous language revitalization efforts.

In 1979 Cummins (2008) coined the terms BICS and CALP, acronyms for "Basic Interpersonal Communication Skills" and "Cognitive Academic Language Proficiency," respectively, to distinguish between the informal, day-to-day social language which usually takes children two years to develop fluency in the target language and the formal, academic language essential for school success which takes between 5 to 7 years for a child to acquire the language to be working at the same level with never-EL peers. Most Native students do speak English as their first language, but as pointed out, they speak an Indian English dialect (Leap, 1993). So, although their BICS may disguise their inadequate foundation in academic English, teachers need to be aware that their CALP may not be fully developed.

LITERACY INSTRUCTION: LEANING TO READ, READING TO LEARN

Developing CALP and being able to read well and comprehend what one is expected to learn is the most demanding academic challenge. Most educators are familiar with the concept of "learning to read" which shifts to "reading to learn" before entering fourth grade. It is important for students to build literacy skills because the research clearly states that if students are not reading proficiently at grade level by the end of third grade, they are going to struggle, to not catch up with their peers, and possibly drop out before graduating (Center for Public Education, 2015; Zehr, 2010).

Teaching reading in kindergarten through third grade usually focuses on the decoding and memorizing of basic words using phonemic awareness and phonics. Students are expected to reach "fluency" by the fourth grade, when they are expected to "read to learn" and use skills to gather information, expand their comprehension in curricular subjects, solve problems and think critically, as well as share their newly acquired knowledge all while tackling increasingly difficult texts.

SUPPORTING AMERICAN INDIAN ELLS

Helping students build literacy skills is the job of all educators. Afterall, no matter what subject or grade level we teach, we are all language teachers. Unfortunately, educators fail to recognize, or appreciate, that reading comprehension is also a function of background knowledge, vocabulary development and life experience. This is a critical issue which must be addressed since low achievement in reading results in school failure as well as long term personal, economic, and societal consequences.

Under both state and federal law, school districts are responsible to identify and provide services for students who are eligible for language assistance. It is necessary to prepare all teachers to integrate content and language objectives so ELLs can achieve academically while simultaneously improving their English literacy. This has proven difficult since, the OPI does not endorse an English as-a-second language (ESL) certificate and related coursework offerings is limited. In 2016 of the 10,560 K–12 Montana teachers, only 52 of them had earned an ESL endorsement (OPI, 2019). Consequently, we are making concerted efforts to support K–12 teachers' professional development in this area.

CONCLUSION

In Montana, there needs to be development and enhancement of a capacity to identify AI/AN ELLs and provide effective instruction and support to these students by acknowledging the damage that has been done through language oppression and discouraging the educational system from causing further harm. It is important to support the teaching and learning of Indigenous languages, the implementation of IEFA, and the integration of culturally responsive pedagogy while also increasing the English language proficiency of students. This is necessary if educators want to assure AI/AN students meet the same standards that all children in Montana's classrooms are expected to meet, including scoring *proficient or above* on the state reading assessments and attaining proficiency in the State approved content area assessments.

REFERENCES

August, D., Goldenberg, C., & Rueda, R. (2006). Native American children and youth: Culture, language, and literacy. *The Journal of American Indian Education, 45*(1), 24–37.

Best, J., & Dunlap, A. (2012). Native-language education: Addressing the interests of special populations within U.S. federal policy. Mid-continent research for education and learning.

Brayboy, B. M. J., & Lomawaima, K. T. (2018). Why don't more Indians do better in school? The battle between U.S. schooling & American Indian/Alaska Native education. *Daedalus, 147*(2), 82–94.

Carjuzaa, J., Jetty, M., Munson, M., & Veltkamp, T. (2010). Montana's Indian education for all: Applying multicultural education theory. *Multicultural Perspectives, 12*(4), 192–198. https://doi.org/10.1080/15210960.2010.527585

Carjuzaa, J., & Ruff, W. G. (2016). American Indian English language learners: Misunderstood and under-served. *Cogent Education, 3*(1), 1–11. https://doi.org/10.1080/2331186X.2016.1229897

Crawley, C. K. (2020). *Native American bilingual education: An ethnography of powerful forces*. Emerald Publishing Limited.

Center for Public Education. (2015). *Learning to read, reading to learn: Why third grade is a pivotal year for mastering literacy.* [White paper]. https://www.nsba.org/-/media/NSBA/File/cpe-learning-to-read-reading-to-learn-white-paper-2015.pdf?la=en&hash=8E0E470C3E263C66E4491EC035224DC9018C6D5F

Cummins, J. (2008). BICS and CALP: Empirical and theoretical status of the distinction. In B. Street & N. H. Hornberger (Eds.), *Encyclopedia of language and education* (2nd ed., pp. 71–83). Springer Science, Business Media LLC.

Demmert, W. G., Jr., & Towner, J. C. (2003). A review of the research literature on the influence of culturally based education on the academic performance of Native American students. Northwest Regional Educational Laboratory. https://educationnorthwest.org/sites/default/files/cbe.pdf

Education Commission of the States & The Progress of Education Reform. (2013). *English language learners: A growing-yet, underserved-student population.* http://www.ecs.org/clearinghouse/01/10/20/11020.pdf

Every Student Succeeds Act (ESSA). (2015). *20 USC 6301.* http://www2.ed.gov/documents/essa-act-of-1965.pdf

Jaime, A., & Rush, R. T. (2012). Standing together: American Indian education as culturally responsive pedagogy. In B. J. Klug (Ed.), *A three-part strategy for ensuring culturally relevant pedagogy for American Indian children* (pp. 149–159). Rowman & Littlefield Publishers, Inc.

Richie, C. & Heape, S. R. (Directors). (2008). *Our spirits don't speak English: Indian boarding school.* Rich-Heape Films.

Holbrook, D. (2011, February 16). *Native American ELL students, Indian English and the Title III Formula Grant.* [Paper presentation]. National Association for Bilingual Education, 40th Annual Bilingual/Multicultural Education Conference, Native American and Alaska Native Pre-Conference Institute, New Orleans, LA, United States. https://ncela.ed.gov/files/uploads/7/Holbrook_NABE2011.pdf

Juneau, D. (2006). *Montana's agenda: Issues shaping our state, Indian education for all.* The University of Montana Press.

Leap, W. L. (1993). *American Indian English.* University of Utah Press.

Littlebear, R. E. (2014, July 18). *Montana takes the lead in Indian education.* Indianz.com. http://www.indianz.com/News/2014/014444.asp

Littlebear, R. E. (2017). A brief history of language and cultural specialists in the state of Montana: Class 7 testing. *Cogent Education.* https://www.tandfonline.com/doi/10.1080/2331186X.2017.1371820?utm_source=CPB&utm_medium=cms&utm_campaign=JQA18406

Lomawaima, K., & McCarty, T. L. (2006). *To remain an Indian: Lessons in democracy from a century of Native American education.* Teachers College Press.

Mahmood, O. (2014). Omar Mahmood: I am Urdu. *The Michigan Daily.* https://www.michigandaily.com/uncategorized/10omar-mahmood-i-am-urdu23/

McCarty, T. (2014). Negotiating sociolinguistic borderlands—Native youth language practices in space, time, and place. *Journal of Language, Identity, and Education, 13*(4), 254–267. https://doi.org/10.1080/15348458.2014.939031

McCarty, T., & Lee, T. (2014). Critical culturally sustaining/revitalizing pedagogy and indigenous education sovereignty. *Harvard Educational Review, 84*(1), 101–124.

Mitchell, C. (2020, February 18). *The nation's English-learner population has surged: 3 things to know.* Education Week. https://www.edweek.org/leadership/the-nations-english-learner-population-has-surged-3-things-to-know/2020/02

Mont. Code. Ann. ttl. 20, ch.1, pt. 5, § 1. Indian Education for All. 1999.

Montana Census and Economic Information Center. (2021). *County populations.* Montana Census and Economic Information Center. https://dataportal.mt.gov/t/DOC/views/MontanaCountyPopulation_Sep2018/PopulationTable?:origin=card_share_link&:isGuestRedirectFromVizportal=y&:embed=y

Montana Office of Public Instruction. (2021). *Montana home language survey updated winter 2021.* http://opi.mt.gov/Portals/182/Page%20Files/Statewide%20Testing/ELP%20Page/2020-2021/APPENDIX%20A_MONTANA%20HOME%20LANGUAGE%20SURVEY.pdf

Montana Office of Public Instruction. (2020). *2020–2021 English learner guidance for school districts.* http://opi.mt.gov/Portals/182/Page%20Files/English%20Language%20Learners/Docs/EnglishLearnerGuidanceForSchoolDistricts.pdf

Montana Office of Public Instruction. (2018). *Montana American Indian student achievement data report fall 2018.* Indian Education Division. https://opi.mt.gov/Portals/182/Page%20Files/Indian%20Education/Indian%20Student%20Achievement/Docs/Data_Report_2018.pdf?ver=2021-03-11-153704-403

Native American Languages Act (NALA), 25 U.S.C. 2903 (1990).

National Center for Education Statistics. (2020.) *Condition of education.* https://nces.ed.gov/programs/coe/

National Center for Education Statistics. (2018). *English language learner (ELL) students enrolled in public elementary and secondary schools, by state: Selected years, fall 2000 through fall 2016.* https://nces.ed.gov/programs/digest/d18/tables/dt18_204.20.asp

National Education Association (NEA) Education Policy and Practice Department. (2020). *English language learners.* National Education Association. https://www.nea.org/resource-library/english-language-learners

Nieto, S. (2006). *Teaching as political work: Learning from courageous and caring teachers.* Child Development Institute, Sarah Lawrence College. https://www.sarahlawrence.edu/media/cdi/pdf/Occasional%20Papers/CDI_Occasional_Paper_2006_Nieto.pdf

Nieto, S., & Bode, P. (2007). *Affirming diversity: The sociopolitical context of multicultural education* (5th rev. ed). Allyn & Bacon.

Northwest Regional Education Laboratory. (2020, June 8). *Strategies for improving the advocacy of Native student identification.* [Video]. YouTube. https://www.youtube.com/watch?v=QI4Hm0eSnTQ

Oesch, D. (1996, March 27–30). *Accommodating difference: Native American English education—Reexamining past assumptions and recognizing sociopolitical influences.* [Paper presentation]. Conference on College Composition and Communication, Milwaukee, WI, United States. https://files.eric.ed.gov/fulltext/ED402598.pdf

Office of English Language Acquisition. (2015). *Fast facts: Profiles of English learners (ELs).* http://www2.ed.gov/about/offices/list/oela/fast-facts/pel.pdf

Reyhner, J., & Hurtado. D.S. (2008). Reading first, literacy, and American Indian/Alaska Native students. *Journal of American Education, 7*(1), 82–95.

Stiffarm, L A., & Stiffarm, J. M. (Na Gya Tha [L. A. Stiffarm, EdD] & Thay Wus [J. M. Stiffarm]). (2017). AA AH NAK. *Cogent Education, 4*(1), 1–6. https://doi.org/10.1080/2331186X.2017.1390821

Stockwell, H., & McCracken, P. (2018). *Helping Montana's poorest performing students: English learners: Final report to the 66th Montana legislature.* Montana Legislature. https://leg.mt.gov/content/Publications/Services/2019-agency-reports/2018-State%20Tribal%20Relations-EnglishLearners.pdf

U.S. Department of Justice and U.S. Department of Education. (n.d.). *Ensuring English learner students can participate meaningfully and equally in educational programs.* http://opi.mt.gov/Portals/182/Page%20Files/English%20Language%20Learners/Docs/EnglishLearnerGuidanceForSchoolDistricts.pdf

Zehr, M. A. (2010, February 22). Study: Language is an issue with some Native American dropouts. Education Week. http://blogs.edweek.org/edweek/learning-the-language/2010/02/study_language_is_an_issue_wit.html?_ga=1.140820210.197222892.1454533460

Chapter 7

Multilingual English Language Learners

A Social Change Perspective

Tamara Collins-Parks, Katie Richards, and Amber Riehman

Participatory professional development helps teachers recognize and build on student assets. This process is illustrated in a two-year study of problem-solving professional development where teachers collaborated in the constructive use of data to support change. Concrete examples of asset-based practices included translanguaging and visual summaries within an iELD (integrated English Language Development) science classroom.

Linguistically diverse students come to school with a wealth of personal, linguistic, and cultural resources (Spycher, González-Howard, & August 2020). However, under the current schooling system in the United States, emergent bilingual students are less likely to meet college and career readiness standards and less likely to graduate from high school than their English only peers (Green & Ochoa, 2020; US Census, 2020). To change this outcome, schools need to change their approach. Collaborative professional development (Musanti & Pence, 2010; Shavard, 2021) and asset-driven instruction (Moll et al., 1992, 2005; Villalobos, 2020) offer solutions. However, there is little literature on this process from the perspective of multilingual/English learner coordinators leading transformative professional development. The following sections provide more background on this issue followed by a model of collaborative professional development and two promising practices, translanguaging and visual summaries. By examining the process as well as key examples of asset-driven instruction, coordinators, administrators, professional learning communities (PLCs), and teacher education professionals can engage in transformative collaborative practice to build on student assets and improve outcomes for emergent bilingual learners.

Note: The authors refer to EL or English learner students as *emergent bilinguals*, an asset-focused term promoted by Garcia, Kleifgen, and Falci (2008).

PROFESSIONAL DEVELOPMENT
FOR EQUITABLE ACCESS

Inequitable results for emergent bilingual students in the U.S. reflect numerous factors, from monolingual schooling that ignores children's roots and resources (Moll et al., 2005) to a patch-work system of school funding that reflects local inequities (EdBuild, 2019). Among other things, emergent bilingual students need more time to acquire English proficiency due to a lack of opportunity to develop literacy skills in their native language and, therefore, may take longer to graduate (Sugarman, 2019). Of these inequalities, it is monolingual schooling that can be most effectively addressed by individual schools and educators via transformative professional development.

The obligation to effectively implement equitable instruction to all learners has a solid foundation in US law (*Castaneda v. Pickard*, 648 F.2d 989, 5th Cir. 1981). To meet this obligation, stakeholders must work together to assess current program practices and identify areas that need special attention (California Department of Education, 2017). Asset-driven instruction and asset-driven professional development are key to this transformation. These approaches are driven by growth and based on "a culture where we acknowledge strengths and expect success" (Villalobos, 2020). Indeed, both Freire's (1970) problem-posing theory outlined in *Pedagogy of the Oppressed,* and the California English Learner Roadmap (California Department of Education, 2017) call on institutions to provide such asset-based instruction.

Educators, like students, need and want to be heard and valued, therefore, the professional development model presented here was designed to affirm the challenges educators face within integrated ELD (iELD) instruction as well as their preexisting knowledge of student supports. This two-year study, based on the implementation of the California English Learner (CA EL) Roadmap through professional development, was conducted at a high school in Southern California that had recently transitioned from tracking to an integrated model. According to the California Dashboard (https://www.caschooldashboard.org/), as of 2019, about half the students (42.5%) at this school site were classified as multilingual/English learners and the majority (94%) were socioeconomically disadvantaged.

Embedded in the transformative paradigm, this study was designed to record and analyze the ongoing implementation of CA EL Roadmap teacher training in hopes to build support for instructional strategies and transform institutional outcomes regarding emergent bilingual student development. As part of the process, the 75 instructors on site completed various surveys and participated in two years of professional development. During the process, instructors identified the challenges they faced with iELD (integrated ELD) instruction and worked to develop solutions to these challenges. This led to instructors sharing best practices. Two particularly promising strategies, visual summaries and translanguaging, are highlighted here.

USING DATA TO SUPPORT CHANGE

Surveys indicated that the staff prided itself in supporting emergent bilingual students but found the population challenging. When surveyed, 75.6% of educators at this site responded that they agreed or strongly agreed that their teaching and learning emphasized engagement, interaction, discourse, inquiry, and critical thinking with the same elevated expectations for emergent bilinguals as for other students. No staff members strongly disagreed with this statement. The majority (90.9%) of the participants at this site also believed that school is affirming, inclusive, and safe. However, most participants in the survey indicated perceived deficits in the students which prevented them, the teachers, from providing effective instruction. The challenges that staff expressed, illustrated in Figure 7.1, can be represented by four major categories: student-centered, teacher-centered, systematic barriers,

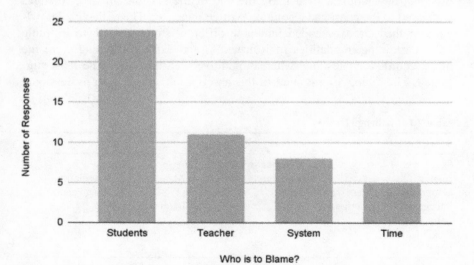

Fig. 7.1. Challenges: Who is to blame?

and time constraints. Despite these educators' high-quality teaching, or perhaps because they believe it to be so, this same group reported that most of the problems they were facing in an iELD environment were student-centered. Indeed, over half of the 41 staff responses indicated that their main challenges are embedded within students' identity, circumstance, and language rather than items with which they struggle.

These challenges were further coded into themes, recorded in Table 7.1. The chief themes that situated blame on students were apathy and skill level. Unfortunately, placing the blame on the student takes away any responsibility of the teacher and the educational system. In an equitable practice model, the teacher would assume the responsibility of filling in background knowledge, foundational skills, and relevant curriculum that engages students in a meaningful way. Once identified, moving the responsibility from the student to the teacher became part of the focus of the professional development. For example, apathy may be reframed as withdrawal due to lack of engagement in the material. Hammond (2015) states, "While on the outside, some teachers interpret this behavior as a lack of motivation and a cultural lack of investment in education. What looks like a lack of motivation is the student losing hope that anything can ever change because the academic hurdles seem insurmountable." This suggests that there needs to be more focus on what students can do and how educators can help rather than what students cannot do yet. Instead of confronting or blaming educators, the coordinator asked them to find solutions.

Identifying solutions proved to be the most powerful piece to this professional development model. By the end of the session, all 41 challenges expressed in the chart had a solution written by a peer. The collective knowledge of the staff was coded into nine different strategies shown in Table 7.2. Scaffolding, modalities of instruction, and explicit teaching were the most recorded suggestions whereas punitive measures were the least suggested. The dialogue promoted in this asset-based approach to professional

Table 7.1. Challenge Themes

Students	Teachers	System	Time
Skill Level	Differentiation	Class Size	Pacing
Apathy	Vocabulary	Reading Materials	Differentiation
Understanding Directions	Apathy	Placement	Grading/Feedback
Background Knowledge		Teacher Training	
Behavior			
Plagiarism			
Speaking in L1			

Note. Challenge themes are categorized by type. Each column is sequential from most to least identified challenges.

Table 7.2. Solution Themes

Most identified	Scaffolding	Modalities	Explicit
to	Student Metacognition	Teacher Collaboration	Formative Assessments
Least identified	PBIS	Differentiation	

development elicited teacher-centered promising practices compared to the student-centered focus recorded in their initial responses.

INCLUSION AND ASSET-BASED STRATEGIES

When asked to develop solutions, teachers didn't focus on what students should do (which is largely out of their control) but rather addressed things they could adjust in their own practice. These solutions are recorded in Table 7.2 "Solution Themes." Four of these strategies, modalities of instruction, student metacognition, teacher collaboration, and differentiation, lend themselves to the goal of being inclusive of students' diversity as well as being asset-based. "Modalities of instruction" is a particularly promising solution as it provides an opportunity to use students' languages and/or cultures to drive curriculum. This assets-based approach is supported by the California English Learner Roadmap and Culturally Responsive Teaching.

Principle 1 of the California English Learner Roadmap (CA EL Roadmap) affirms that students' cultural and linguistic backgrounds are assets that should be built upon. According to Freire's (1970) banking system theory, the traditional teacher "deposits" information into students who in turn become the "receptors." This process dehumanizes both the teacher and student by making them objects. It strips away both creativity and curiosity around learning. In *Culture and Power in the Classroom: Educational Foundations for the Schooling of Bicultural Students*, Darder (2012) adds, "Important to this discussion is the manner in which the dominant school culture functions to support the interests and values of the dominant society while marginalizing and invalidating knowledge forms and experiences that are significant to oppressed groups" (2012, p. 84). To combat this, the CA EL Roadmap suggests that schools should build inclusive and affirming environments (California Department of Education [CDE], 2017).

Principal one of the CA EL Roadmap focuses on assets oriented and needs responsive teaching and element 1A specifically mentions culturally responsive instruction (CDE, 2017). Gay (2010) notes that culturally responsive instruction, where educators use their knowledge of students' cultural backgrounds to guide their lesson plans, is a particularly promising asset-based strategy to meet the needs of emergent bilinguals. DeCapua and Marshall (2015) explain the importance of recognizing students' cultures when they write, "People develop different learning paradigms based on how they have learned to learn. These prior learning experiences have cognitive consequences in terms of how they view the world and understand teaching and learning" (p. 358). To address this concept, DeCapua and Marshall (2015) developed the Mutually Adaptive Learning Paradigm (MALP). This paradigm suggests that lessons written for emergent bilinguals must incorporate interconnectedness between the students, staff, and school, as well as cultural relevance for each lesson topic. Culturally relevant strategies that incorporate asset-based student skills are key to both avoiding the archaic educational banking system and encouraging educators to see students as resources rather than problems. Two particularly promising examples are translanguaging and visual summaries. These assign value to and allow emergent bilingual students to build both their home and target language proficiency.

TRANSLANGUAGING

In their book, *Translanguaging in the Classroom*, García et al. (2017) provide pedagogical processes and lesson planning templates to help teachers incorporate translanguaging into their curriculum. Their study synthesizes former findings that state that both cultural awareness and specific literacy strategies are beneficial to culturally and linguistically diverse students. Flores and Schissel (2014) note that,

> Translanguaging can be understood on two different levels. From a sociolinguistic perspective it describes the fluid language practices of bilingual communities. From a pedagogical perspective it describes a pedagogical approach whereby teachers build bridges from these language practices and the language practices desired in formal school settings. (p. 461–462)

Translanguaging can be used as a strategy wherein students work in homogeneous language groups to analyze information (including classwork as well as additional text or audio) to create multilingual projects. In doing so, students can leverage their biliteracy skills to synthesize information. Beyond the benefit of reaffirming the value of their home language, building skills in a first language creates a stronger and affirming foundation onto which students can apply skills and knowledge in a second language (Cummins, 1979).

For example, an instructor incorporating translanguaging into a unit might take the following steps:

1. Provide students with multilingual supplemental texts and recordings.
2. Place students in homogenous language groups.
3. Ask them to collaboratively create a summative report (infographic, poster, children's book, etc.) that has information in both English and their home language.
4. Encourage them to reflect on their language choices within the project.

Working on this in groups allows students to practice their speaking and writing skills in both languages as can be seen in Figure 7.2. Reflection encourages students to metacognitively consider how language is used for different purposes. Both benefits are in line with DeCapua and Marshall's (2015) MALP as well as the CA Roadmap and serve to celebrate student's assets and prior knowledge.

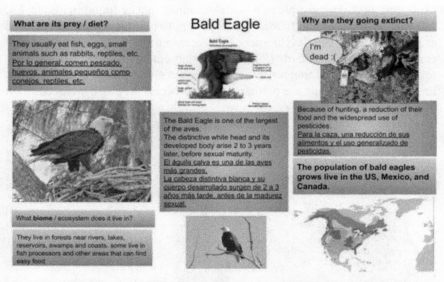

Fig. 7.2. Example of a translanguaging project. Image 1 adapted from *Bald Eagle* **by Los Padres Forest Watch, 2013 (https://lpfw.org/our-region/wildlife/bald-eagle/?hcb=1). Creative Commons Copyright 2013 by Bill Evans. Image 2 adapted from** *Eagle (Bald)* **by Exploring Nature, 2013–2021 (https://www.exploringnature.org/db/view/197). Copyright 2021 by Sheri Amsel. Reprinted with permission. Image 3 adapted from Flickr by U.S. Fish and Wildlife Service Southeast Region, 2013 (https://www.flickr.com /photos/usfwssoutheast/9077880472). Creative Commons Copyright 2013 by U.S. Fish and Wildlife Service.**

VISUAL SUMMARIES

The data collected during the study showed that teachers commented on how students cannot write summaries. This perception focuses on what teachers perceive students cannot do rather than responding to what students can do. Change in modalities, as suggested by peers during the problem-solution professional development offered an assets-based solution. Students may understand but not yet be able to represent their understanding in the target language. Visual summaries remove the linguistic barrier, allowing students to represent their understanding while weaving in their growing vocabulary in the target language.

There are two steps to visual summaries. Students begin by looking at a short block of text (one paragraph or less) where they identify key words and ideas within, translating as needed. Using those key words and important ideas, students then create a sketch that represents the meaning of the passage. In doing so, students practice identifying key information and summarizing the overall meaning of the passage into something simple enough to draw (Mayer et al., 1996). Visual summaries are particularly useful for expository text. An example of a visual summary can be found in Figure 7.3.

Visual summaries and translanguaging were two of the strategies explored as part of professional development at the research site. In additional research conducted on site, Richards (2020) noted that emergent bilinguals studying science using these strategies showed academic growth in content as well as English. Since students are partners in this process, they also weighed in on

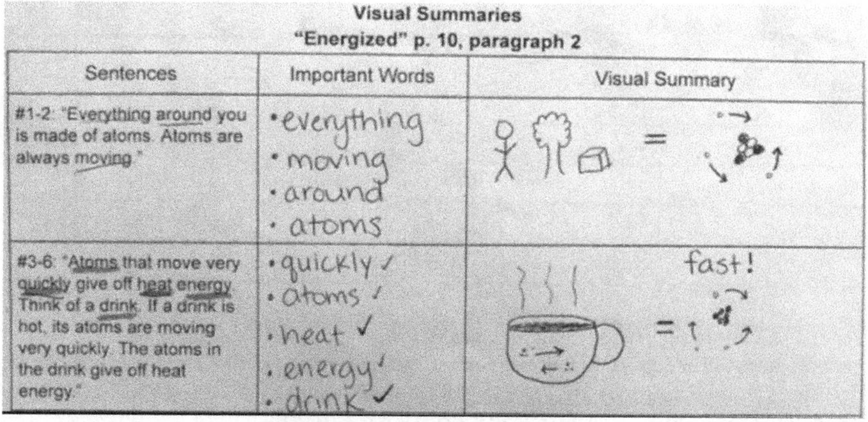
Visual Summaries
"Energized" p. 10, paragraph 2

Sentences	Important Words	Visual Summary
#1-2: "Everything around you is made of atoms. Atoms are always moving."	• everything • moving • around • atoms	=
#3-6: "Atoms that move very quickly give off heat energy. Think of a drink. If a drink is hot, its atoms are moving very quickly. The atoms in the drink give off heat energy."	• quickly ✓ • atoms ✓ • heat ✓ • energy ✓ • drink ✓	fast! =

Fig. 7.3. Example of a visual summary. Text in column 1 adapted from "Language, Literacy & Vocabulary—Reading Expeditions (Physical Science): Energized!" (p. 10) by *National Geographic*, 2007, National Geographic School Pub. Copyright 2007 by National Geographic.

the use of the strategies, the vast majority reporting that the strategies were valuable to their learning (Richards, 2020).

CONCLUSION

Educators and those who work in the education system are tasked with teaching and validating our students. To do so, they must acknowledge that the challenges faced are not necessarily student-centered, though that is often how they are perceived. Educators may see students who are not making quick progress in learning English and blame it on lack of motivation. Educators may observe student apathy toward learning and blame it on student culture. However, to do so is a disservice to those students and to the craft of education. In order to allow transformation in the mindsets of educators, the authors suggest solution-based professional development that allows educators to identify challenges they face, propose solutions that are supported by research (such as the use of translanguaging and visual summaries), and begin to reassess whether the challenges they see are truly student-centered, or whether there are strategies and pedagogical changes that will allow students the means to build their academic and language skills using their linguistic and cultural prior knowledge. These authors suggest that, not only is this pedagogical shift possible, but it is also essential to meet the needs of our students.

REFERENCES

California Department of Education. (2017). English learner roadmap. California Department of Education. https://www.cde.ca.gov/sp/el/rm/

Cummins, J. (1979). Cognitive-academic language proficiency, linguistic interdependence, optimal age, and some other matters. *Working Papers in Bilingualism, 19*, 197–205.

Darder, A. (2016). *Culture and power in the classroom: Educational foundations for the schooling of bicultural students*. Routledge.

DeCapua, A., & Marshall, H. W. (2015). Reframing the conversation about students with limited or interrupted formal education: From achievement gap to cultural dissonance. *NASSP Bulletin, 99*(4), 356–370. https://doi.org/10.1177/0192636515620662

EdBuild. (2019). $23 billion [Report]. https://edbuild.org/content/23-billion/full-report.pdf

Flores, N. & Schissel, J. (2014). Dynamic bilingualism as the norm: Envisioning a heteroglossic approach to standards-based reform. *TESOL Quarterly, 48*(3), 454–479.

Freire, P. (1970). *Pedagogy of the oppressed*. The Seabury Press.

García O., Kleifgen, J. A., & Falci, L. (2008). From English language learners to emergent bilinguals. *Equity Matters: Research Review No. 1.* https://files.eric.ed.gov/fulltext/ED524002.pdf

García, O., Johnson, S. I., Seltzer, K. (2017). *The translanguaging classroom: Leveraging student bilingualism for learning*. Caslon.

Gay, G. (2010). *Culturally responsive teaching: Theory, research, and practice*. Teachers College.

Green, S., and Ochoa, A. (2020). Latinx education achievement report [conference report]. *San Diego County Office of Education, Latinx Education Summit XVIII*. https://www.sdcoe.net/lls/MEGA/Documents/Latinx/LS2020%20Education%20Achievement%20Report.pdf

Hammond, Z. (2015). *Culturally responsive teaching and the brain: Promoting authentic engagement and rigor among culturally and linguistically diverse students*. Sage.

Mayer, R. E., Bove, W., Bryman, A., Mars, R., & Tapangco, L. (1996). When less is more: Meaningful learning from visual and verbal summaries of science textbook lessons. *Journal of Educational Psychology, 88*(1), 64–73.

Moll, L. C., Amanti, C., Neff, D., & Gonzalez, N. (1992). Funds of knowledge for teaching: Using a qualitative approach to connect homes and classrooms. *Theory Into Practice, 31*(2), 132–141. doi:10.1080/00405849209543534

Moll, L., Amanti, C., Neff, D., & González, N. (2005). Funds of knowledge for teaching: Using a qualitative approach to connect homes and classrooms. In N. Gonzalez, L. C. Moll, & C. Amanti (Eds.), *Funds of knowledge: Theorizing practices in households, communities, and classrooms* (pp. 71–88). Lawrence Erlbaum Associates. https://doi.org/10.4324/9781410613462

Musanti, S. I., & Pence, L. (2010). Collaboration and teacher development: Unpacking resistance, constructing knowledge, and navigating identities. *Teacher Education Quarterly, Winter 2010*. https://files.eric.ed.gov/fulltext/EJ872650.pdf

Richards, K. (2020). *Strategies for teaching students with limited or interrupted formal education in content classes*. [Field research project for master's in education, unpublished]. San Diego State University, Department of Dual Language and English Learner Education.

Shavard, G. (2021). From school improvement to student cases: Teacher collaborative work as a context for professional development. *Professional Development in Education*. DOI: 10.1080/19415257.2021.1879216

Spycher, P., González-Howard, M., & August, D. (2020). Content and language instruction in middle and high school: Promoting educational equity and achievement through access and meaningful engagement. In California Department of Education (Ed.), *Improving education for multilingual and English learner students: Research to Practice* (pp. 339–412). https://www.cde.ca.gov/sp/el/er/documents/mleleducationch6.pdf

Sugarman, J. (2019). *The unintended consequences for English Learners of using the four-year graduation rate for school accountability*. Migration Policy Institute.

Villalobos, J. (2020). An asset-based approach to support ELL success. *ACSD Express: Building bridges with ELLS, 15*(10). http://www.ascd.org/ascd-express/vol15/num10/an-asset-based-approach-to-support-ell-success.aspx

US Census. (2020). Educational attainment in the United States: 2019. United States Census Bureau. https://www.census.gov/data/tables/2019/demo/educational-attainment/cps-detailed-tables.html

Chapter 8

Linguistically Sustaining Core Instructional Practices

Supporting Multilingual Learners in General Education Classrooms

Olivia Murphy and Landon Wilson

For over three decades, researchers, teacher preparation programs, educators, and school communities have been working hard to understand and support the unique educational needs of multilingual learners (MLLs). Much of this work, understandably, is targeted towards preparing teachers who specialize in working with MLLs in standalone courses or as classroom co-teachers. However, with almost a quarter of public-school students speaking a language other than English at home (Zeigler & Camarota, 2018), it is becoming increasingly important for *all* classroom teachers to have an asset-based pedagogical toolkit to sustain and educate multilingual students culturally and linguistically. With standardized testing creating de facto language policies that shape how and what teachers teach (Menken, 2006), and many general education classroom teachers reporting feeling ill prepared to adequately support MLL students (Lucas, Villegas, & Martin, 2015), more scholarship surrounding universally applicable linguistically sustaining core practices for general education teachers is needed.

In this chapter we combine core practice scholarship with a language-centered lens on culturally sustaining pedagogy scholarship to create a set of four core instructional practices tailored to address the learning needs of MLL students in general education classes. These practices are aimed for broad use by all educators, and include building classroom relationships, selecting texts, generating authentic and critical discussions, and developing students' social consciousness via critical literacy.

THEORETICAL PERSPECTIVES

Core practices are elements of teaching that are frequently occurring, can be learned, and enacted by any educator in any context, are research based, and allow educators to continue to learn about students and teaching (Grosser-Clarkson & Neel, 2020; Grossman et al., 2009). By design, core practices are widely applicable and designed to help all teachers support all students, and they are meant to be responsive to student needs. However, using core practices within a deeply hegemonic education system *without* having specific discussions of how to implement them in ways that are responsive to the needs of historically marginalized students often means that these very students continue to get overlooked. For this and other reasons, the idea of "core practices" has been criticized for its potential to center certain people and histories while marginalizing others and decentralizing social justice and equity goals (Philip et al., 2019).

We believe that learning about core practices can be a useful way for educators to think about and improve their practice, but also agree with the critiques of the field and find that conversations surrounding core practice techniques like "orchestrating a full class discussion" often exclude nuanced conversations about how to work with different populations of students like MLLs. In response to this discord, we have created a set of core practices for educators that are both widely applicable as well as intentionally curated with the goals of linguistically and culturally sustaining MLL students informed by the principles of culturally sustaining pedagogy.

Culturally sustaining pedagogy builds on other asset-based education approaches like culturally relevant pedagogy (Ladson-Billings, 2014) to assert that not only should academic spaces acknowledge and affirm students' cultures, backgrounds, and languages, but that academic spaces should sustain these elements of student identity by centering them in instruction (Paris & Alim, 2017). Further, culturally sustaining pedagogy calls for guiding students in critiques of dominant power structures through the leveraging of their own cultural and linguistic assets (Paris, 2012). Extant research has found that culturally sustaining methods that incorporate students' linguistic and cultural diversity are not only an important way to counteract hegemonic education norms, but also lead to important learning outcomes specifically for MLL students (i.e., Khote, 2018). Because language is so deeply intertwined with culture, in this chapter, we apply a culturally sustaining lens to our thinking about core practices to create four linguistically sustaining core instructional practices for multilingual learners.

LINGUISTICALLY SUSTAINING CORE INSTRUCTIONAL PRACTICES

Each section below highlights one of four linguistically sustaining core practices: building classroom relationships, selecting texts, generating authentic discussions, and developing students' social consciousness via critical literacy. For each, we ground the practice in relevant literature, and then explore how this practice may be employed to suit the needs of MLL students.

Building Classroom Relationships

Our first core practice involves building relationships. Students enter the classroom with three basic needs—competency, relatedness, and autonomy— that each can be addressed by fostering strong relationships (Deci & Ryan, 2002). As Doherty and Hilberg (2007) report, academic achievement of multilingual learners increases in environments where students can collaborate freely and openly speak to their teachers. We suggest that the culturally sustainable educator consider two main factors in building relationships: the environment and individualized knowledge of the student.

Environment

On average, students spend close to 40 hours a week within school buildings. If these buildings are "aesthetically inclusive" (Emdin, 2016, p. 171), meaning that a student sees themselves and their lived realities displayed authentically, that student is more likely to "show up." Educators who are looking to create an environment that is welcoming of all students should fight the urge to decorate every surface before the first day of school, and instead allow students the opportunity to make the space their own by displaying their contributions. Consider a place in the classroom where students can draw or write freely, where typical classroom posters are replaced with (or at least supported by) popular musicians, cultural icons, or significant, diverse contributors to the content area. In offering these relatable entry points, students can create their learning environment while the educator remains respectful of the ever-changing cultural interests and identities of students (Paris & Alim, 2017). Beyond cultural icons, it is also important that students also see their native languages represented in the classroom. When students can freely bring their linguistic influences into the classroom, their comfort and connection to the environment significantly increases.

Knowing Students

In classrooms that are not engaged with a pedagogy of sustenance, it is likely that the educator may believe that the "get to know you" phase lasts only the first few days of school. This error, however, means missing critical conversations, opportunities, and relationships. When educators get to truly know their whole students—including their home and community languages and cultures—they are better able to invite the whole student into learning experiences.

Inviting students to create introductory videos is an accessible and intimate way to learn about students. Though these videos can create vulnerable moments, when filming may take place within students' living environment, the practice provides the opportunity for educators to get a first-hand glimpse into the student's life beyond the classroom, particularly if the student is asked to share moments or items that are important to their personalities and cultural identities.

As educators connect with students, it is important to also connect with the students' familial communities; educators who are invested in sustaining relationships must consider the cultural dynamics. Cultural expectations in US schools may be significantly different compared to students' or families' home culture or country; for example, a guardian may not feel comfortable reaching out to educators or school administration if that is not a customary practice in their experience (Kugler, 2011). To respect those cultural experiences while also inviting students' caretakers into their educational environment, teachers should communicate regularly with updates and invitations for caretakers to be a part of the classroom environment. If language barriers exist, teachers can rely on the student or other fluent speakers to help translate. Inviting all members to be a part of students' education experience communicates the shared effort among students, families, and educators.

SELECTING TEXTS

Our second core practice addresses the process of selecting texts for classroom use several factors involved in the selection of texts for the classroom, but two practices are particularly important for supporting multilingual MLL students: the first is expanding the traditional understanding of what a "text" is to include multimodal forms, and the second is considering cultural and linguistic representation both in the text itself and its authorship.

Including Multimodal Forms

In many US classrooms, understandings of "literacy" are hegemonic and bimodal: mastering reading and writing via traditional text forms like books and essays in dominant American English is how students succeed and are deemed literate (Metz, 2018). A culturally sustaining approach to literacy, however, requires expanding the way we define words like "text" and "literacy" to include multimodal forms. These forms—including digital media, photos and pictures, videos, and oral stories—combined with traditional dominant print forms offer the MLL student multiple points of entry into content via text forms that are localized and specific to students and their cultures (Cappello et al., 2019). Further, using multimodal texts outwardly challenges dominant expectations about language and literacy in ways that help students feel more comfortable using their own knowledge and language as strengths, which can in turn build bridges towards new academic and language learning (Smith et al., 2020).

Barter-Storm and Wik (2020) explain that multimodal texts diversify the cognitive load of reading, increase reading engagement, and can pique MLL students' emotional interest in ways that prose-only texts cannot. Having content represented in multiple modes simultaneously gives students a variety of entry points to engage with content, as well as helps them use a variety of skills to support both language content development. In their study of teachers' integration of multimodal units in K–12 classrooms, Choi, and Yi (2015) found that not only did incorporating multimodal texts throughout study participants' teaching units enhance students' content-knowledge growth, but it also benefited students' social emotional well-being in the classroom by increasing their academic confidence and self-esteem. Similarly, in an investigation of the impact of digital storytelling on adolescent MLLs, Yi et al. (2017) found that participants not only felt proud and excited about their work, but also learned valuable technology and English language reading, writing, and speaking skills throughout the process.

These studies—as well as an abundance of similar scholarship throughout the past decade—demonstrate the importance of expanding what we use and value as a "text" in the classroom. There are endless multimodal forms that teachers can choose to engage students visually, aurally, and verbally, including photos and photo essays, graphic novels, videos, podcasts, newspapers, social media, storyboards, diagrams, timelines and more. By not only using these texts in the classroom but centering them as anchor texts and primary modes of assessment (as opposed to secondary, optional, or supplemental addendums to prose-only anchor texts), teachers can open new textual avenues that simultaneously support MLL students' content and language acquisition as well as their academic confidence and self-esteem.

Considering Representation

The foundation of culturally sustaining pedagogy is supporting students' local (home/community) cultural and linguistic knowledge, as well as helping them with translanguaging to access dominant cultural and linguistic forms (Paris & Alim, 2017). Especially for MLL students, local cultural and linguistic competence has the powerful ability to support dominant cultural and linguistic growth. Because students are constantly consuming and creating texts in school, considering representation in the content and authorship of texts is a critical step in facilitating this translanguaging process.

The benefits of translanguaging—inviting students to use their complete linguistic repertoires in the classroom instead of enforcing "English only" policies—have been demonstrated to support MLL students' academic and multiple-language learning across the content areas (i.e., Poza, 2018 [science]; Hernandez Garcia & Schleppegrell (2021) [social studies]; Planas & Chronaki (2021) [math]). Choosing multilingual authors and texts as well as allowing students to compose multilingual texts as assessments is an important way to support students' translanguaging, while also helping sustain their home cultural and linguistic competencies (Hill et al., 2020). For teachers, this means selecting and centering multimodal texts written by culturally and linguistically diverse authors, which feature culturally and linguistically diverse subjects or characters, and that authentically incorporate students' local cultures, languages, and literacies. Further, students should be allowed to draw on and incorporate their languages, literacies, and cultures when composing texts and assessments in the classroom. Doing so opens multiple avenues for MLL students to enter content and demonstrate learning while simultaneously sustaining and leveraging their extant knowledges and literacies.

Generating Authentic Discussions

Our third core practice centers on voice and discussions in the classroom. With 79% of US classroom teachers being White (U.S. Department of Education, 2020), the potential for conflict based on cultural communication styles is high: for example, a student may be asked to be quiet or even asked to leave the classroom for communicating in a way that they think is appropriate but that an educator perceives as disruptive or disrespectful. This gesture penalizes the student in a multitude of ways: it communicates that the student's contributions are not important, pushes the student's native communication preference to the margin, and removes the student from an otherwise productive learning opportunity. To sustain and engage all students, educators must reflect on their own teaching practices; call and response (Smitherman,

1977) or signifyin (Gates, 1988) or translanguaging (García, 2009) is not the teacher's preferred way to communicate, but it is authentic to the student's learning and linguistic identity. To invite and encourage student discussion, we propose disrupting the traditional approach to a "co-taught" classroom, which calls for authentic student-centered conversations.

Sustainable Co-Teaching

Multiple educators lead the traditional co-taught classroom. To move into sustainable discussions, however, educators must reframe the co-taught classroom as a space where students are the "experts." This does not mean simply inviting students to share their findings at the front of the class (Emdin, 2016), but to integrate the student as the current subject matter expert. Much like a call and response approach, this shift in power opens the possibility for new understandings, broader participation, and most significantly, authentic communication. This approach also asks students to spend a significant amount of time working through the subject material together, providing holistic opportunities for communication amongst like-minded peers. Additionally, when opening the classroom to include student facilitators, this shift allows, or rather demands, that students are the primary figures in their educational progress. Welcoming communication in its various forms while placing the onus on the student simultaneously addresses different learning needs and preferences and opens a "communal [space]" where all stakeholders are "deeply invested in the emotional and academic well-being of the entire classroom community" (Emdin, 2016, p. 100). This collaborative approach also demands that educators see the student as more than "mere objects" (Ladson-Billings, 2014, p. 76) in their educational experiences.

Educators should ensure there are opportunities in the classroom discussions for students to reflect on the material and experience. This process creates opportunities for the educator to gain important feedback and data from the student while also requiring students to think deeply about their own learning process (Costa & Kallick, 2008). By asking students to consider questions—such as, "What was most memorable about today's discussion?," "What about this lesson was effective?," and "What would you like to do differently next time?"—students are reminded of their role as active participants in their classrooms. Once the reflections are collected and reviewed, the educator must also discuss the feedback with the class. Sharing this feedback anonymously and broadly ensures no student is made uncomfortable; instead, this reflective process validates student opinions, allows students to understand the perspective of their peers, and demonstrates a vulnerability on behalf of the educator, further shifting the traditional power dynamic in the classroom.

Developing Students' Social Consciousness Via Critical Literacy

Our final linguistically sustaining core instructional practice involves adapting a critical literacy lens in the classroom to help build MLL students' social consciousness. Critical literacy theorists and proponents of critical literacy pedagogy have long argued that traditional approaches to school literacy practice are hyperfocused on surface-level comprehension work and the passive decoding and reporting on authors' intentions. When such literacy tasks constitute most of the student's literacy work in the classroom, that student's ability to use a range of knowledges and literacies to engage critically with their worlds is stunted (Luke, 2000). Unfortunately, MLL students are often the most likely to encounter this sort of surface-level literacy work because of linguicism, poorly executed "differentiation," standardized testing pressures, and/or having teachers who either do not know how or are unwilling to try to be responsive to their MLL students' needs. However, critical literacy holds powerful potential to benefit MLL students by connecting their home, community, and academic literacy practices (Haneda, 2006).

Critical literacy is an approach to literacy activities that involves asking students to challenge the idea of absolute or objective knowledge, to evaluate texts for bias, to actively read with an eye towards power and positioning, and to think about how both they and texts are positioned in the world (Vasquez et al., 2019). It also demands the reading, evaluation, and production of narratives and counternarratives that represent a range of perspectives (Behrman, 2006). Because critical literacy inherently requires the incorporation of a variety of voices, it easily creates space to welcome texts that include students' home and community languages, cultures, identities, and perspectives. In response to the affirmation of their identities, languages, and cultures, students not only feel more connected to the work but are also able to leverage their linguistic and cultural capital as legitimized academic knowledge. In turn, they can use that knowledge to bridge to further learning and social justice thinking.

To implement critical literacy in linguistically sustaining ways, teachers must begin with themselves. First, it is important that teachers value linguistic diversity and establish their classrooms as spaces where linguistic diversity is not only allowed but encouraged and respected. Second, teachers must constantly work to build their own sociolinguistic consciousness to appreciate the fact that MLL students' use of language is inextricably linked to their identities and cultures (Shoffner & De Oliveira, 2017). Once these understandings are in place, teachers can then try to learn about their MLL students' languages, cultures, and identities to incorporate these knowledges into instruction. For example, Haneda (2006) details Comber's (2002) work with an ESL teacher who chose to watch (read) a film with her students, guided her students through a conversation and deconstruction of the film and its commentary on multiple identities. Then, the teacher asked her MLL students to combine their own visual, spoken, and print texts into storyboards or short films that told their own (hi)stories and explored their own identities. Throughout the process, students tackled critical literacy skills, language skills across several modalities, and developed their critical consciousness by thinking about identities, representation, and power (Haneda, 2006).

Discussion

As classrooms become increasingly linguistically and culturally diverse, teachers similarly increasingly need to diversify their approaches and be able to teach in ways that sustain and build the identities of their students. Because core practices are a fashionable way of thinking about how to prepare teachers, core practice scholarship also needs to increase to encompass linguistically sustaining strategies. The four linguistically sustaining core practices offered here serve as an entry point for any educator to begin or continue improving their practice to meet the needs of multilingual learners, and as a call for future and further consideration of how culturally and linguistically sustaining approaches can be incorporated into teacher training in useful, applicable ways that specifically meet the needs of historically marginalized student populations.

REFERENCES

Barter-Storm, B., & Wik, T. (2020). Using social justice graphic novels in the ELL classroom. *TESOL Journal, 11*(4), e551.

Behrman, E. H. (2006). Teaching about language, power, and text: A review of classroom practices that support critical literacy. *Journal of Adolescent & Adult Literacy, 49*(6), 490–498.

Cappello, M., Wiseman, A. M., & Turner, J. D. (2019). Framing equitable classroom practices: potentials of critical multimodal literacy research. *Literacy Research: Theory, Method, and Practice, 68*(1), 205–225.

Choi, Y. (2013). Teaching social studies for newcomer English language learners: Toward culturally relevant pedagogy. *Multicultural Perspectives, 15*(1), 12–18.

Choi, J., & Yi, Y. (2016). Teachers' integration of multimodality into classroom practices for English language learners. *Tesol Journal, 7*(2), 304–327.

Costa, A., & Kallick, B. (2008). Learning through reflection. In A. Costa & B. Kallick (Eds). *Learning and leading with habits of mind: 16 essential characteristics for success* (pp. 221–235). Association for Supervision and Curriculum Development.

86 *Olivia Murphy and Landon Wilson*

Deci, E. L., & Ryan, R. M. (2002). Overview of self-determination theory: An organismic dialectical perspective. In E. L. Deci & R. M. Ryan (Eds.), *Handbook of self-determination research* (pp. 3–33). University of Rochester Press.

Doherty, R. W., & Hilberg, R. S. (2007). Standards for effective pedagogy, classroom organization, English proficiency, and student achievement. *The Journal of Educational Research, 101*, 24 – 34.

Emdin, C. (2016). *For white folks who teach in the hood . . . and the rest of y'all too: Reality pedagogy and urban education.* Beacon Press.

Forzani, F. M. (2014). Understanding "core practices" and "practice-based" teacher education: Learning from the past. *Journal of teacher education, 65*(4), 357–368.

García, O. (2009). Education, multilingualism and translanguaging in the 21st century. In A. Mohanty, M. Panda, R. Phillipson, and T. Skutnabb-Kangas (Eds.), *Multilingual education for social justice: Globalising the local* (pp. 128–145). Orient Blackswan.

Gates, H. (1988). *The signifying monkey: A theory of African American literary criticism.* Oxford University Press.

Grosser-Clarkson, D., & Neel, M. A. (2020). Contrast, commonality, and a call for clarity: A review of the use of core practices in teacher education. *Journal of Teacher Education, 71*(4), 464–476.

Grossman, P., Compton, C., Igra, D., Ronfeldt, M., Shahan, E. C., & Williamson, P. (2009). Teaching practice: A cross-professional perspective. *Teaching and Teacher Education, 111*, 2055–2100.

Haneda, M. (2006). Becoming literate in a second language: Connecting home, community, and school literacy practices. *Theory into Practice, 45*(4), 337–345.

Hernandez Garcia, M., & Schleppegrell, M. J. (2021). Culturally sustaining disciplinary literacy for bi/multilingual learners: Creating a translanguaging social studies classroom. *Journal of Adolescent & Adult Literacy, 64*(4), 449–454.

Hill, K., Ponder, J. M., Summerlin, J., & Evans, P. (2020). Two language books: The power and possibilities of leveraging multilingual texts for critical translanguaging pedagogy. *Journal of Higher Education Theory & Practice, 20*(12).

Institute of Education Sciences. (2019). Digest of education statistics 2019. U.S. Department of Education. https://files.eric.ed.gov/fulltext/ED611019.pdf

Khote, N. (2018). Translanguaging in systemic functional linguistics: A culturally sustaining pedagogy for writing in secondary schools. *Educational Linguistics, 33*, 153–178.

Kugler, E. (2011). Is anyone listening to families' dreams? *Educational Leadership, 68*(8), 32–36.

Ladson-Billings, G. (2014). Culturally relevant pedagogy 2.0: Aka the remix. *Harvard Educational Review, 84*(1), 74–84.

Lucas, T., Villegas, A. M., & Martin, A. D. (2015). Teachers' beliefs about English language learners. *International Handbook of Research on Teachers' Beliefs*, 453–474.

Luke, A. (2000). Critical literacy in Australia: A matter of context and standpoint. *Journal of Adolescent & Adult Literacy, 43*(5), 448–61.

McDonald, M., Kazemi, E., & Kavanagh, S. S. (2013). Core practices and pedagogies of teacher education: A call for a common language and collective activity. *Journal of teacher education, 64*(5), 378–386.

Menken, K. (2006). Teaching to the test: How No Child Left Behind impacts language policy, curriculum, and instruction for English language learners. *Bilingual Research Journal, 30*(2), 521–546.

Metz, M. (2018). Challenges of confronting dominant language ideologies in the high school English classroom. *Research in the Teaching of English, 52*(4), 455–477.

National Council of Education Statistics. (2020, April). *Characteristics of public and private elementary and secondary school teachers in the United States.* US Department of Education. https://nces.ed.gov/pubs2020/2020142.pdf

Paris, D. (2012). Culturally sustaining pedagogy: A needed change in stance, terminology, and practice. *Educational researcher, 41*(3), 93–97.

Paris, D., & Alim, H. S. (Eds.). (2017). *Culturally sustaining pedagogies: Teaching and learning for justice in a changing world.* Teachers College Press.

Philip, T. M., Souto-Manning, M., Anderson, L., Horn, I., J. Carter Andrews, D., Stillman, J., & Varghese, M. (2019). Making justice peripheral by constructing practice as "core": How the increasing prominence of core practices challenges teacher education. *Journal of Teacher Education, 70*(3), 251–264.

Planas, N., & Chronaki, A. (2021). Multilingual mathematics learning from a dialogic-translanguaging perspective. In N. Planas, C. Morgan, & M. Schütte (Eds.) *Classroom research on mathematics and language* (pp. 151–166). Routledge.

Poza, L. E. (2018). The language of ciencia: Translanguaging and learning in a bilingual science classroom. *International Journal of Bilingual Education and Bilingualism, 21*(1), 1–19.

Shoffner, M., & De Oliveira, L. C. (2017). Courageous literacy: Linguistically responsive teaching with English language learners. *Voices from the Middle, 24*(3), 44.

Smith, B. E., Pacheco, M. B., & Khorosheva, M. (2021). Emergent bilingual students and digital multimodal composition: A systematic review of research in secondary classrooms. *Reading Research Quarterly, 56*(1), 33–52.

Smitherman, G. (1977). *Talkin' and testifyin': The language of Black America.* Houghton Mifflin.

Vasquez, V. M., Janks, H., & Comber, B. (2019). Critical literacy as a way of being and doing. *Language Arts, 96*(5), 300–311.

Zeigler, K., & Camarota, S. A. (2019, September 19). *Almost half speak a foreign language in America's largest cities.* Center for Immigration Studies. https://cis.org /Report/Almost-Half-Speak-Foreign-Language-Americas-Largest-Cities

Chapter 9

Bilingual Education for African American Students

Where the Resolution at?

Dianisha Lanette Croft

As a Black woman and speaker of Ebonics, alike to many African Americans, the sense of pride that encompasses being *Young, Gifted, and Black* is often overshadowed by the discomfort in *The Skin That We Speak*. According to Du Bois (1903/2019) this disposition of conflict is evident in *The Souls of Black Folks,* which he theorized as double consciousness or the feeling of viewing one's ways of being through the eyes of others; a duality of distinct identities: the African and the American. Exacerbating this twoness, as James Baldwin stated, is the realization that being African American implies being African without memory while simultaneously being American void of privilege (Peck, 2016). Although this statement rings true, there remains a deeply ingrained surviving African cultural marker that has withstood the historical degradation of all things Black: Ebonics aka Black Language (BL). However, as language is viewed as a proxy for identity (Myers, 2020), some educators are determined to extinguish the existence of the native tongue of African slave descendants via anti-Black Linguistic Racism while other educators and political allies seek to sustain this linguistic phenomenon: this chapter is for the latter.

Because language envelops us before we take our first breath, language and identity are inextricably linked. Thus, language expresses identity (Baker-Bell 2020; Freire, 1985; Lavoie, 2018), group and racial solidarity (Baker-Bell, 2020; Baugh, 1999; Koch et al., 2001; Smitherman, 1998a), social prestige (Delpit, 2002; Stubbs, 2002), culture and thinking (Fanon,

1952/2008), and defines the speaker even when the speaker refuses to be defined by a language that refuses to acknowledge her (Baldwin, 1979/1997).

However, language also defies social constructs. As Fanon (1952/2008) concluded, "There is nothing more sensational than a Black man speaking correctly, for he is appropriating the white world" (Fanon, 2008, pg. 19). One might question speaking correctly according to whom, and why would African Americans appropriate the White world via language? While the former question involves unpacking beyond the scope of this chapter, Fanon's theory of epidermalization or the unconscious training of Blacks to embody a perspective of "to be black" is to be deficient and "to be white" is to be right provides a plausible answer to the latter (Baker-Bell, 2020). This internal conundrum is symbolic of the duality espoused by Du Bois's theory of double consciousness (Myers, 2020), and is an ever-present reality for many African American students.

Being well versed in both Ebonics and what Paris (2009) referred to as White Mainstream English (WME) presents an internal warring of language ideologies. On the one hand you have the language of your soul, your native tongue, and on the other you have the language of power. Reconciling the two is no easy feat, and the native tongue is often relegated to second-class citizenry as the language of power is deemed the standard of linguistic success. Accordingly, Dowdy (2002) suggested that success comes by besting the language that was used to enslave one's ancestors which is a "painful strategy of survival" (Dowdy, 2002, pg. 7). Yet another reminder of the linguistic brutality endured by surviving descendants of enslaved Africans.

Although the U.S. has yet to designate English as the official language (Baker-Bell, 2020), WME is the language of media, politics, and public institutions. As a result, African American students, despite resilient linguistic histories, are required to speak and subsequently think in WME without regard to their identity, psychological and academic well-being. Thus, purpose of this chapter is to reignite a vision for bilingual education perspective for African American students via Antiracist Black Language Pedagogy. This scholarship offers critical discourse interrogating US language education through a lens of Anti-Black Linguistic Racism and provides implications for practice for educators who serve African American students.

IF EBONICS ISN'T A LANGUAGE, THEN TELL ME, WHAT IS?

Contrary to colonizers and people who currently seek American citizenship, enslaved Africans did not choose to make America their land nor did they receive the liberty that is stressed in the national anthem. Africans shipped like chattel to the United States were stripped of all cultural markers (Smith, 1998b). Enslaved Africans were intentionally dispersed to ensure the impossibility of communication; it is worthy to note that this linguistic segregation was also enforced via segregation from native speakers of English (Baugh, 1999). As a result, African ancestors retained African language systems in the context of America, which is not only an artifact of survival, demonstrating the resiliency of the African tongue, but also a tool for thinking and learning.

Although it is rare to find Americans who have preserved their ancestral language(s) after three generations (Baugh, 1999), Ebonics continues to thrive despite attempts of linguistic genocide, and serves as the primary language of 80–90% of African Americans (Smitherman, 1998a). Extant scholarship on the language reveals many monikers (e.g., Negro English, Black English, Ebonics, African American vernacular English, African American English, African American language, and Black language), however, for the purposes of this chapter, the terms Ebonics and Black language (BL) are used interchangeably in solidarity with the Black intellectuals that preceded this author.

Coined by Dr. Robert L. Williams in 1973, Ebonics rejected former deficit laden terminology utilized by White linguists of the era to describe the language of African Americans (Smitherman, 1998a; Yancy, 2011). A portmanteau of the word's ebony and phonics (i.e., Black sounds), Ebonics, espoused Black language from a Black perspective, which, according to Dr. Williams, posed a threat to White America because African Americans cultivated and defined their own linguistic reality. This linguistic phenomenon, originating from West African and Niger-Congo languages connects Africans in America to the African diaspora and supports the decolonization of the "psycholinguistically maimed psyche" of Black Americans (Smitherman, 1998b, pg. 30). Likewise, Black language is similarly described by Africologists as a continuum of African languages in an American sociocultural context, a distinct language rather than a dialect of English (Kifano & Smith, 2003). This perspective presents a point of contention among linguists and has spurred fiery public debate (Myers, 2020).

With the intent to develop teacher capacities for instructing African American students in their primary language in addition to WME, the infamous 1997 Oakland Resolution is one point in history that sparked public controversy surrounding the legitimacy of Ebonics as a language. Rather than focusing on the school board's goal of educating teachers to support African American student achievement by way of sustaining their primary language while acquiring WME, critics defamed the resolution by denigrating and interrogating the legitimacy of Ebonics as a language.

Linguists have argued that classifications of varieties as a dialect or language are often determined on sociopolitical grounds (Boutte & Johnson, 2013b; Longres & Harding, 1998; Rickford, 1998; Williamson-Ige, 1984).

American society operates within paradigm of White linguistic supremacy thus it is clear why the media and public gravitated to dismantling the Oakland Resolution by asserting Ebonics as a dialect rather than focusing on the attempt to improve the educational outcomes for African American children. Given the negative attitudes associated with dialects (Fogel & Ehri, 2006; Rickford, 1998; Smitherman, 1998a), in addition to scholarship that revealed attitudes shape expectations, and teacher expectations shape student performance (Martinez, 2017; Rickford, 1998) one must critically examine the roots of the issue: Anti-Black Linguistic Racism reflected in policy, pedagogy, and teacher attitudes.

THE ENEMY IS THE ELEMENTARY SCHOOL TEACHER

What happens when the language spoken in the home does not meet the language expectations of school? Does the home language dry up like a raisin in the sun as one attempts to assimilate to the cultural and linguistic demands of the classroom?

Despite linguistic diversity represented in American classrooms, stark differences exist between the perceptions of Black language and other non-mainstream languages (i.e., Hmong, Spanish). For example, Spanish, Mien, Hmong, etc., speaking students are afforded opportunities to sustain their primary language while learning English via bilingual or English as a second language supports. Reifying Anti-Black Linguistic Racism within educational policy, bilingual programs for African American students do not exist, although the literacy achievement of African American students in relation to their non-Black peers is publicized. Unfortunately, Sung (2018) found that when Black students were provided an opportunity to participate in English language support courses, teachers reasoned that Black students "struggled because they were Black" (Sung, 2018, pg. 652). These attitudes pervade US classrooms thus one must critically interrogate educational systems and attitudes of teachers supporting African American students.

Fogel and Ehri (2006) conducted a study with the intent to educate, sensitize, and prepare in-service teachers to instruct speakers of Ebonics. Post attitude surveys revealed that teachers retained negative attitudes towards BL regarding the language as ungrammatical slang that needed to be censored. Similarly, the research of Thibodeaux and colleagues (2020) demonstrated that 68% of pre-service teachers in the study viewed speakers as less intelligent. Unfortunately, attitudes towards language reflect historical socially ingrained roots that can be difficult to change, thus educators must be knowledgeable of their personal, explicit, and implicit biases towards language (Cheatham et al., 2009; Costner et al., 2010). Without regard for entrenched biases, attitudes may manifest themselves in a multitude of ways such as low expectations of African American students (Beneke & Cheatham, 2015; Costner et al., 2010; Fogel & Ehri, 2006), rejection of BL as linguistically valid, incessant correction (Fogel & Ehri, 2006; Martinez, 2017), and revoicing of speech acts (Martinez, 2017).

Unfortunately, African Americans also exhibit adverse biases towards Ebonics (Baker-Bell, 2020; Boutte & Johnson, 2007; Koch et al., 2001; Martinez, 2017; Rosenthal 1977). Delpit (2002) concluded that America's perceptions and attitudes attaches inferiority to all aspects of Blackness. Furthering this notion, Baker-Bell (2020) affirmed that the policing, stereotypes, and exploitation of Black language derive from policy and practice of anti-Blackness that is intended to sustain White supremacy.

According to Jefferies (2014), the "anti" in anti-Blackness reflects the denial of Black people's ways of knowing, being, and ultimately their right to life. Baker-Bell (2020) conceptualizes Anti-Black Linguistic Racism as the denial of Black students' right to utilize their native language to support their language and literacy learning which is antithetical to literacy development as language is foundational to literacy growth (Baker-Bell, 2020; Smitherman, 1997).

Reverberating the sentiments of Smitherman (2020), why do speakers of Black Language have to be bilingual when speakers of WME continue to be monolingual? Reflecting on linguistic experiences, one Black student commented, "Black vernacular, it's not seen as a cultural expression, it's seen as a speech problem. You're just punished for expressing your Black culture . . . you're just constantly forced to take on the culture of White America" (Feagin, 1992, p. 552).

Similarly, another student commented, "And everything is predicated on a White norm, so that when the student is in the environment, he is in a situation where the norm is the thinking, the philosophy, the feelings, the attitudes of Whites, and if you deviate from that norm, you're wrong" (Feagin, 1992, p. 577).

It is worthy to note that the "White norm" encompasses WME which Kiki, a middle school participant in the study of Hill (2009), explained that she was able to fit in with the White students at her school by "talking like them" (Hill, 2009, p. 126). Surviving in an educational system that fails to acknowledge your language and linguistic competence reinforces Anti-Black Linguistic Racism without regard for the damage done, thus one must question, what tools can be used to dismantle the systemic issue of linguicism in US schools?

WHERE THE RESOLUTION AT?

Although scholars (Baker-Bell, 2020; Delpit, 1998; Ladson-Billings, 1994/2009; Smitherman 1997/2003) have outlined how to approach the rich linguistic repertoires of African American students, the American education system has failed to recognize Black language and develop strategies to sustain the linguistic diversity presented among African American students (Ladson-Billings, 2009). The current scholarship proposes that teacher preparation programs critically challenge Anti-Black Linguistic Racism that plagues institutions by adopting a bilingual perspective when educating future teachers on the linguistic needs of African American students. Supporting this proposition, Kiramba and Oloo (2017) argued that "drawing upon student strengths and the linguistic capital they possess is an empirically effective way to support and enable academic excellence and better educational outcomes in general" (Kiramba & Oloo, 2017, p. 24).

Therefore, this work must begin within the walls of colleges and universities. For example, in 1980 language researcher Robert Berdan following an observation of in-service teachers, applied the observed teaching behavior of hypercorrection with his college students (Delpit, 1998). Alike to K–12 students, college students became hesitant, questioning their abilities which resulted in the silencing of their voices. This activity provided an opportunity for students to engage in critical dialogue around the practice, and students were able to get a sense of what it felt like to be hypercorrected because of the language (i.e., WME) they spoke. Consequently, teachers must be able to critically analyze what it means to speak inside and outside the box of American educational systems. Supporting this study, Greene and Walker (2004) affirmed that examining cultural differences enable teachers to be more reflective and reexamine their beliefs about language. Given the diversity of US students one would assume that cultural and linguistic studies would be an integral part of teacher education programs. Unfortunately, this is not the case, therefore pedagogical change must also be considered.

Bilingual education for African American students must center the linguistic legacy of African Americans utilizing tools, such as *Antiracist Black Pedagogy* (Baker-Bell, 2020) to critique hegemonic language policy and practice. As means to move beyond approaches that merely highlight differences between BL and WME, Antiracist Black Language Pedagogy supports student learning of Black language via Black language to dismantle mainstream narratives that perpetuate racial injustice. Ten framing ideas (see Baker-Bell, 2020, p. 4) were presented that advocated for linguistic justice for African American students. Crucial to the current scholarship are the following framing ideas that demanded BL education to: (1) center the literacy needs of African American students, (2) work to dismantle normative practices of Anti-Black Linguistic Racism, (3) raise consciousness of the origins of Black language, and (4) utilize Black linguistic traditions to develop linguistic flexibility.

To illustrate these framing ideas, consider the English Language Unity Act (2021) H.R. 997, a bill that seeks to designate English as the official language of the U.S. An educator interested in exacting antiracist Black pedagogy would consider the need for African American students to be able to critically analyze policy and practice that may cause them harm. To introduce the topic of race, identity, language and power, the educator could use Angie Thomas' novel *The Hate U Give* and watch Jamila Lyiscott's *3 Ways to Speak English*. Following the absorption of literacies, the educator could facilitate an open dialogue questioning the language choices of the authors and the origins of Ebonics. Possible questions could be: (1) What language(s) do you speak, (2) What is the origin of your language, (3) How did the characters use Ebonics to navigate social settings, (4) How do you use language to negotiate identity, (5) What does language say about one's identity, and (6) Who decides what language is appropriate for social, public, and educational settings? Posing questions and allowing students to think and respond in their language of choice will prepare them to interrogate systems that perpetuate linguistic oppression.

Following several discussions on the topic, educators could introduce H.R. 997; reading sections collectively in class followed by a student led discussion. Students could formulate questions about the bill, agree or disagree with the bill, or hold a schoolwide debate, but to exact antiracist pedagogy African American students must be involved in dismantling oppressive practices. This will look differently for each student. Some suggestions include orchestrating and recording a schoolwide cipher for public viewing, constructing a poem or rap in their home language expressing their views of the bill, or creating social media posts so that others can become informed about the bill. Notice that the possibilities are not limited to traditional forms of communication (i.e., writing an essay), but open to a variety of literacies and languages for learning. Because policies such as H.R. 997 stifle the creativity inherent in the language of African Americans, the resolution will not be televised. As evidenced by the Oakland School Board Resolution, it should not be televised, rather it must be internalized.

WHAT DO YOU CALL A BLACK LANGUAGE SPEAKER? BILINGUAL WITH NO ACCOMMODATIONS

Could you imagine having a story to tell or a song to sing but couldn't because there was no way to say it in the language of power (Scott, 2017)? If enslaved Africans used a deadly situation to retain a linguistic system to express their thinking, to collectively triumph and overcome the perils of slavery, then why wouldn't this same language be used as a tool to create knowledge, struggle for justice, and to define their educational achievements from the Black perspective just as their ancestors before them? One might suggest that the educational system is a reproduction of times past reflecting the inequitable practices of linguistic slavery. Forcing children to assimilate and incorporate the code of the master without regard for their academic well-being, identity, their school of thought, or realities of the systems in which they operate. African American students need a chance to explore and relish in their linguistic realities. An opportunity to think in Black, to learn in Black, to speak Black language without fear of remediation, hypercorrection, or translation of their ways of knowing, being, and becoming so that it fits some hypothetical standard. If you haven't noticed Black students aren't standard, but if given the opportunity they can and will exceed standards. What other people you know created a language where there wasn't one under the hand of master? Teacher-educators and teachers must internalize a bilingual perspective while utilizing antiracist Black language pedagogy to uplift African American student voice and achievement.

REFERENCES

Baldwin, J. (1998). If Black English isn't a language, then tell me, what is? In T. Perry & L. Delpit (Eds.), *The real Ebonics debate: Power, language, and the education of African American children* (pp. 67–70). Beacon Press.

Baker-Bell, A. (2020). *Linguistic justice: Black language, literacy, identity, and pedagogy*. Routledge.

Baugh, J. (1999). *Out of the mouths of slaves*. University of Texas Press.

Beneke, M., & Cheatham, G. (2015). Speaking up for African American English: Equity and inclusion in early childhood Settings. *Early Childhood Education Journal*, *43*(2), 127–134. https://doi-org.csu.ezproxy.switchinc.org/10.1007/s10643-014-0641-x

Boutte, G. S. (2007). Teaching African American English speakers: Expanding educators and student repertoires. In M. E. Brisk (Ed.), *Language, culture, and community in teacher education* (pp. 47–70). Routledge.

Boutte, G. S., & Johnson, G. (2013a). Do educators see and honor biliteracy and bidialectalism in African American language speakers? Apprehensions and reflections of two grandparents/professional educators. *Early Childhood Education Journal*, *41*(2), 133–141. https://doi-org.csu.ezproxy.switchinc.org/10.1007/s10643-012-0538-5

Boutte, G., & Johnson, G. (2013b). Funga Alafia: Toward welcoming, understanding, and respecting African American speakers' bilingualism and biliteracy. *Equity & Excellence in Education*, *46*(3), 300–314. https://doi.org.csu.ezproxy.switchinc.org/10.1080/10665684.2013.806850

Cheatham, G. A., Armstrong, J., & Santos, R. M. (2009). "Y'all listenin'?" Accessing children's dialects in preschool. *Young Exceptional Children*, *12*(4), 2–14. https://doi.org.csu.ezproxy.switchinc.org/10.1177/1096250609337588

Costner, K. L., Daniels, K., & Clark, M. T. (2010). The struggle will not continue: an examination of faculty attitudes toward teaching African American students. *Journal of Black Studies*, *41*(1), 40–55.

Delpit, L. (1998). What should teachers do? Ebonics and culturally responsive instruction. In T. Perry & L. Delpit (Eds.), *The real Ebonics debate: Power, language, and the Education of African American children* (pp. 17–26). Beacon Press.

Delpit, L. D. (2002). Introduction. In L. Delpit & J. K. Dowdy (Eds.), *The skin that we speak: Thoughts on language and culture in the classroom* (pp. xv–xxvi). The New Press.

Dowdy, J. K. (2002). Ovuh dyuh. In L. Delpit & J. K. Dowdy (Eds.), *The skin that we speak: Thoughts on language and culture in the classroom* (pp. 3–13). New Press.

Du Bois, W. E. B. (2019). *Souls of Black folk*. G&D Media. (Original work published 1903)

English Language Unity Act, H.R. 997, 117th Cong. (2021). https://www.congress.gov/bill/117th-congress/house-bill/997/text

Fanon, F. (2008). *Black skin, White masks*. (R. Philcox, Trans.). Grove Press. (Original work published 1952)

Fogel, H., & Ehri, L. C. (2006). Teaching African American English forms to standard American English-speaking teachers: Effects on acquisition, attitudes, and responses to student use. *Journal of Teacher Education*, *57*(5), 464–480. https://doiorg.csu.ezproxy.switchinc.org/10.1177/0022487106294088

Freire, P. (1985). *The politics of education: Culture, power, and liberation.* Bergin & Garvey Publishing.

Greene, D. M., & Walker, F. R. (2004). Recommendations to public speaking instructors for the negotiation of code-switching practices among Black English-speaking African American students. *The Journal of Negro Education*, *73*(4), 435–442. https://doi:10.2307/4129627

Hansberry, L. (2011). *To be young gifted and Black.* New American Library. (Original work published in 1969)

Hill, K. D. (2009). Code-switching pedagogies and African American student voices: acceptance and resistance. *Journal of Adolescent & Adult Literacy*, *53*(2), 120–131. http://www.jstor.org/stable/40344357

Jefferies, M. (2014, November 28). Ferguson must force us to face anti-Blackness. *Boston Globe*. https://www.bostonglobe.com/opinion/2014/11/28/ferguson-must-force-face-anti-blackness/pKVMpGxwUYpMDyHRWPln2M/story.html

Kifano, S. & Smith, E. (2003). Ebonics and education in the context of culture: Meeting the language and cultural needs of LEP African American students. In D. J. Ramirez, T. Wiley, G. de Klerk, E. Lee, & W. E. Wright (Eds.), *Ebonics: The urban education debate* (pp. 62–95). Multilingual Matters LTD.

Kiramba, L. K. & Oloo, J. A. (2017a). Multilingual literacies: Invisible representation of literacy in a rural classroom. *Journal of Adolescent & Adult Literacy, 61,* 267–277. https://doi.org.csu.ezproxy.switchinc.org/10.1002/jaal.690

Koch, L., Gross, A., & Kolts, R. (2001). Attitudes toward Black English and codeswitching. *Journal of Black Psychology, 27,* 29–42. https://doi:10.1177/0095798401027001002

Ladson-Billings, G. (1995). Toward a theory of culturally relevant pedagogy. *American Educational Research Journal, 32,* 465–491.

Ladson-Billings, G. (2009). The dreamkeepers: Successful teachers of African American children. Jossey-Bass.

Lavoie, C. (2018). "Hey, teacher, speak Black please": The educational effectiveness of bilingual education in Burkina Faso. *International Journal of Bilingual Education & Bilingualism, 11*(6), 661–677. https://doi.org.csu.ezproxy.switchinc.org/10.2167/beb475.

Longres, J. F., & Harding, S. (1997). Ebonics and social work education. *Journal of Social Work Education, 33*(2), 222–224. https://doiorg.csu.ezproxy.switchinc.org/10.1080/10437797.1997.10778865

Martinez, D. C. (2017). Emerging critical meta-awareness among Black and Latina/o youth during corrective feedback practices in urban English Language Arts classrooms. *Urban Education, 52*(5), 637–666. https://doi.org/10.1177/0042085915623345

Myers, T. K. (2020). Can you hear me now? An autoethnographic analysis of code-switching. *Cultural Studies ↔ Critical Methodologies, 20*(2), 113–123. https://doi.org/10.1177/1532708619879208

Paris, D. (2009). "They're in my culture, they speak the same way": African American Language in multiethnic high schools. *Harvard Educational Review, 79*(3), 428–447. https://doi-org.csu.ezproxy.switchinc.org/10.17763/haer.79.3.64j4678647mj7g35

Paris, D. (2012). Culturally sustaining pedagogy: A needed change in stance, terminology, and practice. *Educational Researcher, 41*(3), 93–97. http://www.jstor.org/stable/41477769

Peck, R. (Director). (2016). *I am not your Negro* [Film]. Magnolia Pictures.

Rickford, J. (1998). Holding on to a language of our own: An Interview with Linguist John Rickford. In T. Perry & L. Delpit (Eds.), *The real Ebonics debate: Power, language, and the Education of African American children* (pp. 59–66). Beacon Press.

Rosenthal, M. S., ERIC Clearinghouse on Early Childhood Education, C. I., & ERIC Clearinghouse on Languages and Linguistics, W. D. (1977). *The magic boxes: Children and Black English.* https://eric.ed.gov/?id=ED136553

Scott, K. D. (2016). Young, shifting, and Black: Leaving the language of home and back again a cautionary tale of crossing race and gender borders. *Qualitative Inquiry, 23*(3), 119–129. https://doi.org/10.1177/1077800416655824

Smitherman, G. (1997). Black language education: One mo once. In D. J. Ramirez, T. Wiley, G. de Klerk, E. Lee, & W. E. Wright (Eds.), *Ebonics: The urban education debate* (pp. 49–61). Multilingual Matters LTD.

Smitherman, G. (1998a). What go round come round. In T. Perry & L. Delpit (Eds.), *The real Ebonics debate*: *Power, language, and the Education of African American children* (pp. 163–171). Beacon Press.

Smitherman, G. (1998b). Black English/Ebonics: What it be like? In T. Perry & L. Delpit (Eds.), *The real Ebonics debate: Power, language, and the Education of African American children* (pp. 29–37). Beacon Press.

Smitherman, G. (2020). Foreword. In A. Baker-Bell. (2020), *Linguistic justice: Black language. Literacy, identity, and pedagogy* (pp. xii–xvii). Routledge

Stubbs, M. (2002). Some basic sociolinguistic concepts. In L. Delpit & J. Dowdy (Eds.), *The skin that we speak: Thoughts on language and culture in the classroom* (pp. 63–85). New Press.

Sung, K. K. (2018). Raciolinguistic ideology of anti-Blackness: Bilingual education, tracking, and the multiracial imaginary in urban schools. *International Journal of Qualitative Studies in Education (QSE), 31*(8), 667–683. https://doiorg.csu.ezproxy.switchinc.org/10.1080/09518398.2018.1479047

TED. (2014, June 19). *3 ways to speak English* [Video]. YouTube. https://www.youtube.com/watch?v=k9fmJ5xQ_mc&t=81s

Thibodeaux, T., Curette, D., Bumstead, S., Karlin, A., & Butaud, G. (2020). Gauging pre-service teachers' awareness of dialectical code switching in classroom settings. *Journal of Education, 200*(2), 120–129. https://doi.org.csu.ezproxy.switchinc.org/10.1177/0022057419877399

Thomas, A. (2017). *The hate u give.* Walker Books.

Williamson-Ige, D. (1984). Approaches to Black Language studies: A cultural critique. *Journal of Black Studies, 15*(1), 17–29. http://www.jstor.org/stable/2784114

Yancy, G. (2011). The scholar who coined the term Ebonics: A conversation with Dr. Robert L. Williams. *Journal of Language, Identity & Education, 10*(1), 41–51. https://doi.org.csu.ezproxy.switchinc.org/10.1080/15348458.2011.539967

Chapter 10

Equitably Assessing Emergent Bilinguals

Altheria Caldera, Carol Revelle, and Freyca Calderon-Berumen

Preservice teachers often fall short in planning and implementing lessons that are sensitive to the needs of *emergent bilinguals*. The use of the term *emergent bilinguals* shifts the focus away from the deficit model implied with English Language Learners (ELLs) or English as a Second Language (ESL) and instead frames the second language as an asset owned by the learner. The ongoing use of deficit models can be partly attributed to lack of intention and attention in teacher preparation programs. Pressured by time and content restraints, teacher educators often fail to do more than loosely address tested objectives in order to help teacher candidates pass certification exams. Recognizing this need for asset-based language and corresponding practices, Texas recently became the first state to replace limited English proficient in its education code (Texas Legislature Online, 2021). This shift holds implications for other states, many of which still see using non-English home languages as obstacles to overcome.

The need to better prepare teachers to assess emergent bilinguals is supported by translanguaging, a strategic approach for instruction that provides space for students to draw from all of their resources in both English and their other language(s) to best learn and demonstrate their knowledge and skills without being limited to the English language alone. Additionally, when we extend this idea of flexible demonstration of understanding through multimodality, learners can use other representations beyond oral and written language including art, graphs, media, and other forms of new literacy, to process and demonstrate learning.

REVIEW OF ASSESSMENT PERSPECTIVES

Translanguaging assessment practices provide authentic, performance-based opportunities for students to demonstrate both their content and language learning "using the full features of the linguistic repertoires" (Garcia, Johnson, & Seltzer, 2016, p. 80). These appropriate assessments may also include perspectives of the student's learning from multiple points of view with the teacher, the family, and even the students themselves participating in the evaluation process. Additionally, students may demonstrate their learning using dynamic performances, by providing various outputs that meet the linguistic needs of the student while measuring learning and/or language objectives. When students are not allowed to translanguage, they are forced to suppress their idiolect putting them at a disadvantage compared to their monolingual peers in traditional whole-class assessments (Otheguy, Garcia, & Reid, 2015).

When monolingual teachers with limited experiences in their students' culture evaluate learning, they may not award credit for cultural ideas and values represented in translanguaging Corrientes when students express complex learning and may need the support and perspectives of the students and their families to assess the learning of emergent bilingual students in a fair way. When teachers consider that the goal of assessment is the development and growth of the learner and not the grades in the gradebook, they make space for more dynamic assessment practices. For example, increasingly, translating software provides the literal translations of text into English, so teachers can interpret a student's non-English responses, but idiomatic and metaphoric representations rarely translate accurately. Taking the time for students to share their work with members of their family prepares the students to demonstrate their understanding in conferences with their teacher and for the teacher to review the feedback provided by family members on almost any written, visual, or oral assignment.

A family's perspective of its emergent bilingual student is more complete than the teacher who only observes the student in a classroom setting. Families see the students interacting in the community and at home using their authentic language skills. Furthermore, assignments that privilege family interactions provide students an opportunity to tap into the families' funds of knowledge. These assignments value the family as peer teachers that work with the school to fully develop the students' language repertoires.

Alternative collaborators may also include the students' peers and the students themselves. In the end, the teacher must assign the grades, but these should be done in collaboration with others who know the students well and have perspectives on the students' growth and learning outside class.

Dynamic assessment takes time, but it provides a truer picture of the students' overall development. A standardized assessment takes far less time, but it is limited in its scope, and these limits create inequitable assessments for emergent bilingual students. Because of the time that these assessments take, teachers will likely need to rotate students through these practices, maybe only doing these once during a grading period, so that only a few students at a time are working through this multi perspective model.

These culturally responsive approaches can take many forms depending on what they are assessing. They provide emergent bilingual students opportunities to participate in authentic assessment. By taking the curriculum and standards of a course, a teacher can create a continuum of learning by placing the big skills and understandings into rubrics that describe the growth of skill development and knowledge acquisition for the course. As the students demonstrate proficiency, the teacher moves the student along the continuum of learning providing flexibility over the rigid practice of assessing a skill with a single measurement and moving forward. With these continuums, a teacher can give the student credit for the learning as they are able to demonstrate understanding.

When the goal of the assessment is to ascertain the understanding of content knowledge, teachers need different tools than can be used to collect information on language development. Yet these two objectives are often conflated in assessment practices when teachers do not provide opportunities for students to use their full language repertoire in assessment. During assessment, equitable practices allow students to use all of their resources, both internal and external—the language they need to demonstrate their understanding and classroom resources that help them perform tasks and communicate their learning. Some of these resources are physical resources: dictionaries, anchor charts, word walls, images, and gestures; while others are social resources, such as a class friend, group partner, or digital support.

However, inevitably, all assessments measure language in some way (AERA, APA, NCME, 2014). So, to deny students access to the language supports they need to demonstrate their understanding of content is not only inequitable, penalizing students for not having the English language to demonstrate their understanding, but also inaccurate, providing poor data to teachers for planning future instruction. As teachers design their lessons, separating their content and language objectives make it easier to assure content assessments explicitly measure content learning. An example can be found in Table 10.1.

Table 10.1. Separating Content and Language Objectives

Initial Objective: The student will identify and explain the stages of the water cycle by presenting the cycle with an authentic example to the class.

Content Objectives: The student will identify and explain the water cycle. The student will present an example of the water cycle to the class.	The student will read and learn the vocabulary associated with the water cycle. The student will develop a presentation using content-specific vocabulary and share it orally in English.

Translanguaging Objective: The student will determine when to use both English and Spanish to learn about and present their understanding of the water cycle.

EQUITABLE PRACTICES FOR EMERGENT BILINGUAL ASSESSMENT

Because language and content proficiency are intertwined in diverse ways, practicing a combination of multimodal approaches to formative assessment that provide teachers with language-specific information to record the student's progress is essential to equitable assessment. Emergent bilingual students benefit from teacher-designed formative assessments. Formative assessments are "designed to diagnose, reveal, and prepare students for mastery of learning outcomes" (Caldera, 2020). Because they are designed by teachers for a specific purpose, these assessments can reflect the distinct language practices of emergent bilinguals. One of the main purposes of assessment is to gather information that helps teachers guide, redirect, or adjust their practice to improve teaching and learning. In gathering this information, it is essential to use a variety of sources from diverse situations, at different times, and in response to students' needs.

In designing formative assessments, teachers should be aware of multimodal approaches. All communicative practices have multimodal aspects, such as writing and speech being linked to other modes of expression, for example, gesturing. Consequently, assessment should reflect a multitude of ways students make meaning and represent learning. Multimodal assessment can be a useful tool when working with students whose language practices do not hold the "privileged position of English" and whose preferred expressions include "images, music, movement" (Darvin, 2015, p. 591). The next section lists practices that represent the principles.

- Authentic assessment refers to activities or tasks demonstrated in real life contexts or with a meaningful application of essential knowledge or skills. Authentic assessment drives the curriculum and pedagogical approaches to it. It helps students to be engaged and innovative in their demonstrations, as well as build upon their translanguaging practices. These assessments provide opportunities for students to use their cultural capital to make connections to the content as they share their personal, cultural, and community experiences in their demonstrations of learning. Examples of authentic assessments may often be multimodal and include biographical narrative writing, family interviews, and local examples of content drawn from the community. Multimodal assessments may include a variety of writing genres including new literacies such as social media posts and memes. Or students may find that they can use visual representations of their learning like photo essays or paintings. Put together, written and visual elements can provide a clearer understanding than a single mode of writing.

- Performance-based assessments involve asking "students to perform to demonstrate their knowledge, understanding, and proficiency" (McTighe, 2015, para. 1) as an accurate evidence of their learning. Performances may include a specific activity using a skill, a creative product, artistic performance, or a tangible outcome. Performance-based assessments are particularly favorable for situations with a single "right" answer. They are open-ended and/or multifaceted. So, it is usually helpful to determine the evaluation criteria using a rubric specific to the content. Adding a double column rubric could collect evidence of student learning as it is demonstrated in both languages, so teachers can give credit for the content learned as they track language development.

- Portfolios are a collection of students' work organized in a systematic way to show their learning progress relevant to the curriculum. Teachers and students together should decide the content of the portfolio. In that way, this is an opportunity for both to reflect on the learners' goals and improvements in all areas. Portfolios focus on individual progress rather than comparing it with another student. The portfolio may also include anecdotal or other types of narrative records from the teacher and journals or reflections from the student. A continuum of learning may be used to track content development with learning standards and language development. Garcia suggests a dynamic progression that includes entering, emerging, developing, expanding, and commanding (Garcia, 2017, p. 85). Moreover, EBs might build a multi-year language portfolio that goes with them throughout their school years (see Celic & Seltzer, 2012).

- Project-based learning (PBL) is a great approach to help emergent bilingual students to learn and use academic language in a rigorous yet engaging way. PBL supplies EB students opportunities to practice their language and literacy skills in authentic contexts, making the learning process more meaningful. Assessment is an ongoing activity throughout the project, emphasizing student's self-assessment in relation to the project's learning target, checking for understanding, and finishing with a product or performance inviting other teachers, parents, and community members.

- Service learning (Blodgett, 2017) is another opportunity for students to prove their learning outcomes after a combination of assignments with a specific purpose. A key part of service-learning projects is self-reflection and metacognition, in addition to developing their literacy and oral fluency. Thus, allowing students to decide how they choose to show their personal learning in the project is part of dynamic assessment. Teachers might offer a list of options for students to choose, such as posters, performances, videos, reflective writing, oral presentation, among others.
- Teacher observation/documentation is one of the most important tools for gathering information for assessment purposes. Observation could be used for formal and informal assessments. Teachers observe students all the time, yet not all the information gets recorded or documented. There are multiple ways to organize teachers' observations such as vignettes, checklists, photographs, work sampling, or mind-mapping, among others. Systematic observation could be challenging. It is important to include students' information in individual and group settings, from different situations, times of the day, and subject-content; and even gather information regarding EB's cultural and background knowledge that is relevant to their progress.
- Assessing from many perspectives provides students additional feedback from different points of view. Starting with the self, a student becomes involved in evaluating their own development using the language they produced to complete the assignment. Peer assessment with language-paired partnerships may reveal learning to a teacher when the teacher is limited in the student's second language. When a teacher includes members of the family in the evaluation process, long-term growth and development, mitigating factors, and cultural values may be revealed in the demonstration of learning as family members bring a complete understanding of the student to the process.

Summarily, these practices include a dynamic approach to assessment based on the idea of Vygotsky's (1997) zone of proximal development that focuses not only on what the student can do independently, but more specifically on what he or she can do with the assistance of others, not only in their content learning but also in their language development. Moreover, these recommendations should not be interpreted as invitations for teachers to lower assessment expectations of emergent bilinguals based on perceived cultural deficits. To the contrary, they can perform well on assessments when given the opportunity to represent their learning in ways that privilege their cultural expressions.

CONCLUSION

Standardized assessments deprive emergent bilinguals of the opportunity to convey their knowledge and skills in culturally responsive ways (Montenegro & Jankowski, 2017). These assessments create "achievement gaps" between Whitestream students and emergent bilinguals. Because of cultural differences and other factors, there is a risk that even with adaptations to standardized tests, assessment results are unreliable (Spinelli, 2008). Consequently, it is important that educators "be steadfast in developing other means of assessing student knowledge and skills" (Howard, 2020, p. 13). Traditional approaches to assessment, limited in their ability to recognize the diverse ways students exhibit a myriad of skills including creative and artistic ability (Howard, 2020), create inequitable learning environments for emergent bilingual students.

REFERENCES

American Educational Research Association, American Psychological Associations, & National Council on Measurement in Education (AERA, APA, & NCME). (2014). *The standards for educational and psychological testing.* American Psychological Association.

Blodgett, J. (2017). Taking the class out of the classroom: Libraries, literacy, and service learning. In *The experiential library* (pp. 43–52). Chandos Publishing.

Caldera, A. (2020). The power of formative assessment: Using Classroom Assessment Techniques (CATs) to promote learning. In A. M. Quinzio-Zafran & E. A. Wilkins (Eds.), *The new teacher's guide to overcoming common challenges: Curated advice from award-winning teachers* (p. 178). Routledge.

Celic, C., & Seltzer, K. (2012). Translanguaging: A CUNY-NYSIEB guide for educators. *CUNY-NYSIEB.* New York.

Darvin, R. (2015). Representing the margins: Multimodal performance as a tool for critical reflection and pedagogy. *TESOL Quarterly, 49*(3), 590–600.

Garcia, O., Ibarra Johnson, S., & Seltzer, K. (2016). *The translanguaging classroom: Leveraging student bilingualism for learning.* Caslon Publishing.

Howard, T. C. (2020). *Why race and culture matter in schools: Closing the achievement gaps in America's classrooms.* Teachers College Press.

Knoester, M., & Meshulam, A. (2020). Beyond deficit assessment in bilingual primary schools. *International Journal of Bilingual Education and Bilingualism.* DOI: 10.1080/13670050.2020.1742652

Martinez, D. C., & Martínez, R. A. (2017) Researching the language of race and racism in education. In K. King, Y. J. Lai, and S. May (Eds.), *Research methods in language and education. Encyclopedia of language and education* (3rd ed.). Springer. https://doi.org/10.1007/978-3-319-02249-9_37

McTighe, J. (2015). Performance task Pd with Jay Mctighe—Blog. https://blog .performancetask.com/

Montenegro, E., & Jankowski, N. A. (2017). Equity and assessment: Moving towards culturally responsive assessment (Occasional Paper No. 29). National Institute for Learning Outcomes Assessment (NILOA).

Otheguy, R., Garcia, O., & Reid, W. (2015). Clarifying translanguages and deconstructing named languages: A perspective from linguistics. *Applied Linguistic Review, 6*(3), 281–307.

Spinelli, C. G. (2008). Addressing the issue of cultural and linguistic diversity and assessment: Informal evaluation measures for English language learners. *Reading & Writing Quarterly, 24*(1), 101–118.

Texas Legislature Online. (2021). S.B. No. 2066. Retrieved from https://capitol.texas .gov/tlodocs/87R/billtext/pdf/SB02066F.pdf#navpanes=0.

Valdés, G., & Figueroa, R. A. (1994). *Second language learning. Bilingualism and testing: A special case of bias.* Ablex Publishing.

Vygotsky, L. S. (1997). *The collected works of LS Vygotsky: Problems of the theory and history of psychology* (vol. 3). Springer Science & Business Media.

Chapter 11

We Are All Language Teachers

Lessons Learned From a Japanese Bilingual Program

Andrea Allen

The number of English Language Learners (ELLs) enrolled in US public schools is increasing at a considerable rate, with a 5 million student increase in the last decade alone (National Center for Education Statistics [NCES], 2018). According to the National Education Association (2020), 1 out of 4 students across the nation will be categorized as an ELL by the year 2025. As student demographics continue to change, attention has turned to narrowing the achievement gap growing between ELLs and their native English-speaking counterparts. While there are existing policies in place to ensure school districts identify, place, and monitor the progress of ELLs, they have proven insufficient in meeting the academic and socioemotional needs of these students. The all-English policies and transitional programs that hold dominance in most states, subtract students' language and culture from their learning and ultimately limit their chances for success (Valenzuela, 2017). Without native language support and familiar cultural exemplars, students are less likely to achieve English language proficiency at the standards required for them to transition out of exclusive programs. This chapter aims to provide more holistic strategies for serving ELLs by illustrating how one school's bilingual program operates from a social justice standpoint to foster the personal and academic growth of its students. The bilingual program, while situated in Japan, serves as an example of how US policies and practices can be reconstructed to be more inclusive of ELLs and the student body at large.

AN ISSUE OF SOCIAL JUSTICE

Adopting social justice as a lens through which to centralize the needs of ELLs is an avenue through which to narrow the achievement gap maintained by current policy and practice. Social justice refers to the reconstruction of a given space to ensure equity, recognition, and inclusion (Bell, 2016). When this definition is applied to the schooling of students whose first language is not English, educational systems that intentionally segregate students based on differences in language and culture must be eradicated to provide ELLs with the same educational opportunities as native English-speaking students. It is often assumed that social justice must correlate with controversy or overtly political issues, however social justice practice occurs when participants are equipped with the knowledge and skills necessary to critically analyze the world around them (Dewhurst, 2010). Once educators recognize that improving circumstances for ELLs is an issue of social justice, they are better able to develop more inclusive behaviors in themselves and their school communities (Bell, 2016).

CONTEXT

Taking into consideration that creating a socially just environment is dependent on factors unique to particular people and places, this section aims to provide educators with a general sense of what social justice education can look like in practice. Situated in a Japanese high school, observations of equitable school culture and inclusive practice are described in relation to how they contribute to the personal and academic success of ELLs on their campus.

The Bilingual Program

The junior and senior high school, located about an hour south of Tokyo, provides students the opportunity to study the English language through a bilingual program. Students who do not wish to study English have the option to take regular-track courses taught in Japanese. The program serves nearly all Japanese and native Japanese speakers with a small percentage of students coming from bicultural families in which one of the parents is a foreign national. Ten to twelve international teachers are employed in the bilingual program and come from predominately English-speaking countries, such as the U.S., Canada, Australia, New Zealand, and Great Britain. All teachers are required to have a teaching license and extensive teaching experience.

Numerous classes within the program are taught in English, with the exception of physical education and Japanese. Language acquisition, however, is not the only goal of the program. Japanese students are expected to maintain high standards of their Japanese language and scholastic achievement while achieving functional competence in the English language. Additionally, the program aims to foster global citizens who are globally minded and interculturally aware while maintaining their Japanese cultural identity.

Equitable School Culture

The program goals listed above reflect those of additive bilingual programs that have been shown to be more effective for academic achievement than the all-English instructional methods predominately utilized in the U.S. (Han & Park, 2017). Additive bilingual programs intentionally include students' culture and language as tools for language acquisition and content learning. This approach positions students' languages and cultures as central aspects of their educational experience, which can lead to more inclusive learning environments and higher levels of achievement (Theoharis & O'Toole, 2011). Considering that the bilingual program described above is in a Japanese school serving primarily Japanese national students, it's understandable that adopting an additive approach may be more easily achievable than it is for US schools serving more diverse populations. However, the success of students graduating from this program underlines the need to reform current practice and policy that hinders students' success in the U.S.

Student Experience

Students enrolled in the bilingual program are actively involved in all aspects of school life. They have unrestricted access to extracurricular activities and whole-school programs that allow them to share experiences and build friendships with students studying in regular-track Japanese courses. Encouraging an inclusive school culture in which both the bilingual students and staff interact regularly with the Japanese students and staff mitigates feelings of isolation and promotes solidarity. Social ties among students greatly influence their feelings about schooling, which in turn affects academic achievement and graduation rates (Valenzuela, 2017). Not only are the program goals of helping students learn English while maintaining their Japanese language and cultural identity achieved, but graduates from this program are truly global citizens who go off to study in universities all over the world.

Teacher Expectations

Another notable factor that contributes to the success of the students and the program is the quality and training of the teachers. The literature has established that teachers of ELL students are often underprepared to provide equitable educational opportunities and lack the knowledge and skills necessary to address structural inequities (Oliveira, 2013). The international teachers in the bilingual program, however, are well versed in school structures and instructional expectations before they even enter the classroom. During the hiring process, teachers are evaluated on their experience teaching ELL students as well as provided with a handbook outlining the skills and mindset necessary for success in the program. Teachers are expected to be flexible, open, patient, and understanding, alongside their ability to assess language needs and maintain a rigorous curriculum. To support these attributes, international teachers collaborate with Japanese faculty in lesson planning and are provided with professional development opportunities that target instructional methods for teaching ELL students specifically. There is a communal awareness that both the teacher's and student's linguistic, national, and cultural identities are all factors in the learning process, which creates a classroom environment rooted in inquiry and exploration. Further, all content teachers are also considered language teachers and are required to incorporate both content and language objectives when lesson planning and during instruction.

Inclusive Practice

A lesson on aesthetics gives an example of how content is presented with students' language and culture in mind. This lesson was implemented in a secondary art class within the bilingual program. Mirroring the demographics of the overall program, the class consisted of nearly all Japanese national students with a handful of bicultural students who had parents from the Philippines, Great Britain, and the U.S. The teacher was a US national and identified culturally as Mexican, Filipino, and American.

When teaching through a social justice lens, inclusive practice begins while lesson planning. It is through lesson development that teachers must think critically about the knowledge they are presenting and how that knowledge is influenced by their personal experiences and beliefs (Sensoy & DiAngelo, 2017). In reference to the aesthetics lesson, the teacher planned for students to discuss a set of questions that would not only give them time to practice speaking and listening in English but also think critically about their own knowledge construction. Introducing a new topic with discussion rather than lecture encourages learners to reflect on their own identities, experiences, and interests that shape the world around them. This meaningful reflection then contributes to students feeling more connected to the subject and their work moving forward (Dewhurst, 2010).

The discussion questions included were: "What is your idea of a successful artwork?," "What is the function of an artwork?," "What do people in your country think is beautiful?," and "Does art have to be beautiful?" Images of works created from around the world, with intentional inclusion of Japanese art, were presented alongside these questions. With the knowledge that the use of students' first language can promote higher levels of proficiency in their second language when learning new content, the teacher asked students to discuss these questions with their peers in Japanese before presenting their ideas in English. This exercise enables students to create a network of context clues that can help them make references to new meanings and structures in English (MacSwan et al., 2017).

After time to share in Japanese, the teacher transitioned students into a whole-class discussion in English. Within minutes it was evident that not all students agreed on what made an artwork successful or functional and had different ideas about beauty. For instance, some students thought bright colors and expressive lines made an artwork interesting, while others thought realistic depictions of nature and people signified a successful work of art. Inclusive practice requires making room for multiple voices to promote the idea that diverse positions can coexist (Nordlund et al., 2015). Therefore, to encourage critical thinking about personal beliefs in relation to those of others, the teacher invited students to identify factors that may influence their perspectives around beauty and art.

Some Japanese students attributed their preferences to their culture's deep connection to nature or made references to pop culture. Bicultural students made references to their experiences living in different countries or participating in cultural traditions that differed from those celebrated in Japan. The lesson's objective to have students think critically of their knowledge construction was ultimately achieved when students realized that no knowledge is neutral. All knowledge, however, is shaped by personal experience and context. Keeping this in mind, students can be more critically conscious of their roles in society and become active participants in their own learning.

CONCLUSION

Throughout this chapter, it is maintained that current all-English and transitional programs limit access to a quality education for ELLs in the U.S. To counter these practices, social justice is suggested as a framework from which to reconstruct existing systems to be more accessible and inclusive. A description of a bilingual program and a sample lesson taught within it provide examples of how principles of social justice can be implemented to develop more equitable learning environments for all members of the school community. With nearly 25% of students being negatively impacted by injustices within the US education system, it is critical to view differences in language and culture as complementary rather than restrictive factors in the advancement of society.

REFERENCES

Bell, L. (2016). Theoretical foundations for social justice education. In M. Adams & L. Bell (Eds.), *Teaching for diversity and social justice* (3rd ed., pp. 3–26). Routledge.

Nordlund, C., Speirs, P., & Stewart, M. (2010) An invitation to social change: Fifteen principles for teaching art. *Art Education, 63*(5), 36–43.

de Oliveira, L. (2013). Perspectives and lessons learned about teacher education for social justice. In C. de Oliveira (Ed.), *Teacher education social justice: Perspectives and lessons learned* (pp. 1–10).

Dewhurst, M. (2010) An inevitable question: Exploring the defining features of social justice art education. *Art Education, 63*(5), 6–13.

Han, J., & Park, K. (2017). Monolingual or bilingual approach: The effectiveness of teaching methods in second language classroom. Purdue Languages and Cultures Conference.

MacSwan, J., Thompson, M., Rolstad, K., McAlister, K., & Lobo, G. (2017). Three theories of the effects of language education programs: An empirical evaluation of bilingual and English-only policies. *Annual Review of Applied Linguistics* (37th ed., pp. 218–240).

National Center for Education Statistics. (2018). *English language learners in public schools.* U.S. Department of Education. Retrieved from https://nces.ed.gov/programs/coe/pdf/2021/cgf_508c.pdf

National Education Association. (2020). English language learners. Retrieved from https://www.nea.org/resource-library/english-language-learners.

Sensoy, O., & DiAngelo, R. (2017). *Is everyone really equal? An introduction to key concepts in social justice education* (2nd ed.). Teachers College Press.

Theoharis, G., & O'Toole, J. (2011). Leading inclusive ELL: Social justice leadership for English language learners. *Educational Administration Quarterly, 47*(4), 646–688.

Valenzuela, A. (2017). Subtractive schooling, caring relations, and social capital in the schooling of U.S.-Mexican youth. In D. Flinders and S. Thornton (Eds.), *The curriculum studies reader* (5th ed., pp. 267–278). Routledge.

Chapter 12

Toward a Glocalized and Translingual Perspective on Emerging Bilinguals

Ashley Karlsson

The idea of glocalization (Roudometof, 2016; Lam & Warriner, 2012), a portmanteau of two words "globalization" and "localization," offers a helpful frame for examining the universalities of educating multilingual learners while also attending to the significance of locally situated characteristics. This chapter argues that there are indeed universal principles and practices that all teachers of emerging bilinguals should know, and at the same time, all teachers need to be prepared to contextualize those global ideas with explicit attention to local spaces and identities. As part of the argument for a glocalized perspective on emerging bilinguals, this chapter calls into question the construction of the English Language Learner label (Motha, 2014), provides insights that complicate an essentialist view of multilingual students, and offers a more responsive framework for understanding and supporting the strengths and needs of this diverse student group through pedagogies centered around translanguaging.

As with many institutional labels, the phrase "English Language Learner" represents a paradox in educational equity. The socially constructed nature of this phrase and its ubiquitous use in education warrant a closer look at both the construction of the phrase itself and its alternatives. On the one hand, the phrase "English Language Learner" has offered teachers and schools an opportunity to move towards greater equity by enhancing the visibility of a particular group of students (Johnson & CAAL, 2017). Because students identified as English Language Learners are a federally recognized student group, the disaggregation of data using this term has surfaced school-level practices that disadvantage and marginalize students within this group (Motha, 2014). While the English Language Learner label and accompanying federal education policy may represent movement towards educational justice, there is still a long way to go to decouple current practices, policies from assimilationist and deficit-based views of students learning English. The ongoing marginalization of multilingual learners compels evolvement not only in praxis, but in the language used to talk to and with students and families.

An examination of language use in praxis demonstrates opportunities to continue advancing social justice for multilingual learners. The labels used in education spaces carry constructed meanings, and the phrase "English Language Learner" centers the English language in a way that reinforces the hegemony of English and positions students through a deficit lens. As a result, it is easy for teachers and schools to take up discourse that pathologizes emerging bilinguals (Motha, 2014). Students learning English as an additional language become part of a problematique that teachers and schools aim to solve through clearly explicated service models and comprehensive curriculum programs. This positioning fails to recognize the cultural and linguistic capital that emerging bilinguals bring with them into classrooms every day.

As more scholars and practitioners begin to conscientize the assets of this student population, the phrase "English Language Learner" is gradually being supplanted by more asset-based phrases like multilingual learner and emerging bilingual (Viesca et al., 2019, Machado & Hartman, 2019). This chapter uses both "multilingual learner" and "emerging bilingual" throughout in an intentional effort to decenter English and bring to the fore the linguistic assets of this growing student group.

An additional set of factors that influence the language and labels used in education revolve around policy and politics. At the national level, federal education policy has played a significant role in coalescing public discourse around particular terms and titles within education. For many years, the landmark civil rights legislation known as the Elementary and Secondary Education Act (ESEA) referred to multilingual learners as "limited English proficient," often initialized as LEP. In the 2001 reauthorization known as No Child Left Behind (NCLB), assessment data for students identified as LEP was required to be disaggregated within state accountability systems. While this federal distinction raised conversations about educational opportunities for emerging bilinguals, the word "bilingual" was largely erased from federal policy during this era and replaced by calls for English proficiency. The use of the term "LEP" and the strong focus on learning English with little regard for home languages reinforced assimilationist and hegemonic orientations towards English.

At the federal level, the label LEP was eventually replaced by English Language Learner (ELL) or the truncated English learner (EL) which now appears in the most recent 2015 reauthorization of ESEA as Every Student Succeeds Act (ESSA). In some federal databases and in some local policy documents, however, deficit-oriented labels still appear (Villegas & Garcia, 2021). Continuing to frame multilingual learners through the lens of "limited" proficiency problematizes not only the language learning process, but students themselves as in need of remediation. Policymakers and school leaders should be vigilant to ensure that references to LEP as a label for emerging bilinguals are revised with haste. The glacial speed at which language change takes hold in federal policy means that while LEP is still being phased out, more recent terms like EL are already partially outmoded by ongoing scholarship and quotidian practices within schools. While the pace of language shift can be a source of frustration for some educators, attending to conversations about language and labels is one way to shift public conversation and elevate the assets of multilingual learners.

Pollock (2017) reminds educators that the language and labels used in schools can serve to help or harm the students they serve. Confronting this distinction necessitates an understanding that the specific language and labels used to refer to groups of students within school settings should be used to amplify the strengths and needs of the group and not in ways that lead to collective dehumanization or pathologization. Using labels to identify emerging bilinguals for the purpose of evaluating the impact of institutional programming is a much different conversation than using family language backgrounds to profile students in need of remediation. Shifting language can play a role in shifting teacher dispositions, and subtle but explicit changes can recast conversations about multilingual learners in significant ways. With that said, language change absent tangible redistribution of resources amounts to performative rhetoric that only serves to maintain the status quo. In the fight for social justice, the decision to use the phrase "English learner" or "emerging bilingual" ultimately matters less than the ways in which instructional time and resources are being equitably allocated within the school system.

Increases in the number of emerging bilinguals within the United States have been concomitant with increases in the literature that attempts to offer strategies and practices specific to multilingual learners. Without explicit attention to the heterogeneous nature of emerging bilinguals, literature in this area runs the risk of essentializing a highly diverse population of learners. Even with some of the established categorizations like long-term English learners, students with interrupted formal education (SIFE), and recently arrived English learners, educators must recognize the ways in which these groups are themselves heterogeneous and dynamic and how these tailored labels can also perpetuate deficient orientations towards language learners. In

order to address the strengths and needs of emerging bilinguals more effectively, literature on emerging bilinguals needs to move away from reduction-
ist portraitures and towards a more multiscalar representation that honors the
complexities and intersectionalities of locally situated language identities.
A more developed view of emerging bilinguals must address differences in
language proficiency and multiliteracies that are borne out of differential
experiences with diverse educational systems while also turning attention
to data beyond proficiency and literacy scores (New London Group, 1996;
García & Kleifgen, 2019).

Current practices in supporting emerging bilinguals often place significant
weight on static data from federally required English proficiency assessments. A social justice perspective on multilingual learners questions the
deceptive simplicity of these representations of student language. Proficiency
scores, especially those from annual accountability tests represent a snapshot of student language during a given time. Making sense of these scores
requires contextualizing any particular language performance with additional
information that can create a more holistic and humanizing picture of student
strengths, needs and lived experiences. Static proficiency scores should not
be the only indicator used to determine the specifics of placement and programming for emerging bilinguals. The weight of such decision-making is
better supported with myriad sources of data, including input and engagement
with students, families and communities. Working towards equity with student placement means ensuring that opportunities for students are not limited
based on proficiency measures and that when proficiency scores are used,
they are used in a way that connects students with the resources they need to
continue expanding their linguistic repertoire,

When it comes to universalities about language and language development, one theory that can offer significant support to more dynamic perspectives on emerging bilinguals is that of translanguaging. The development
and theory of translanguaging parallels other concepts that seek not just to
cross, but to transcend socially constructed borders and boundaries. Terms
like "transnationalism" (Douglas Fir Group, 2016) and "transdisciplinary"
(Larsen-Freeman, 2012) move beyond the familiar, bounded concepts of
multinationalism and multidisciplinary. The concept of translanguaging
originated from the perspective of minoritized populations and is considered
by some to be a polysemic term (Leung & Valdés, 2019). Related terms
include "global Englishes, flexible bilingualism, hybrid language practices,
polylingual languaging, transidiomatic practices, code meshing, translingual
practice, and metrolingualism" (Poza, 2017). These terms share a sense of
flexibility within and between named languages.

While the general population may see language alternation as a coping
strategy to cover language gaps, translanguaging recognizes that the choices

individuals make to deploy different elements of their linguistic repertoire are more systematic in nature (Durán & Palmer, 2014). Translanguaging shifts away from static assumptions and orientations towards language by asserting that students have a dynamic and unitary linguistic repertoire (Orellana & García, 2014). The notion of a unitary linguistic repertoire contrasts with traditional views of language in which bilingualism has been socially constructed as two discrete language systems. Translanguaging also moves beyond traditional views of language by positioning language as a sympoetic process. In a sympoetic process, elements of language are co-organized and produced in relation to each other (Viesca et al., 2019). Translanguaging asserts that languages expand one another, not interfere with one another (Orellana & García, 2014).

The term "translanguaging" views language "with an epistemology that differs from that produced and normalized by the processes of nation building and colonialism" (García & Kleifgen, 2019, p. 555). Translanguaging goes beyond the use of conventional and bounded language domains of listening, speaking, reading and writing to include other multimodal communicative practices (Poza, 2017). Within the theory of translanguaging, multilingual students and adults are positioned as agential decision-makers who operate a complex, unitary linguistic repertoire (Durán & Palmer, 2014; Orellana & Garcia, 2014). The linguistic complexity recognized by translanguaging is concomitant with a recognition of the social and political complexities of language and identity. Another essential element of translanguaging is the development of critical language awareness (Orellana & García, 2014) through which students understand the social and political influences on the decisions they make both inside and outside the classroom. Promoting translanguaging in schools is a complex endeavor, one that requires vigilance in ensuring that the aims of linguistic justice are not diluted.

A more expansive view of students' languaging practices requires attention to the myriad factors that influence emerging bilinguals in classroom settings, including educational and literacy experiences as well as student identities. These identities can include not only the sociopolitical constructions of language, race, gender, and class, but also the hopes, goals, and dreams that students have for themselves and for their communities (Salazar, 2013; Lazar & Schmidt, 2018). In addition to static language proficiency scores, fully supporting emerging bilinguals requires understanding and appreciation for cultural funds of knowledge, family languaging practices, and lived experiences in community languages. The extension of student portraitures beyond quantitative measures is one way to humanize education practices and policies for multilingual learners. By including student interests and experiences as part and parcel of scholastic representations, educators are able to move away from essentializing approaches to language education and towards pedagogies that recognize assets both collectively and individually.

Given the complex and hybrid nature of students' linguistic identities, any approach to teaching and learning in support of emerging bilinguals must eschew the notion of a pedagogical panacea and instead recognize the complementarities of global principles in combination with locally contextualized strategies (Beech, 2011). A glocalized and translingual framework for teaching emerging bilinguals includes universal dispositions and quintessential knowledge co-organized with a diversity of pedagogical strategies to address unique student strengths and needs. The last few decades have seen the emergence and proliferation of myriad educational frameworks that have been implemented in support of multilingual learners. These frameworks can include specific programming structures, strategies for planning, instruction and assessment, as well as particular curricular materials. Evidence on the efficacy of certain frameworks continues to be collected, interpreted and extended across different settings.

When it comes to identifying strategies that have global applicability to support teaching and learning for emerging bilinguals, there are some themes with consistent evidence across theory and practice. These universals include an emphasis on meaningful relationships between teachers and students and an orientation towards multilingualism as an asset. In addition, advocacy for ongoing home language development, explicit attention to the language demands of academic tasks, and catalytic awareness of the role of social interaction in language learning all contribute to a framework of globally effective practices (Lucas, Villegas, & Freedson-Gonzalez, 2008). While the specific strategies used in service of these goals may vary, the core tenets represented in these concepts have both endurance and leverage. Constructing a pedagogical repertoire that is flexible enough to address the dynamic strengths of multilingual students requires attending to global themes while also tailoring practices to individual identities.

To accomplish these overlapping goals of globalization and localization alongside more fluid conceptualizations of language is a bold endeavor that necessitates action across multiple fronts. Teachers and education leaders must learn more about intersectional identities and lived experiences of the students they serve. Educational labels must be used in ways that lead towards greater equity by focusing attention and resources on marginalized populations without framing those populations as deficient in any way. Instruction should be designed to attend to dynamic identities within dynamic contexts, and all students should be encouraged to expand their language repertoires. Multilingualism and translanguaging should be normalized in educational spaces through both policy and practice. Positioning localized strategies in a supporting role to more expansive ideologies materialize a glocalized and translingual perspective on emerging bilinguals that advances social justice for culturally and linguistically diverse students.

REFERENCES

Beech, J. (2011). *Global panaceas, local realities: International agencies and the future of education* (Comparative studies series). Peter Lang.

Douglas Fir Group (2016). A transdisciplinary framework for SLA in a multilingual world. *Modern Language Journal, 100*(S1), 19–47. https://doi.org/10.1111/modl .12301

Durán, L., & Palmer, D. (2014). Pluralist discourses of bilingualism and translanguaging talk in classrooms. *Journal of Early Childhood Literacy, 14*(3), 367–388. https://doi.org/10.1177/1468798413497386

García, O., & Kleifgen, J. A. (2019). Translanguaging and literacies. *Reading Research Quarterly, 55*(4), 553–571. https://doi.org/10.1002/rrq.286

Johnson, A., & Coalition of Asian American Leaders (CAAL). (2017). *Minnesota multilingual equity network: English learner-every student succeeds act initiative.* Minnesota Education Equity Partnership.

Lam, W., & Warriner, D. (2012). Transnationalism and literacy: Investigating the mobility of people, languages, texts, and practices in contexts of migration. *Reading Research Quarterly, 47*(2), 191–215. https://doi.org/10.1002/RRQ.016

Larsen-Freeman, D. (2012). Complex, dynamic systems: A new transdisciplinary theme for applied linguistics? *Language Teaching, 45*(2), 202–214. https://doi.org /10.1017/S0261444811000061

Lazar, A., & Schmidt, P. (2018). *Schools of promise for multilingual students: Transforming literacies, learning, and lives.* Teachers College Press

Leung, C., & Valdés, G. (2019). Translanguaging and the transdisciplinary framework for language teaching and learning in a multilingual world. *Modern Language Journal, 103*(2), 348–370. https://doi.org/10.1111/modl.12568

Lucas, T., & Villegas, A. M. (2011). A framework for preparing linguistically responsive teachers. In *Teacher preparation for linguistically diverse classrooms: A resource for teacher educators* (pp. 76–93). Taylor and Francis.

Machado, E., & Hartman, P. (2019). Translingual writing in a linguistically diverse primary classroom. *Journal of Literacy Research, 51*(4), 480–503. https://doi.org /10.1177/1086296X19877462

Motha, S. (2014). *Race, empire, and English language teaching: Creating responsible and ethical anti-racist practice.* Teachers College, Columbia University.

The New London Group (1996) A pedagogy of multiliteracies: Designing social futures. *Harvard Educational Review, 66*(1), 60–93. https://doi.org/10.17763/haer .66.1.17370n67v22j160u

Orellana, M., & García, O. (2014). Conversation currents: Language brokering and translanguaging in school. *Language Arts, 91*(5), 386–392. https://www.jstor.org/ stable/24575550

Pollock, M. (2017). *Schooltalk: Rethinking what we say about and to students every day.* The New Press.

Poza, L. (2017). Translanguaging: Definitions, implications, and further needs in burgeoning inquiry. *Berkeley Review of Education, 6,* 101–128. https://doi.org/10.5070/B86110060

Roudometof, V. (2016). *Glocalization: A critical introduction.* Routledge.

Salazar, M. (2013). A humanizing pedagogy: Reinventing the principles and practice of education as a journey toward liberation. *Review of Research in Education, 37*(1), 121–148. https://doi.org/10.3102/0091732X12464032

Viesca, K. M., Strom, K., Hammer, S., Masterson, J., Linzell, C. H., Mitchell-Mccullough, J., & Flynn, N. (2019). Developing a complex portrait of content teaching for multilingual learners via nonlinear theoretical understandings. *Review of Research in Education, 43*(1), 304–335. https://doi.org/10.3102/0091732X18820910

Villegas, L. & Garcia, A. (2021). *A federal policy agenda for English learner education.* New America. https://www.newamerica.org/education-policy/reports/a-federal-policy-agenda-for-english-learner-education/

Chapter 13

Who Are the Students Learning English and How Do We Talk About Them?

Rachael Dektor and Kip Téllez

Teachers and others who work directly with children and youth do not have to wrestle with terms referring to students who share some demographic connection, learning characteristic, or other feature. They can call students by their names and their knowledge of the students' backgrounds and learning needs come clearly (or should come clearly) into view. As former teachers in elementary and secondary schools, we remember the names of many of our former students—Roberto, Anh, or Nayeli, for example—and when we called them by their name, they looked at us, and when we referred to them by name with our colleagues, we knew the students about whom we were talking.

We are not suggesting that all teachers know every important characteristic of their students; we admit openly that we did not. But we knew our students by their name, their face, and their families. It was only when we became researchers and advocates of educational policies that we needed terms to refer to students who shared some characteristics we considered important. In our new roles, we are forced to refer to students not by the name their parent(s) lovingly gave them but rather by some impersonal reference that coarsely groups them together. We are forced to do this because, in most cases, we do not know their names. And even if we did, we would not be allowed to use their names in our publications.

So, like every researcher and policy advocate, we must use terms for students that clearly and fairly identify the characteristic(s) important to our investigations or policy recommendations. In our case, we must arrive at an unbiased, asset-based term that describes students who are learning English.

Moreover, we must also operationally define students who are learning English; that is, when does a student know enough English to lose the designation? Or, if a student was once an English learner (EL) or English Language Learner (ELL), does the designation remain (e.g., "ever" an English learner)? These questions point out the difference between identifying students learning English and many other important student characteristics, such as ethnicity, which does not change over time.

In 2008, Durán, citing a report from the National Research Council, suggested "that ELLs are not a true demographic population that can be unambiguously defined by a set of well-defined indicators that are reliably measurable in an all-or-none way" (p. 300). We wondered if conditions had changed since 2008 and believed a new exploration on the topic was warranted. Like Durán, we are limiting ourselves to defining students learning English in the U.S. while recognizing that China educates, by far, the most students learning English (Na, Gregory & Téllez, 2021). We begin by analyzing four US states' policies to determine who receives English instruction (the "operational" definition portion of our chapter). We follow this analysis by exploring the terms researchers and policymakers have suggested, paying particular attention to those developed in the past decade.

ENGLISH LEARNER IDENTIFICATION
PROCEDURES IN FOUR STATES

In the U.S., the federal government must count the number of students learning English for at least one simple reason: since 1968, it has given school systems funding for each student learning English. In recent years, that amount has been about $125 (Williams, 2020). Despite this fiscal responsibility, the US Department of Education (US DOE) has allowed states to determine which students require English instructional services and then sends funding based on the number of students the states report. Neither the US DOE nor the states have paid much attention to the potential inequities that might result from this policy, primarily because $125 per student is equal to approximately three hours of instruction, a very small contribution considering most states are currently spending about $13,000 per student/year (National Center for Education Statistics, 2020).

Nevertheless, we have chosen to explore four states' criteria for determining how students initially qualify for special instruction in English and how they are "exited" after they gain sufficient English skills. Our four state cases (California, Texas, Arizona, and North Carolina) represent the states with the largest number of students learning English and one (North Carolina) with rapid growth. Notice that we have simply copied the terms used by the US

DOE in our analysis, saving the history and analysis of these terms for later in our chapter. The following table reports on each states' identification, assessments, "exiting" protocols and monitoring.

California, Texas, Arizona, and North Carolina all use the federally mandated home language survey to identify students who speak a language other than English at home (see Henry et al., 2017 for a review). Subsequently, the four states utilize a standardized test to determine each student's English proficiency. Students who, according to the test, are not proficient in English, are given the ELL label and are given a standardized test each year to demonstrate growth and/or English proficiency. All four states have a protocol for "exiting" students out of the ELL designation including demonstrating proficiency on the state mandated test which is followed by monitoring of student progress for varying numbers of years. Ultimately, all four states follow what seems to be a relatively standardized practice of identifying, tracking, "exiting" and monitoring their ELLs.

Table 13.2 illustrates the common features of the assessment states are using to designate students as English learners.

Tables 13.1 and 13.2 reveal that the process for identifying, assessing, exiting, and monitoring students from ELL programs are relatively consistent across all four states as well as being consistent with federal expectations. In addition, the assessments used to identify, place, and exit students from language instruction programs assess the same four skills (also according to federal guidelines), categorizes students into (between four and six) skill levels, and are developed by outside testing entities who appear to follow earlier test constructions (e.g., Language Assessment Scale). This finding is not surprising because all states are (fiscally) incentivized to adhere closely to the federal guidelines. We would also point out that additional research could determine if the states' tests are measuring the same constructs (as we suspect) via a straight-forward test "equating" procedure (see Kolen & Brennan, 2014). Such an analysis is, however, beyond the scope of our chapter.

Our analysis of four states' processes suggests that contrary to Durán's 2008 publication, we do indeed have reliable systems in place for determining who is categorized as an ELL in the U.S. We now turn our attention to a messier problem: What term do we use to refer to students learning English? In the following sections, we explore the various labels used to refer to those learning English, beginning with state policy language and ending with the newest terms.

Table 13.1. ELL Identification, Assessment and Exiting Protocol by State

State	ELL Identification	Assessments	Exiting Protocol	After Exiting
California (CA Department of Education, 2021)	Home Language Survey	ELPAC	Score of 4 on all domains, demonstration of basic skills relative to English proficient students through SBAC, Teacher evaluation, parent consultation/ opinion	4 years of monitoring after RFEP
Texas (Texas Education Agency, n.d.)	Home Language Survey	State Approved Identification Test and Language Proficiency Assessment Committee (LPAC) review, parent notification/ approval	Texas English Language Proficiency Assessment System (TELPAS) score of Advanced High Score in the 4 domains, state standardized reading assessment, teacher evaluation	2 years of monitoring from LPAC after reclassification

Arizona (Arizona Department of Education, 2013)	Home Language Survey	Arizona English Language Learner Assessment (AZELLA), parent accepts or declines services	Annual student assessment using AZELLA, score of "Overall Proficiency Level of Proficient"	2 years of monitoring after RFEP
North Carolina (Public Schools of North Carolina, 2020)	Home Language Survey	W-APT/WIDA test or Assessing Comprehension in English State-to-State for ELLS (ACCESS for ELLs)	Students exit EL identification by scoring a 4.8 composite score on ACCESS for ELLs	Subgrouped as Monitored Former English Learners for 4 years

"ELL" DEFINITIONS BY STATE

The development and use of the terms used to label and categorize the ELL population can be traced through policies such as the Elementary and Secondary Education Act of 1965 (ESEA), No Child Left Behind (NCLB) (2002), and the 2015 Every Student Succeeds Act (ESSA). In the ESEA and NCLB documents, language learners are consistently referred to as limited-English-proficient (LEP) however the 2015 ESSA, a reauthorization of ESEA, documents the shift of terminology from LEP to EL. The U.S. Department of Education defines ELL as "A national-origin-minority student who is limited-English-proficient. This term is often preferred over LEP as it highlights accomplishments rather than deficits" (2020, para. 2). Throughout the various policies, EL and ELL are used interchangeably and, while replacing the deficit based LEP label, LEP has not been eliminated.

We now turn to several state definitions to understand what label is being taken up and used across the country. According to California law an English Learner is "a pupil who is 'limited English proficient' as that term is defined in the federal No Child Left Behind Act of 2001" (California Legislative Information), thus relying on federal policy and definitions to inform state level decisions. The Texas Administrative Code uses the terms ELL and EL interchangeably. The terms, the code suggests, "are synonymous with LEP student" (2020). Arizona's laws are similar. The North Carolina Department of Public Instruction (NCDPI) uses ELL with the term "limited English

Table 13.2. Publisher Information, Skills Assessed, Level of Proficiency, and Frequency of Assessments

State	Publisher/ Developer	Skills Assessed	Levels	Frequency of assessments
California (California Department of Education, 2021)	Educational Testing Services	Listening, Speaking, Reading, Writing	The initial ELPAC assessment levels students as initially fluent English proficient, intermediate English learner, or novice English learner. The summative ELPAC assessment levels students 1–4.	Administered as initial assessment and as an annual summative assessment
Texas (Texas Education Agency, n.d.)	Texas Education Agency developed TELPAS to meet federal testing requirements of NCLB. (Busby, 2021)	Listening, Speaking, Reading, Writing	Beginning, Intermediate, Advanced, Advanced High	Administered annually
Arizona (Arizona Department of Education, 2021)	Harcourt Assessment Business (now part of Pearson PLC) (Lawton, 2009)	Listening, Speaking, Reading, Writing (Bruen et al., 2012).	Pre-Emergent/ Emergent, Basic, Intermediate, Proficient (Arizona Department of Education, 2016)	Initial placement test followed by annual assessments
North Carolina (Public Schools of North Carolina, 2020)	Wisconsin Center for Education Research	Listening, Speaking, Reading, Writing	Levels 1–6 (entering, emerging, developing, expanding, bridging, reaching) (Board of Regents of the University of Wisconsin System, 2021)	Initial (screening) assessment followed by annual assessment

proficient." While all four states have slightly differing definitions, they essentially define and characterize the population in the same way.

HISTORY OF ENGLISH LEARNER AS A TERM

The previous section demonstrates that the term most widely used by state agencies to refer to students who speak a language other than English at home is EL, which has largely replaced LEP (U.S. Department of Education, n.d.). As federal policy has shifted to the use of EL and ELL, we see a consistent use of the term across the four states we have examined demonstrating that, in contradiction to Durán's (2008) assertion, ELLs are a demographic that is determined across states in generally the same way and defined by generally the same terms. In the previous section we analyzed ELL definitions across four states but want to recognize and address the shortcomings of previous terms.

As the U.S. DOE (n.d.) explains, ELL has replaced LEP, but some researchers and policy makers argue that the ELL label is still deficit based. (It is also worth noting that "ELL" ignores the fact that even native speakers of English can be logically described as ELL.) For example, Ennser-Kananen & Leider (2018) explain that bilingual students are continuously labeled and identified based on what they cannot do (e.g., read at grade level). ELL, they argue, still points out what students cannot do instead of recognizing what students *can* do.

García (2008) proposed the term "emergent bilingual," maintaining that bilingualism is a resource that should be recognized, encouraged, and developed. Categorizing students as emergent bilinguals has many positive implications for students, including a focus on linguistic potential, the use of home language practices in the class, and the implementation of teaching strategies and practices that support bilingual practices. While "emergent bilingual" is certainly a shift towards an asset-based label, it too has shortcomings. To begin, it is grammatically incorrect. The term "emergent" generally means something arising unexpectedly or calling for prompt action. Indeed, two decades before García suggested "emergent," Téllez (1998) proposed the term "emerging bilingual," which is grammatically more accurate, but which also failed to recognize that some students, especially those attending dual language programs, might be learning more than two languages. In fact, any term using the word bilingual will face a similar fate.

Webster and Lu (2012) point out the terms designed to avoid the limitations of "bilingual": (a) dual language learners (Gutiérrez et al., 2010), (b) second language learners, (c) English as a second language learners, (d) language minority students, and (e) culturally and linguistically diverse students, each of which they argue fail in precision and learner assets. Instead, they suggest Learner of English as an Additional Language (LEAL), noting that person-first language is important. In fact, person-first terms are now routine in the special education community (i.e., "a learning-disabled student" becomes "a student with a learning disability"). The term LEAL, Webster and Lu argue, also recognizes that learning language is a dynamic process that utilizes *all* a learner's linguistic repertoires. Despite these advantages, LEAL is not (or not yet) widely used by policymakers or researchers. Many contemporary advocates of language programs prefer the term emergent bilingual, despite the shortcomings we noted above.

TOWARDS NEW TERMS

The language teaching community is currently embroiled in discussions regarding what is meant by a person's linguistic resources, and the term "translanguaging" has become the symbol of the controversy (see Castillo, 2021; Cummins, in press; MacSwan, 2017 for reviews). We believe that translanguaging might point to a new term because it implies that language learners "engage in *multiple discursive practices* . . . in order to *make sense of their bilingual worlds*" (García, 2009, p. 45). These practices challenge the belief that languages are learned and spoken separately. Instead, students draw on multiple linguistic repertoires for communicative and sense-making purposes. Translanguaging practices should be capitalized on as a resource for students learning English along with any other languages they may be learning.

Translanguaging also seems to mirror the growing number of dual language education programs (Kim et al., 2015) or maintenance bilingual education (Téllez, 2018), in which students are taught two languages for their entire schooling career, unlike, for example, transitional bilingual education, which ends native language instruction as soon as possible. Seltzer and García (2017) argue that translanguaging should be encouraged by teachers, even in classrooms or programs that want to keep language use separate. They suggest that a focus on translanguaging enables "authentic bilingual performances that give life to minoritized languages" (p. 2).

Translanguaging, as its adherents point out, promotes the view that (a) students' linguistic repertoire is for meaning-making purposes, (b) frames minoritized languages as assets instead of problems, (c) affirms student identity, and (d) offers a more holistic view of language learners. We suggest that translanguaging might be used to identify ELLs. For all the reasons translanguaging is a beneficial practice in the classroom, labeling children "students who translanguage" is attentive to the complex and dynamic process happening as children learn a new language along with their home language.

Instead of reducing students to "not-yet-proficient" learners as past terms have done, we need one that honors the diverse linguistic backgrounds of students and encourages multilingualism. Referring to learners as "students/learners who translanguage" or simply as "translanguagers" does just that and might prove to be the second-best term. The best, as we noted at the beginning of the chapter, is a student's name.

REFERENCES

Arizona Department of Education. (2013). *Procedures for identifying English language learner (ELL) students.* Arizona Department of Education. https://www.azed.gov/sites/default/files/2015/04/procedures-for-identifying-ell-students.pdf?id=55411316aadebe0b186bcbcd

Arizona Department of Education. (2016). *AZELLA proficiency scale and cut scores.*

Arizona Department of Education. (2018). https://www.azed.gov/sites/default/files/2017/10/AZELLA_ProficiencyScaleandCutScores_2pages_May2018.pdf?id=59f256793217e10b1c173f1c

Arizona Department of Education. (2021). *AZELLA assessment.* Arizona Department of Education. https://www.azed.gov/assessment/azella

Board of Regents of the University of Wisconsin System. (2021). *Access for ELLs interpretive guide for score reports: Grades K-12 spring 2021.* WIDA. https://wida.wisc.edu/sites/default/files/resource/Interpretive-Guide.pdf

Bruen, C., Nedrow, B., Scott, J., & Van Moere, A. (2012). *AZELLA development: The inside story* [PowerPoint slides]. OELAS Conference. https://www.azed.gov/sites/default/files/2016/12/AZELLA%20Development%20The%20Inside%20Story.pdf?id=585073f6aadebe0988f82be7

Busby, D. (2021). *What is TELPAS? What is ESL?* Haslet Elementary. http://northwesthaslet.ss10.sharpschool.com/staff_directory/donna_busby/what_is_t_e_l_p_a_s__what_is_e_s_l_

California Department of Education. (2021, June 16). *Reclassification.* U.S. Department of Education. https://www.cde.ca.gov/sp/el/rd/

Castillo, J. G. (2021). *Student and teacher translanguaging in dual language elementary mathematics classrooms: An exploration of beliefs, responses, and functions.* Unpublished doctoral dissertation, University of California, Santa Cruz.

Commissioner's Rules Concerning State Plan for Educating English Learners, Tex. Admin. Code § 19.89–1203. (2020). http://ritter.tea.state.tx.us/rules/tac/chapter089/ch089bb.html

Cummins, J. (in press). Translanguaging: A critical analysis of theoretical claims. In P. Juvonen & M. Källkvist (Eds.), *Pedagogical translanguaging: Theoretical, methodological and empirical perspectives.* Multilingual Matters.

Durán, R. P. (2008). Assessing English language learners' achievement. *Review of Research in Education, 32*, 292–327.

English Learner Portal. (2019). Texas Education Agency. https://www.texl.org/

Ennser-Kananen, J., & Leider, C. M. (2018). Stop the deficit: Preparing pre-service teachers to work with bilingual students in the United States. In P. Romanowski & M. Jedynak (Eds). *Current research in bilingualism and bilingual education. Multilingual education* (p. 26). Springer, Cham.

García, O. (2009). *Bilingual education in the 21st century: A global perspective.* Blackwell Publishing.

García, O. (2009). Emergent bilinguals and TESOL: What's in a name? *TESOL Quarterly, 43*(2), 322–326.

Procedures for Identifying English Language Learner (ELL) Students. (2013). Arizona Department of Education. https://www.azed.gov/sites/default/files/2015/04/procedures-for-identifying-ell-students.pdf?id=55411316aadebe0b186bcbcd

Reclassification-English Learners (CA Dept of Education). (2021). California Department of Education. https//www.cde.ca.gov/sp/el/rd/

Téllez, K. (1998). Class placement of elementary school emerging bilingual students. *Bilingual Research Journal, 22*(2–4), 279–295

Téllez, K. (2018). Maintenance Bilingual Education (MBE). *The TESOL Encyclopedia of English Language Teaching*, 1–6.

Guidelines for Testing Students Identified as English Learners. (2020). Public Schools of North Carolina. https://www.dpi.nc.gov/media/8789/open

Gutiérrez, K., Zepeda, M., & Castro, D. C. (2010). Advancing early literacy learning for all children: Implications of the NELP report for dual language learners. *Educational Researcher, 39*(4), 334–339.

Henry, S. F., Mello, D., Avery, M.-P., Parker, C., & Stafford, E. (2017). *Home language survey data quality self-assessment (REL 2017–198).* U.S. Department of Education, Institute of Education Sciences, National Center for Education Evaluation and Regional Assistance, Regional Educational Laboratory Northeast & Islands. Retrieved from http://ies.ed.gov/ncee/edlabs.

Identification of English Language Learners, Arizona Revised Statutes. §15–756. (2020). https://www.azleg.gov/viewdocument/?docName=https://www.azleg.gov/ars/15/00756.htm

Kim, Y. K., Hutchinson, L. A., & Winsler, A. (2015). Bilingual education in the United States: An historical overview and examination of two-way immersion. *Educational Review, 67*(2), 236–252.

Kolen, M. J., & Brennan, R. L. (2014). *Test equating, scaling, and linking: Methods and practices.* Springer Science & Business Media.

Lawton, S. B., (2009). *Use and impact of English-language learner assessment in Arizona* [White paper]. Arizona State University. https://files.eric.ed.gov/fulltext/ED530047.pdf

MacSwan, J. (2017). A multilingual perspective on translanguaging. *American Educational Research Journal, 54*(1), 167–201. https://doi.org/10.3102/0002831216683935

Na, L., Gregory, J. C., & Téllez, K. (2021). English language standards in California, China, and Mexico: History, comparison, and analysis. *Interchange*, 1–20.

Public Schools of North Carolina. (2020). *Guidelines for testing students identified as English learners.* North Carolina Department of Public Instruction. https://www.azed.gov/sites/default/files/2015/04/procedures-for-identifying-ell-students.pdf?id=55411316aadebe0b186bcbcd

Seltzer, K., & García, O. (2017). *Topic brief: Translanguaging and dual language bilingual education classrooms.* CUNY-NYS Initiative on Emergent Bilinguals.

Texas Education Agency. (n.d.). *English learner (EL) identification/reclassification flowchart.* Texas Education Agency. https://www.txel.org/media/p22bsjuc/english-learner-identification-reclassification-flowchart.pdf

Texas Education Agency. (n.d.). *What is TELPAS?* Texas Education Agency. https://tea.texas.gov/sites/default/files/Final_English_TELPAS%20FAQ.PDF

U.S. Department of Education. (2020, January 16). *Developing programs for English language learners: Glossary.* U.S. Department of Education. https://www2.ed.gov/about/offices/list/ocr/ell/glossary.html

U.S. Department of Education. (n.d.). *Ensuring English learner students can participate meaningfully and equally in educational pPrograms.* U.S. Department of Education. https://www2.ed.gov/about/offices/list/ocr/docs/dcl-factsheet-el-students-201501.pdf

U.S. Department of Education, National Center for Education Statistics, Common Core of Data (CCD), National Public Education Financial Survey, 2017–2018. (This table was prepared October 2020.)

Webster, N. L. & Lu, C. (2012). "English language learners": An analysis of perplexing ESL-related terminology. *Language and Literacy, 13*(3), 83–94.

Williams, C. P. (2020, March 31). *The case for expanding federal funding for English learners.* The Century Foundation. https://tcf.org/content/commentary/case-expanding-federal-funding-english-learners/?agreed=1&agreed=1

Chapter 14

Translanguaging as a Tool for Social Justice

Marta Carvajal-Regidor and Leah Mortenson

In this chapter, we provide insights into the ways that translanguaging—the notion and practice that centers emergent bilinguals' (EBs') language practices as fluid, heteroglossic, and holistic can serve as a tool for social justice by prioritizing students' whole linguistic repertoires when engaging with curricular materials in the classroom. The discussions in this chapter advance both knowledge and capacity for practitioners working with EB students by demonstrating that translanguaging resists nationalist and linguistic ideologies that otherize multilinguals as subaltern, thereby opening avenues of opposition. Furthermore, we demonstrate that the social justice angle of translanguaging advances multicultural education by highlighting the enmeshment of multiculturalism with multilingualism. We also comment on how translanguaging works as a practical tool, even in the context of standardized curricula and external, institutional pressures that place a high value on student performance via measurable output. Readers will come away with a deeper knowledge of the tenets of translanguaging and its relevance to all educators interested in promoting a more equitable environment for their learners.

Because teaching is never and can never be neutral (Dewey, 1938) and therefore must be acknowledged as a political act (Buchanan, 2017), teachers' choices in the classroom are fundamentally important for either maintaining or disrupting the status quo of the educational system (hooks, 1994). Therefore, it is imperative to interrogate instructional practices and strive to utilize those that promote social justice, since classrooms serve as "mini societies" whose makeup reflects or refracts the makeup of society writ large (Kumaravadivelu, 1999). In the following section, we explore the practice of translanguaging and discuss how it can be used to promote social justice when working with EB students.

ORIGINS OF TRANSLANGUAGING

The term translanguaging was coined by Cen Williams in 1994 and comes from the Welsh *trawsieithu*. Williams used the term to refer to a pedagogical practice where students are asked to switch languages according to receptive and productive uses (García & Li, 2014). For example, students may have been asked to read in Welsh and write in English. This practice of translanguaging was noticed by Williams (1994) through Welsh revitalization programs. There were concerns about how to keep both Welsh and English alive and functional, rather than students being reliant only on English. Williams framed these fluid language practices as positive, building from learners' and teachers' linguistic resources, instead of viewing these exchanges as negative practices due to the mixing of languages (Li & Ho, 2018).

Since Williams described translanguaging in the Welsh context, it has been used and expanded by several scholars. Translanguaging works both as an "act of bilingual performance and a bilingual pedagogy for teaching and learning" (García & Leiva, 2014, p. 199). It is an oppositional practice that relates to power, legitimacy, and authenticity to language repertoire (de Certeau et al., 1980). It works to question and problematize conceptions and definitions of language (García & Li, 2014) by demonstrating that bilinguals do not separate languages into distinct codes and instead, utilize one repertoire to communicate that consists of dynamic language practices (Kleyn & García, 2019). These dynamic language practices emphasize the agency of language users and help EBs develop as agentive members through their own language learning and language experiences. Thus, translanguaging challenges the idea that one thinks in named languages (although awareness of the political entities of named languages is present) and instead centers individual idiolects (a holistic linguistic repertoire) that are influenced by geography, social class, age, and gender (Li, 2018).

According to Gal and Irvine (1995), language ideologies are processes that both create and separate differences through socially constructed hierarchies. These hierarchies establish social practices around language- how it is used, what is constructed as "normal" or "standard," and what is constructed as "abnormal" or a deviation from the established norm. These linguistic scales are social constructs built around non-neutral language ideologies that underlie identity development, discourse construction, and the processes and practices of teaching and learning. These ideologies manifest through habitus and capital (Bourdieu, 1986), and ultimately have an impact on the kinds of opportunities one is given and the ways one's language use may be viewed as legitimate or illegitimate, which has both material and symbolic consequences that then produce and reproduce existing language ideologies.

Encompassing much more than simply shifting between two languages, translanguaging offers a way through which the creation and recreation of linguistic normalcy may be disrupted and reimagined, as it highlights the construction of speakers interrelated and complex discursive uses and practices that may not necessarily be categorized under the traditional definition of language. Translanguaging acknowledges that language is not fixed or neutral, but is instead heteroglossic, an ongoing process existing in context and shaped by complex histories of use. Translanguaging creates new discourses that critically question societal patterns to change such practices invested in the reproduction of inequitable frameworks (Garcia & Leiva, 2014).

It can be used to refer to the intermixing of language varieties, text types, symbols, discourses, and other modes of communication, and one of its aims is to position such dynamic practices as communicational norms rather than as separate and/or codified. Translanguaging pushes us to consider the socio-political context in which communication occurs, and it shifts teaching and learning away from existing as fixed products towards acting as processes to aid in meaning-making construction.

Li (2018) shows that using translanguaging as a theoretical frame may allow for both students as well as teachers to transform existing power dynamics. Everyone utilizes language in a variety of ways to communicate, so in a classroom context, this necessitates teachers' willingness to be vulnerable and open to encourage students to use all of their language capabilities, even if the teacher is not familiar with them. These changes can help progress language users' ability to transcend traditional understandings of language use to create meaning-making practices that are authentic to them. It provides a space for learners to practice their languages, question authoritative definitions of knowledge, capital, and identity to transform the status quo and reimagine representations of reality. It redefines belonging, language use, and ways of participating in society towards more fluid markers, and it pushes language use towards expanded notions of legitimacy and authenticity. In all the ways just described, translanguaging serves as a mechanism for social justice as it aids in rethinking language definitions and hierarchies that have historically valued some more than others, and it moves us towards more equitable orientations.

SOCIAL JUSTICE PEDAGOGY (SJP)

Social justice pedagogy (SJP) is a liberatory teaching practice in which educators acknowledge that injustice is real and that in order to build a more equitable society, we must revise our practices towards equitable orientations that recognize the impact of systemic injustice on students' lives. In practice, SJP understands education to be a means through which societal transformation is made possible (Zeichner, 2003), as students may be prompted to see themselves as agents of change whose actions within their own community's matter (Parker, 2006). SJP requires that teachers commit to: (1) Destabilizing the status quo and promoting visibility of marginalized individuals and communities through their teaching and actions and (2) Standing against oppression in all forms. In this way, SJP requires one's ethics to be put into practice through everyday reflection and action (Cumming-Potvin, 2009). Within an educational system that is deeply entrenched in inequities, SJP requires courage to go against the grain and be willing to turn inward and reflect on the prejudices, biases, and internalized "-isms" one may have absorbed through growing up in an "-ist" society.

Transformative teaching may only occur if both teachers and students are co-creating knowledge such that the hierarchies traditionally existing in PK–12 U.S. classrooms begin to dissolve. In contrast to the banking model of education which sees learners as empty vessels to be filled with knowledge, scholars like Freire (2010) and hooks (1994) view teachers and students as co-conspirators of knowledge creation who must co-engage in critical inquiry. Other scholars such as Adams and Bell (2016) describe the ways in which practicing SJP can result in communities where both students and teachers are learning subjects who reflect on their own and others' beliefs, backgrounds, and values to co-construct understandings of current structural systems as well as imagine and actualize new and more radical visions rooted in equity. Teaching is inherently political (Heybach, 2014; Journell, 2011), so the everyday choices we make in our classrooms contribute to or disrupt the existing makeup of society. hooks (1994) identifies that "the cozy, good feeling [of being a passive recipient of knowledge] may at times block the possibility of giving students space to feel that there is integrity to be found in grappling with difficult material" (p. 154). We who believe our current educational and societal structures could be better must teach in accordance with these beliefs.

TRANSLANGUAGING AS A TOOL
FOR SOCIAL JUSTICE

Translanguaging can be used by teachers as a pedagogical practice for social justice for those who face language marginalization by centering language users' flexible linguistic resources that enable them to engage in meaning-making experiences without dictating when and where they can use a specific language (García & Kleifgen, 2010). Furthermore, translanguaging positions language users and learners as multilingual speakers with rich and developed linguistic cultural resources and abilities that they use for communication (and thus as resourceful). This pushes back against a view of English language learners as deficient non-native speakers which is often what is perceived from a monolingual perspective (Kleyn & García, 2019).

Translanguaging is not simply about celebrating the use of different languages. Instead, it is "part of a moral and political act that links the production of alternative meanings to transformative social action" (García & Li, 2014, p. 37). This is a crucial aspect of translanguaging which demonstrates how language users' practices can lead the way in finding avenues of representation for those that have been and continue to be marginalized. Additionally, as a pedagogical practice, translanguaging helps question the long-held assumption that using the home language when learning a second or additional language is problematic, which still often dominates policy, practice, and the assessment of learning outcomes in second language education. Thus, translanguaging represents a pedagogy of empowerment that does not place one language above another in a hierarchical system and centers adaptability and cooperation of language and not competition or deficiency through a separation of language systems.

PEDAGOGICAL APPLICATIONS

As a pedagogical practice, translanguaging works to empower EB students by centering their fluid language practices as resources in learning. Thus, it is a pedagogical practice that can be used in all classroom settings. Below we offer some example applications of translanguaging within K–12 classrooms.

Using Translanguaging in English Language
Arts Classes

By implementing translanguaging as a pedagogical tool, English language arts teachers can help students incorporate their first and additional languages. For example, if students speak something other than English at home and the task is a creative writing assignment, allowing students to use a combination of languages throughout their writing assignment can help students express and learn about how thoughts and ideas may or may not be expressed in the same way in different languages. Scaffolding and allowing the use of different modalities as students work on drafting, editing, and revising can also work to further incorporate students' fluid communicative practices. Incorporating different languages within a school writing assignment can also work to empower students by allowing them to see that their language practices are important, effective, and valuable.

Using Translanguaging in Math Classes

For newcomers, word problems can also be difficult to decipher due to the use of culturally specific vocabulary. The use of translation can often serve as a first step to helping students understand the task at hand (in this case, the word problem). For example, if a student speaks Punjabi at home with their parents but no one in the school speaks Punjabi, the teacher can implement the use of Google Translate to try to help the student familiarize themselves with the word problem. Of course, the translation may not be precise, but this pedagogical practice can help the student get more meaning out of the word problem and the vocabulary. Implementing students' additional languages can also be beneficial for learners who have parents at home helping them with homework in a language other than English.

DISCUSSION

Implementing translanguaging as a pedagogical tool can help expand teachers' curricular practices by developing empathy and strengthening relationships with students. Even for a monolingual instructor who may not share language practices with students, translanguaging helps position students as teachers and facilitators and can encourage students to share what they know using their language practices. Additionally, it promotes critical thinking, collaboration, and problem solving. As a pedagogical practice, translanguaging can also help teachers who do not share students' additional languages be more attuned to students' body language and emotions, since not speaking the same language requires greater attention to these elements to reach understanding. This can lead to deeper reflections of how students are reacting and connecting (or not) to the curriculum and further show students' strengths and challenges and how to address those. Importantly, implementing translanguaging and the use of students' language practices reflects and values the diversity of cultural backgrounds and languages present in today's schools and can further help teachers and administrators develop practices and curriculum that helps engage and empower students.

Moreover, validating students' use of translanguaging within the classroom is also imperative within social justice education. Indeed, translanguaging demonstrates that teachers should develop their pedagogical practices on the whole of their students' abilities and skills, rather than demanding that they suppress linguistic features that might actually help them to communicate and construct knowledge. This allows students to feel ownership over their language abilities and use, rather than ceding control of them to an external authority such as the teacher, school, or state (García & Kleyn, 2016). Thus, we offer some simple ways teachers can validate students' use of translanguaging in the classroom:

- Create democratic spaces that allow for equal participation and create equity among various languages and cultures that are present
- Maintain high expectations for risk-taking, hard work, and use of rigorous content
- Support students to experience quality interactions and share ideas using flexible language abilities
- Develop students' identity investment in content by attending to what is most relevant to their lives (García et al., 2013)
- Allow multiple points of entry that allow students to access content through a variety of media and conceptual approaches
- Accept use of vernacular languages
- Implement instructional planning that is collaborative and cooperative: look at your curriculum through a multicultural lens

CONCLUSION

Translanguaging works as a tool for social justice because it foregrounds ways of creating an educational system that is equitable for all students. Students' use of translanguaging highlight the need to create environments that promote equitable playing fields; teachers' valuing this practice as a pedagogical, curricular, and social tool is one way to do so. The use of translanguaging in the classroom encourages teachers to create assignments and learning experiences that allow emergent bilingual students to use the diverse array of language with which they are equipped and build on existing skill sets rather than holding all students to the same inequitable standard.

REFERENCES

Adams, M., & Bell, L. A. (2016). *Teaching for diversity and social justice.* Routledge.

Bourdieu, P. (1986). The forms of capital. In J. Richardson (Ed.), *Handbook of theory and research for the sociology of education* (pp. 241–258). Greenwood.

Buchanan, R. (2017). Teaching as a political practice. *Literacy in Composition Studies, 5*(1), 76–80.

Cumming-Potvin, W. (2009). Social justice, pedagogy, and multiliteracies: Developing communities of practice for teacher educators. *Australian Journal of Teacher Education, 34*(3), 81–99.

De Certeau, M., Jameson, F., & Lovitt, C. (1980). On the oppositional practices of everyday life. *Social Text, 3*, 3–43.

Dewey, J. (1938). *Experience and education.* Macmillan.

Freire, P. (2010). *Pedagogy of the oppressed* (30th anniversary ed.). Continuum.

Gal, S., & Irvine, J. T. (1995). The boundaries of languages and disciplines: How ideologies construct difference. *Social Research, 62*(4), 967–1001.

García, O., & Kleifgen, J. (2010). *Educating emergent bilinguals: Policies, programs, and practices for English language learners.* Teachers College Press.

García, O., & Kleyn, T. (2016). *Translanguaging with multilingual students: Learning from classroom moments.* Routledge.

García, O., Woodley, H. H., Flores, N., & Chu, H. (2013). Latino emergent bilingual youth in high schools: Transcaring strategies for academic success. *Urban Education, 48*(6), 798–827.

García, O., & Leiva, C. (2014). Theorizing and enacting translanguaging for social justice. In A. Blackledge & A. Creese (Eds.), *Heteroglossia as practice and pedagogy* (pp. 199–216). Springer.

García, O., & Li, W. (2014). *Translanguaging: Language, bilingualism, and education.* Palgrave Macmillan.

Heybach, J. (2014). Troubling neutrality: Toward a philosophy of teacher ambiguity. *Philosophical Studies in Education, 45*, 43–54.

hooks, B. (1994) *Teaching to transgress: Education as the practice of freedom.* Routledge.

Journell, W. (2011). The disclosure dilemma in action: A qualitative look at the effect of teacher disclosure on classroom instruction. *Journal of Social Studies Research, 35*(2), 217–244.

Kleyn, T., & Garcia, O. (2019). Translanguaging as an act of transformation: Restructuring teaching and learning for emergent bilingual students. In L. C. de Oliveira (Ed.), *The handbook of TESOL in K–12* (pp. 69–82). John Wiley and Sons Ltd.

Kumaravadivelu, B. (1999). Critical classroom discourse analysis. *TESOL Quarterly, 33*(3), 453–484.

Li, W. (2018). Translanguaging as a practical theory of language. *Applied Linguistics, 39*(1), 9–30.

Li, W., & Ho, W. J. (2018). Language learning sans frontiers: A translanguaging view. *Annual Review of Applied Linguistics, 38,* 33–59.

Parker, W. C. (2006). Public discourses in schools: Purposes, problems, possibilities. *Educational Researcher, 35*(8), 11–18.

Williams, C. 1994. Arfarniad o ddulliau dysgu ac addysgu yng nghyd-destun addysg uwchradd ddwyieithog [An evaluation of teaching and learning methods in the context of bilingual secondary education]. University of Wales. (Unpublished PhD thesis).

Zeichner, K. (2003). The adequacies and inadequacies of three current strategies to recruit, prepare, and retain the best teachers for all students. *Teachers College Record, 105*(3), 490–519.

Chapter 15

English Language Learner
as sCHOLArs

Who Counts as a Scholar in
a Charter Public School?

Izamar D. Ortíz-González

This chapter will outline how a Spanish teacher supported her English Language Learners in a charter school operationalizing neoliberal market approaches within its academics and school policies. It will set the stage by describing the school before detailing the neoliberal policies pushed forth by the school administrators and then implemented by novice teachers. The policies that explicitly impacted English Language Learners (ELLs) dealt with those promoting scholar behavior. Amidst this context, it will document the steps taken by a Spanish high school teacher to foster a learning environment that integrates the community cultural wealth of her ELL students. As a high school teacher and an advisor to an after-school club, *Movimiento Estudiantil Chicanx/de Aztlan,* this educator worked with most of the English Language Learner students at this school. The lessons from this teacher's experiences and actions will be helpful for teachers who are navigating school stringent expectations and policies that leave English Language Learners alienated. This chapter also hopes to be helpful to administrators who want to enact school policies that incorporate the community cultural wealth of their English Language Learners.

This chapter will be grounded on Tara J. Yosso's community cultural wealth theory (2005) and Dolores Bernal Delgado's Latinx critical theory (2002). Additionally, these theories will be paired to Zaretta Hammond's brain on culture analysis to unpack the importance of the school environment and context in shaping how youths' brains engage with their learning. Overall, these theories will unpack the importance of using the cultural wealth of English Language Learners' (ELLs) to help them recognize themselves as knowledge holders.

Lastly, it will offer the steps that a Spanish teacher undertook for her ELLs students to recognize themselves and their culture in their school, curriculum, and neighboring community. The teacher intentionally aimed to cultivate the cultural wealth of English language learners to help them see themselves as scholars despite not fitting the mold pushed forth by their school, and thereby thrive in a charter school environment that espouses neoliberal school policies that isolate English language learners from their peers.

BACKGROUND OF SCHOOL

Their school is part of a small charter school system consisting of three schools, an elementary, a middle school, and a high school in California. Esperanza Network (a pseudonym) enticed families to enroll students for its high student college enrollment data. The schools in this network have historically outperformed the local public schools; the high school reports a student college enrollment data of 97%, and high standard test scores for middle school math and English language arts. The one exception? Their performance with English Language Learners. Despite this discrepancy, Esperanza Network uses these numbers to construct a narrative that their charter school system better prepares students through their K–12 schooling and college. This narrative fits into a larger dominant narrative that school reforms that employ market-based approaches are more efficient at addressing education disparities (Apple, 2006; Scott et al., 2016)

However, the numbers the school uses to tell this story do not gauge the English Language Learner experience at this school. These numbers do not reveal the student turnover rate and student reports of voice suppression. English Language Learners at Esperanza Network have significantly decreased enrollment over the years. Equally important, using in-state standardized exams, English Language Learners' scores are the lowest compared to other peers and are no better than other public schools. In California, English Language Learners continue to underperform in English and math compared to other learners (California Assessment of Student Performance and Progress). In this remark, Esperanza network's high school is not the great equalizer relative to neighboring schools.

This school operates within a neoliberal education context. *Neoliberal education* is the movement that promotes market-based approaches, like school choice, anti-teacher union policies, and the high use of standardized testing, to shift the blame for the disparities in education outcomes to students, teachers, and community (Apple, 2006; Lipman 2013; Scott et al. 2016; Montaño, 2015; Horsford et al. 2018; Mayorga et al., 2020). Esperanza Network embodies this context in that it has a CEO, employs Teach for America, and relies on high stakes testing to hold students and teachers accountable. These charter schools have become notorious for adopting a "no-excuses" policy towards student behavior and learning. White (2020) describes these no-excuse charter schools as "heightened emphasis on behavior, longer school days. A relentless focus on test scores and the use of data to drive instruction" (p. 151). Esperanza Network equipped all their classrooms with a "no-excuses" sign and "data-driven" as a slogan for promotion and recruitment.

Further, Esperanza Network also integrated neoliberal school policies to push for "scholar" behavior on students. Bettina Love claims these types of schools as merely offering a *Character education* (2019). *Character education* are the "gimmicks" that push for grit, hard work, character traits that supposedly enable students to take accountability for their conduct, and their academics. These gimmicks are all in the vein of promoting professionalism and personality traits espoused as scholarly and professional. Character education operates under the assumption that students lack morality or the proper character traits that serve as the key to success is the adaptation of these traits---this is important because adapting this stance ignores students' lived experiences. Further, these traits, "scholar" in Esperanza Network, are typically centered on Whiteness. Among its pillars of citizenship—leadership, commitment, high expectations, and data—this school specifies that scholars must model professionalism. A scholar does not wear red or blue. A scholar does not use artificial color on their hair; a scholar does not use "excessive jewelry. The characteristics of a scholar they promote alienate my students. The model they present as a scholar does not embody a person of color and instead embodies the standards devoid of my students' culture.

COMMUNITY CULTURAL WEALTH

Who Counts as a Scholar?

Besides stringent expectations of character, the academic content provided for students in a stringent classroom setting rarely acknowledges their ethnic histories and language as scholarly. This serves to isolate students further because, as Zertta Hammond indicates in her book, *Culturally Responsive Teaching and the Brain,* students' brains will not connect if they do not feel valued. Instead, they shut down in an environment it perceives as threatening and unwelcoming (2005). The body's nervous system is hardwired

to detect safety or threats in the environment. Thus, the learning environment of English language learners matters. Hammond highlights this point:
"relationships are at the intersection of mind-body" (p. 45), meaning that
students' brains will learn invested within relationships. What happens in
an environment where the image of a scholar serves to isolate the students?
What happens when the school policies pushed forth by administrators and
implemented by teachers trigger students' safety-threat detection system? At
best, students become disengaged; at its worst, a student is escorted to the
dean's for "clowning around."

The educator in this chapter used *community cultural wealth* theory
grounded in *Latino critical race* theory to construct a learning environment
that would foster relationships and dissuade any activation of a student's
alarm-threats system. *Community cultural wealth* is a theory that focuses on
the assets that individuals outside the dominant society bring into their learning and schooling (Yosso, 2005). This theory builds on *Latino critical race
theory* which holds that the knowledge of Chicanx, now often referred to as
Latinx, also counts as legitimate knowledge (Delgado Bernal, 2002).

These theories help explain why the standards espoused by the charter
school described in this paper do a disservice to ELL speakers of Latinx
backgrounds. The scholar traits that the school pushed for, that focused on
leadership, service and professionalism were devoid of any resemblance to
Latinx culture. Further, the school administrators asked teachers to be vigilant about uniforms, hair style, and aesthetics in order to teach these students
about professionalism. Students were constantly sent to the deans for infring-
ing on these policies, and these in turn kept students from learning and engaging in classroom curriculum. Community cultural wealth and Latino critical
race theory support and provide a roadmap for educators to implement in the
classroom.

BRIDGING THEORY TO PRACTICE

Know Your Community

Latinx epistemology acknowledges students' lived experiences as knowledge—hence the Spanish teacher purposely sought to understand the lived
experiences of students within the community itself. She started with the
school's demographics before planning her curriculum and the schooling
experience that would be culturally engaging. The school collects demographic data that may be too general to gauge the differences in individual
students' backgrounds. For this reason, the teacher utilized student and family
surveys—provided in English and Spanish—to understand the origin of her

English language learners. From these surveys, and eventually, through the relationships fostered between youth and teacher, she recognized that she had Afro-Latinx students, students from Guatemala and El Salvador, and México.

Against this backdrop, the teacher sought opportunities for English language learners to redefine what it means to be a "scholar." She started with the curriculum students received. Most of her ELLs did not have a strong foundation in their native tongue or English. Most of her ELLS were first-generation students with solid speaking abilities in Spanish but low writing and reading abilities. However, about 10% of her English language learners were newly immigrated. This information served as the basis for her curriculum decisions.

Counterstories in a Spanish Classroom

Counterstories tell stories of the marginalized, the minoritized, the often-excluded stories omitted from the dominant curriculum in schools (Yosso, 2006). In order to shift the paradigm of what it means to be a scholar or scholarly, the teacher purposely used counterstories throughout her curriculum. The use of counterstories allowed the teacher to teach a curriculum that defies stereotypes and narrates the omitted stories from mainstream narratives. For this reason, this teacher intentionally chose a curriculum that permitted the telling of stories of people whose own stories were those of the oppressed and minority. She did this using the second language acquisition theory of teaching proficiency through reading and storytelling (TPRS). This language theory aims to expose language learners to as much comprehensive language input as possible using stories in written form, songs, and video (Alley and Overfield, 2008). Therefore, students are listening, reading, and writing stories from the very beginning. This teacher did this in three primary ways (1) through novels specifically created to teach Spanish through TPRS to beginners and advanced speakers, (2) songs, and (3) content lessons highlighting the counterstories of Latinx in US society.

With TPRS novels, the instructor was able to plan lesson plan units that scaffolded for the English language learners who were heritage speakers while centering the counterstories of Spanish speakers of the novels. The teacher chose two novels, one centered on the immigrant refugee plight of a Guatemalan family set in the 1980s, *Esperanza* by Carol Gobb, and the other novel, *Vida y Muerte* by Anonymous. These novels allowed the teacher to highlight the resiliency of the characters who had to escape the caracal state in Guatemala to seek refuge in Mexico and then the United States. More importantly, the teacher asked students to draw parallels between the characters' lives to the students' lives—what were the characters' fears? What were the fears of students? What were the dreams of characters, and what were their dreams? The teacher then used the resilience and ingenuity of the characters and asked them to identify these traits within their own lives, within their families' lives. In this way the educator was asking students to constantly acknowledge the wealth that stems from their own cultures and communities.

During the start of the COVID-19 pandemic, these readings were chunked into small sections, and the questions attached were reflective—students were asked to relate to the experiences of the novel with their own lived experiences. Students responded well, and the teacher had over 70% response rate—this response rate was the second highest in the school grade level at the school. Lucky for this teacher, charter schools love quantifying data.

Along with the novels, the teacher opened her unit lessons with songs that resonated with the novels and highlighted the culture of ELLs—since most of them are Latinx, these songs were chosen to reflect the diversity of Latinx students present. *Caminos de La Vida, La Bamba, Soy America* were chosen to highlight the significant influence of Afro-Latinx on the music industry and culture. Again, the purpose was to constantly tell a counter-story even within the stories I shared of what and who was Latinx/Mexican/Chicanx. Students also reflected the lyrics of the song to their own lives, and therefore constantly recognized their lived experiences as legitimate knowledge worthy of scholarship.

The Spanish curriculum infused civic action: students wrote letters supporting immigrant issues, uniform policies, and other civic issues. Curriculum units dealt with stereotypes and the constant story of the outsider and insider—from the zoot suits of the 1950s to indigenous struggles for autonomy in Mexico. The lessons highlighted the civic action characters in the novel and historical figures who undertook to organize and unionize. The curriculum units asked students to reflect on the obstacles that hinder the actualization of their aspirations—to recognize that these obstacles reflect systemic structures that alienates them and not a deficit characterization of their identities. They also created poster messages that were then used to participate in the Women's March and the Martin Luther King Walk. Encouraging students to participate in these walks was meaningful in that it enabled students to connect their learning with the occurrences of their community.

Healing Through Culture

The instructor intentionally exposed students to community leaders who reflected their identity. First, she had to send that email and outreach with local professors and community organizers. She immersed herself in the community outside of school and recognized a neighborhood group composed of community college professors, restaurant owners, and artisans who yearly planned a Day of the Dead procession and transformed the neighborhood blocks into a celebration honoring the neighborhood's ancestors. Before the educator in this paper was hired as a Spanish teacher, the school had no participation in these neighborhood celebrations.

Through an after-school club and my content, the teacher provided a space for students to learn the celebration's origins. In the after-school space, students came into the classroom to prepare a much larger *ofrenda* or altar. Through the conversations in this space, students shared the loss of siblings and parents with other students and teachers. They brought pictures of the lost ones as a remembrance. The instructor and students-built community through remembrance, and learned stories of each other, they did not otherwise share during the school day. The students then built an ofrenda on the main street of the school's neighborhood. Students invited their friends and families to share their ofrendas through the celebration that ended late in the evening. This learning experience, besides allowing students to share how they remember their loved ones that passed away, connected them with community leaders outside of the school. It showed them that their culture also made them scholars.

La Loteria

Similarly, the educator partnered up with a professor at the local state college to participate in an art workshop on La Lotería. This workshop offered students an opportunity to reflect on the strengths of their families and themselves to overcome obstacles to be in this country. Through this experience, the educator could get students to reconnect with scholars outside of school who were like them and labeled as English language learners when they attended K–12 schools and had succeeded through academia to earn a PhD and be a professor while maintaining his Latinx culture and values. Thereby modeling for students what it means to redefine what it meant to be a sCHOLAr.

CONCLUSIONS

Despite the restrictive environment imposed by Esperanza Network's school policies and student expectations, this instructor was able to leverage the cultural wealth of the school's community to foster a positive understanding of students' identities as scholars. First, the professor sought to understand the community, demographically, the neighborhood, and the classroom. She then taught Spanish using counterstories through the TPRS method. Finally, she outreached to community leaders who were professors at the local universities and community colleges for students to be exposed to scholars who, like them, were Latinx and did not fit the rigid expectations imposed by their charter school.

REFERENCES

Alley, D., & Overfield, D. (2008). An analysis of the teaching proficiency through reading and storytelling (TPRS) method. *Dimension*, 13–25.

Apple, M. W. (2006). *Educating the "right" way: Markets, standards, God, and inequality*. Taylor & Francis.

Apple, M. W. (2006). Understanding and interrupting neoliberalism and neoconservatism in education. *Pedagogies: An International Journal, 1*(1), 21–26. https://doi .org/10.1207/s15544818ped0101_4

Bernal, D. D. (2002). Critical race theory, Latino critical theory, and critical raced-gendered epistemologies: Recognizing students of color as holders and creators of knowledge. *Qualitative Inquiry, 8*(1), 105–126. https://doi.org/10.1177 /107780040200800107

California Assessment of Student Performance and Progress. (n.d). *English language arts literacy and mathematics: Smarter balanced summative assessments.* https://caaspp-elpac.cde.ca.gov/caaspp/PerformanceTrendReportsSB?ps=true &lstTestType=B&lstGrade=11&lstFocus=a

Hammond, Z. (2014). *Culturally responsive teaching and the brain: Promoting authentic engagement and rigor among culturally and linguistically diverse students*. Corwin Press.

Horsford, S. D., Scott, J. T., & Anderson, G. L. (2018). *The politics of education policy in an era of inequality: Possibilities for democratic schooling*. Routledge.

Lipman, P. (2013). *The new political economy of urban education: Neoliberalism, race, and the right to the city*. Taylor & Francis.

Love, B. L. (2019). *We want to do more than survive: Abolitionist teaching and the pursuit of educational freedom*. Beacon Press.

Montaño, E. (2015). Becoming unionized in a charter school: Teacher experiences and the promise of choice. *Equity & excellence in education, 48*(1), 87–104.

Scott, J. T. (2011). Market-driven education reform and the racial politics of advocacy. *Peabody Journal of Education, 86*(5), 580–559. https://doi.org/10.1080 /0161956X.2011.616445

Scott, J., Trujillo, T., & Rivera, M. D. (2016). Reframing Teach for America: A conceptual framework for the next generation of scholarship. *Education Policy Analysis Archives, 24*. https://doi.org/10.14507/epaa.24.2419

Yosso, T. J. (2005). Whose culture has capital? A critical race theory discussion of community cultural wealth. In *Race Ethnicity and Education, 8*(1), 69–91. https:// doi.org/10.1080/1361332052000341006

White, T. (2020). Charter schools: Demystifying whiteness in a market of "no excuses" charter schools. In E. Mayorga, U. Aggarwal, & B. Picower (Eds.), *What's race got to do with it? How current school reform policy maintains racial and economic inequality* (2nd ed.). Peter Lang.

Chapter 16

Building Transfer Partnerships to Increase Culturally and Linguistically Diverse Student Access and Success

Amanda R. Morales, Elvira J. Abrica, Brenee King, Linda P. Thurston, and Beth Montelone

Within the stratified system of higher education, 4-year universities and 2-year community colleges are often discussed as independent entities. Yet, the success of both sectors (and those students learning within them) rests, at least in part, in their ability to collaborate and partner with one another (Phelps & Prevost, 2012). Partnerships between 4-year institutions and 2-year community colleges are especially critical to establishing and maintaining viable pathways for historically underrepresented student groups (Crisp & Nuñez, 2014).

For example, first-generation, low-income, and minoritized students are more likely to begin their post-secondary education experience at the community college (Ma & Baum, 2016; National Student Clearinghouse Research Center, 2017). Yet, their successful access to and completion of the bachelor's degree has been historically hindered in large part by ineffective communication within and across education institutions (K–16), cumbersome college transfer policies, and outdated articulation agreements between 2-year to 4-year institutions leading to credit loss (AAC&U, 2016; Bailey, Jeong, & Cho, 2010; Monaghan, & Attewell, 2015; Johnson, Starobin, & Laanan, 2016; Zeidenberg, 2012; Zamani, 2010). This is in addition to the often chronic and compounding disparities created by economic and educational resource gaps between these students and their predominantly White, and middle-class counterparts (Carter, Welner, & Ladson-Billings, 2013; Zamani, 2010).

Successful partnerships between 4-year universities and 2-year community colleges consider these myriad issues and the complex impacts they have on educational policy, practice, and program design (Herrera, Morales, Holmes, & Herrera-Terry, 2011; Lohfink, Shroyer, Morales, & Yanke, 2011; Starobin, Smith, & Laanan, 2016; Wilcox, Wyn, & Fyvie-Gauld, 2006). Regardless of student type, and whether it is a selective research university or an open-admissions community college, institutions understand that in order to meet student success outcomes, they must address student access, experience, and information gaps at varying levels (Hoffman, Starobin, Laanan, & Rivera, 2010; Kift, Nelson, & Clark, 2010). Doing so necessitates increased investment of time and resources to accommodate the economic, academic, and social-emotional needs of today's college student (Wilcox et al., 2006).

As such, this article documents the work of one institution, a public, 4-year, research university (from here on referred to as High Plains University), and its community college, Hispanic Serving Institution (HSI) partners over the past 20 years as they engaged in equity-oriented, cross-institutional collaborations in their predominantly rural state. It discusses how partners approached the work of increasing Culturally and Linguistically Diverse (CLD) students' engagement and success, particularly in the high-demand/ shortage areas of teacher education and STEM (science, technology, engineering, and math).

In the sections to follow, the authors first explain the need for cross-institutional collaboration, introducing and defining the concept of "partnership capital" (Amey, Eddy, & Ozaki, 2007) as a conceptual framework for structuring effective partnership efforts. Secondly, they provide context for the study and describe the various partnership projects and their development. Thirdly, the authors briefly articulate key lessons learned from the study. Finally, they provide conclusions and considerations for others who might be interested in engaging in similar work.

RESEARCH ON CROSS-INSTITUTIONAL PARTNERSHIPS

Partnerships between 2-year community colleges and 4-year institutions have been considered previously by scholars, particularly by Marilyn Amey and her colleagues (2007, 2010), Carrie Kisker (2007, 2016), L. Allen Phelps and Amy Prevost (2012), and Eboni Zamani (2010). This body of research has yielded important information about the specific dimensions of cross-institutional partnerships that support effective student transfer pathways (such as a focus on increased cohesion and alignment, and the identification and dismantling of historically-problematic structural barriers), as well as the integration of high impact practices such as establishing bridge programs, undergraduate research experiences, living-learning communities, and campus engagement experiences (Contreras, 2011; Hatch, 2017; Kuh, 2008; Kuh & Kinzie, 2018).

Some studies have highlighted multifaceted collaborations making strides particularly towards equity-oriented, systemic improvement related to CLD student engagement and success (Amey, Eddy, & Campbell, 2010; Baxter, 2008; Lohfink et al., 2011; Phelps & Prevost, 2012). The above-mentioned studies affirm the increasingly relevant role that community colleges play in CLD student degree completion and overall workforce development in high-demand fields (Hagedorn & Purnamasari, 2012; Hoffman et al., 2010).

It is important to note that although such partnerships have the potential to contribute to collective goals by leveraging the strengths of each institution (Armistead, Pettigrew, & Aves, 2007; Kisker, 2007; Vidotto, 2014), there are often longstanding challenges to such partnerships (at both the state and institutional levels). For example, incongruent power relations, differences in intentions, poor/ inefficient communication, geographical isolation, and unequal resource distribution between research universities and community colleges can profoundly hinder effective partnership development and sustainment (Amey et al., 2010; Shroyer, Yahnke, Morales, Dunn, Lohfink, & Espinoza, 2009).

As with any type of cross-institutional partnership is more effective when issues are made transparent, when there is strong, action-oriented, distributed leadership, and when each institution is seen as an equal contributor (Farrell & Seifert, 2007). Often, an investment of time and energy towards true relationship building, both at the individual and institutional level, is necessary in order to develop trust across a partnership (Kezar & Lester, 2009; Knackendoffel, Dettmer, & Thurston, 2017). Understandably, this kind of investment leads to increased respect and understanding of the unique organizational cultures of each institution and their potential contributions to the collective work (Cohen, Brawer, & Kisker, 2014). Therefore, literature indicates that if the overarching goal of cross-institutional partnerships is CLD student engagement, success, and degree completion, each partner must be opened to learning *from and with* each other (Gonzales & Terosky, 2016; Phelps & Prevost, 2012; Shroyer, Morales, Yahnke, & Bietau, 2013).

While this growing body of literature is helpful, much of this partnership literature suffers from three central limitations. First, the extent to which community colleges are often positioned as inferior is not well-documented or interrogated (Amey et al., 2007; Amey et al., 2010; Lohfink et al., 2011), even though research universities are historically and widely characterized as elitist from within and outside academia.

Second, given that geography is among the most salient factors that shape college opportunity in the United States (Hillman, 2016), it is problematic that the existing research has focused primarily on urban areas and/or regions with relatively stable demographic change. Meanwhile rural areas, particularly in the Midwest, are witnessing more rapid demographic shifts comparatively (Katisiaficas et al., 2015). With simultaneous increases in (im)migrant and multilingual population settlement and mobility (Hatch, Garcia, & Sáenz; Hamann et al., 2002), in these regions, institutional partnerships become even more essential, yet complicated to navigate. Third, there is limited literature that explores the ways in which systemic and structural racism, classism, and linguicism in higher education impact cross-institutional partnership development and success (Gist, Bianco, & Lynn, 2019; Jain, Herrera, Bernal, & Solórzano, 2011; Morales & Shroyer, 2016).

Despite gains in understanding institutional partnerships, Kisker (2016) posits that there remains a critical need to better identify and understand the real "factors that may be barriers or aids to achieving partnership goals" (Kisker, 2016, p. 283), especially within contexts. Kisker (2016) pointed to the need for a deeper understanding of the "processes by which community college—university transfer partnerships can be created and sustained" (Kisker, 2016, p. 283). As such, this brief chapter seeks to address, at least in part, these identified needs within a Midwest context.

CONCEPTUAL FRAMEWORK

Marilyn Amey and her colleagues, through extensive research on educational collaborations and community college partnerships, have developed a partnership model that accounts for the potential assets (or different types of *capital*) that institutions contribute to collaborative efforts (Amey et al., 2007; Amey et al., 2010). They identify how an understanding of institutions' (a) *social capital*—their connections, relationships, and individual reputations; and (b) their *institutional capital*—their "available resources, trustworthiness for follow-through, and genuineness of mission and goals" can shape partnership development (Amey et al., 2010, p. 338). The authors argue that these two forms of capital, when understood and leveraged correctly, can maximize what they call, *partnership capital*.

In their 2010 study, Amey and colleagues point to several key questions that should be considered to understand the "meaning, relevance, and utility of educational partnerships" (Amey et al., 2010, p. 335–336). Those questions include: (a) what was the impetus to initiate the partnership; (b) what is the context of the partnership; (c) how is the partnership understood by others; (d) what is the role of leadership in framing the partnership for constituents;

(e) what are the outcomes, benefits, and costs of the partnership; and (f) what is required to sustain the partnership or to let is dissolve? (Amey et al., 2010).

Engaging university stakeholders and potential community college partners in discussions around these questions at the development phase of a partnership allows members to better understand each partner's role(s) and responsibilities and can start from a clearer vantage point. These discussions allow for a more transparent process, demystifying political/ economic forces and potentially uneven power relations involved. The concept of partnership capital as a theoretically defined and empirically established construct by Amey et al. (2007) and Amey et al. (2010) served as a useful initial lens for analyzing, defining, and interpreting the various skills, resources, and relationships that were brought to bear within the collaborative partnership in this study.

CONTEXT FOR THE STUDY

In the region of the state where the HSI partners are located there is an increased need for systemic skilled workforce development (Kefalas & Carr, 2001; Morales, 2011; Rooks, 2018). The cattle and poultry production industries in the area, and the labor demands they create, have required *rural dexterity* (Morales, 2019) as communities reimagine social, public health, and educational infrastructures to meet new needs. The schools in the region continue to have increased enrollments of CLD students, Latino/a/x students. With over 65% of the K–12 student population identifying as a race/ethnicity other than White and close to 50% of them being English language learners (State Department of Education, 2020), the schools in this historically White, remote, southern part of the state have been grappling with how to respond effectively.

These shifts have and continue to impact more than the K–12 education systems, as they have direct implications for *how* and *who* post-secondary institutions are recruiting, supporting, and graduating at the collegiate level. Boot Hill Community College, Oasis Community College, and Grasslands Community College (pseudonyms provided) are all Hispanic Serving Institutions (HSIs) in the region and have a great deal of experience serving the needs of their Spanish speaking CLD student populations. While the support systems and resources these community colleges have developed and provide to their communities are arguably robust, due to sheer geographic remoteness, their students still struggle with limited exposure to career options and limited access to baccalaureate-granting institutions (Hatch et al., 2016; Schmitt-Wilson, Downey, & Beck, 2018), making university partnerships both strategic and vital for workforce development (Morales, 2011).

As such, in collaboration with K–16 educational partners in the region, numerous departments within High Plains University designed and implemented targeted pathway programs focused on CLD student access and success in higher education, particularly within the high-demand fields of K–12 (English to Speakers of Other Languages [ESOL]) education and STEM. The present study sought to document this process and the insights gained along the way.

This critical self-study employed life and professional story methodologies (Goodson & Sikes, 2001/2010). Given their long history at the university and their direct involvement with the partnership projects included in this study, the authors of this chapter were both researchers *and* participants. As participant observers, the researchers engaged in ongoing dialogs among themselves and with partnership colleagues, drawing upon contextualized and dialectic methods of data collection and analysis to interpret individual narratives and collective experiences over time. Using a partnership capital model (Amey et al., 2010) as a guiding framework, the authors sought to better understand how partnerships contributed to effective, collaborative, cross-institutional work, particularly as it is related to successful CLD transfer student recruitment, retention, and engagement. Before identifying and discussing the lessons learned across the partnerships, the following section briefly describes the various partnership projects (in both teacher education and STEM) as further context to understand their features and the processes involved in their development.

TEACHER EDUCATION PARTNERSHIPS

BESITOS Program and Affiliated Projects

In 1999, the Center for Intercultural Multilingual Advocacy (CIMA) within the College of Education at High Plains University launched a comprehensive recruitment and retention program focused on increasing the number of bilingual/ bicultural students in teacher education.

The Bicultural Education Students Interacting to Obtain Success (BESITOS) program began with Department of Education (DoE) funds that allowed the university to hire a full-time coordinator and project staff dedicated to the comprehensive support of CLD students in the program. Additionally, this program provided tuition scholarships, targeted tutoring, and intrusive/ holistic advising as well as support for students' sociocultural and linguistic needs and professional development. This initial, highly effective program served as a model for several additional federal- and state-funded projects within the college (e.g., Project Synergy, Chrysalis, and AccessUS) over the next

15 years (Herrera et al., 2011; Holmes, Fanning, Morales, & Herrera, 2012). Though each project had some of its own unique characteristics, they were all designed after the original BESITOS model.

Equity & Access K-16 Partnership

The above-described teacher education programs were built upon/ utilized the well-established professional development school (PDS) partnership between High Plains University and regional K–12 districts, which began in the late 1980s. However, it was through a DoE-funded Teacher Quality Enhancement grant that the university's college of education was able to forge deeper and more sustained partnership relationships within the predominantly Latino/a/x communities that were home to the HSI community colleges. This partnership, called the Equity & Access Partnership (E&A), strengthened the college of education's ability to transform programs to better recruit, retain, prepare, and place bilingual graduates in these high-needs districts as teachers.

STEM PARTNERSHIPS

Bridges to the Future, Pathways to Public Health, and Developing Scholars Programs

The college of engineering and several departments within the college of arts & sciences at High Plains University have longstanding partnerships with these HSI community colleges as well. Through several National Science Foundation (NSF) and National Institute of Health (NIH) funded projects, STEM student recruitment and retention has been a targeted area for growth. Beginning 2003, programs such as Bridges to the Future and Pathways to Public Health (beginning in 2010) were designed/implemented to increase the number of underrepresented students with baccalaureate degrees in the biomedical and behavioral sciences, and in public health.

Ultimately, the long-term goals of such programs were/is to increase the number of CLD students enrolling and graduating with bachelor's, master's, and doctoral degrees in STEM-related fields. The Bridges program supported CLD students in their transition out of the partnering HSI community colleges into High Plains University and connected them with programs and resources at the university in their given field. Once at the university, Bridges students were folded into the successful and institutionalized Developing Scholars Program (DSP). As part of the DSP, students engage in direct research in their STEM area of interest and have numerous professional development opportunities with faculty mentors, graduate students, and program staff.

Louis Stokes Alliance for Minority Participation in STEM Project (LSAMP)

In 2012, faculty and administrators across both the college of education and the college of arts and sciences at High Plains University began interdisciplinary discussions regarding CLD student success across their programs. These leaders realized that while the universities in the state had a long history of impactful programs in specific areas, many CLD and first-generation college students in the state were not entering or persisting in post-secondary education. Therefore, they sought to pool intellectual and human resources to develop more generally, a comprehensive recruitment and retention pathway initiative for CLD and first-generation college students coming from ethno-racially diverse and remote areas of the state.

The first developmental priority was to connect with individuals and institutions whose mission and commitments aligned. A corps of faculty and administrators from education, engineering, biology, veterinary medicine, and agriculture emerged. As this interdisciplinary team began reaching out to transfer institutions, the three, long-time HSI community college partners and one minority-serving transfer institution from the eastern side of the state were eager to work together in program conceptualization.

Once identified, partners from all institutions connected via conference call weekly to discuss needs and ideas for the partnership project. Each institution was encouraged to contribute their perspectives regarding strengthening college access pathways, particularly for CLD students interested in STEM-related degrees. Each partner determined site-specific goals as well as how their institution would contribute to the larger goals of the project. The funding source they pursued and received was the Louis Stokes Alliance for Minority Participation in STEM (LSAMP) program through the NSF. This 4-year project, awarded to and equally distributed to High Plains University and its alliance of HSI partners, leveraged the historic relationships and institutional and social capital existing within/across the partnership.

LESSONS LEARNED

As the researchers in this study looked across the various recruitment and retention, and transfer partnership projects that Great Plains University engaged in over the past 20 years, there were broad, fundamental factors that determined the level of effectiveness of partnership goal achievement. More specifically, participant narratives pointed to institutional characteristics, programmatic considerations, and personnel decisions that directly impacted outcomes for culturally and linguistically diverse student recruitment, retention, and graduation within these collaborative efforts.

Findings from this critical self-study indicated explicit factors, such as cumbersome, outdated, and exclusionary policies, the low expectations for CLD students held by some faculty, and high turnover rates among community college personnel created tensions and challenges. However, (a) fostering authentic and strategic relationships around a common vision, (b) maintaining effective communication and continuous learning, and (c) identifying obstacles, being flexible, and striving for innovation were foundational elements for building strong cross-institutional partnerships in support of CLD student success.

AUTHENTIC & STRATEGIC RELATIONSHIPS AROUND A COMMON VISION

The value of critical *authentic relationships* built around a common vision could not be understated. The concepts of "trust building" and "deep relationships" was reiterated numerous times within the participant narratives. Across each of the transfer partnership projects, the ability of the collaborators to successfully implement program goals was often shaped by the relational commitments of the stakeholders involved. Participants indicated that they grew to understand the importance of "knowing your partners" and "finding your people"—or those who understood the real purpose behind the work.

To minimize historic issues that hinder CLD student success and serve as roadblocks to project outcomes, participants spoke about a need for *systems thinking*. One project leader said, "we all had to be deliberate in everything," which took a commitment to flattening hierarchies, reaching beyond administrators and project managers, and making direct connections with potential "gatekeepers" at various levels within and across institutions (financial aid and admissions staff, professors, etc.). Participants indicated this included fostering "authentic relationships" with both formal and informal leaders, as well as identifying and/or hiring project personnel at each institution who were like-minded, student-focused, equity-oriented, and best suited to the project work at hand.

EFFECTIVE COMMUNICATION AND CONTINUOUS LEARNING

Clear and consistent communication across partner institutions also proved vital. Maintaining regular check-ins with partners and the CLD students and keeping a formalized and up-to-date *communication protocol* across offices at all institutions was essential. This allowed project-associated personnel from each site to stay abreast of student and overall project progress and to know exactly whom to contact in each office for specific answers to questions and concerns. In order to reach collective outcomes, it was important to clarify expectations and voice concerns promptly and directly, while also listening to the needs and expectations of others in the partnership. Participants indicated that when they took time to listen for understanding they were more capable of empathizing and working towards real solutions.

Additionally, in several of the partnership projects, co-learning through *cross-institutional professional development* was an important element built into their design. These professional development sessions proved highly effective for two reasons. First, they provided structured time for project leaders, student services staff, instructional faculty, and administrators to collaborate on specific project-related tasks as well as to address important structural issues and to focus on the larger goals of the partnership. Second, they served as an ideal venue to introduce faculty, staff, and administrators to important research and practices related to diversity, equity, and inclusion, as well as critical pedagogies such as culturally responsive teaching and sheltered instruction for multilingual learners.

IDENTIFYING OBSTACLES, BEING FLEXIBLE, AND STRIVING FOR INNOVATION

Even the most well-intended and thoughtfully designed partnership project encounters obstacles. Participants described that they learned the importance of implementing safeguards against common pitfalls (geographic distance, technology, funding, and high turnover of personnel) early on. In addition to the more logistical and pragmatic issues, narratives indicate that establishing and sustaining the institutional relevance of the program across campus communities required persistent effort and intentionality.

To make a lasting impact, participants indicated that they needed to be flexible, attentive, and brave enough to challenge the status quo. While the partnership projects incorporated important high impact practices such as faculty and graduate student mentorships (social capital) and undergraduate research experiences (institutional capital), participant narratives suggest that some of the most innovative programs and meaningful outcomes of partnership projects occurred when project members were attuned to the historic and emergent needs of CLD students.

For example, this meant *being culturally responsive, not reactive*. Participants indicated a clear commitment to going beyond providing basic student support services. The most successful projects incorporated overt programming to address the academic, sociocultural, and linguistic needs of their primarily first-generation, CLD students. This included providing structured *literacy seminars* (Herrera et al., 2011). Much more than just tutoring, literacy seminars allowed the multilingual/ELL students the opportunity to work together on their academic language proficiency with knowledgeable, multilingual education staff and their multilingual peers. Students were coached specifically on writing and test taking skills in their second language.

Many of the projects also incorporated ongoing *identity seminars* (Herrera et al., 2011) where sociocultural aspects of the students' experiences provided the primary content of focus. In these seminars, students were given the space and time to reflect on and unpack their cultural identities and developing identities as CLD college students within a PWI. Given that Great Plains University lacked ethno-racial diversity writ large, project leaders used such seminars as important mechanisms for historically minoritized transfer students to develop a sense of community within the larger predominantly White campus context.

Finally, participants described *cross-institution faculty collaboration* as another significant innovation they saw develop as a result of the cross-institutional partnerships. Related to the professional development offerings already described faculty members from the university and the community colleges had opportunities to collaborate with each other in meaningful ways. Some examples included co-teaching courses, co-developing research proposals, etc. As a result, participants indicated that mutual respect developed. Though traditionally slow to acknowledge that universities have things to learn from community colleges, university faculty acknowledged that community college faculty often had more localized knowledge of the CLD students they were serving (social capital), and often had better expertise and flexibility in understanding and meeting students' needs.

Conversely, through these partnerships, narratives indicate that the community college faculty gained perspective as they were able to better appreciate and utilize the physical and human resources (institutional capital) available at the research university level and were more knowledgeable and enthusiastic when sharing information with their CLD community college students about future opportunities at the university level.

DISCUSSION AND CONCLUSION

As outlined in the literature, effective models of higher education that support today's college student must go beyond addressing basic needs in isolation (Kanno & Harklau, 2012; Soria, 2015). Given the increasingly complex characteristics and enrollment patterns of students, to be effective institutions must move beyond traditional models of recruitment and retention and use innovative and strategic approaches to implement engaging, relevant, and culturally responsive pathway programs (Holmes et al., 2012). The findings from this critical self-study illustrate the utility of cross-institutional transfer partnerships for implementing such programs that can collectively contribute to local, regional, and state-wide goals not attainable by one institution alone.

It is clear from the lessons learned described above, the longstanding partnership relationships forged were about more than just enrollments. They were about partners developing a genuine understanding of systemic needs, each other (at both the institutional and faculty level), and the populations they serve. Within such deepened relationships, partners were able to maximize both their social and institutional capital to achieve outcomes and respond to students' needs more efficiently and long after targeted funding ended.

This study showed that when partners are committed to a clear vision, effective communication, ongoing learning, and openness to innovation, they can leverage their partnership capital in creative ways to provide students more effective, meaningful, and sustained opportunities. Furthermore, in partnership, institutions can become more robust and strategic. For example, they are better able to tailor programs and services to specific needs, to position themselves for new opportunities, and to take innovative risks; knowing that partners are there to inform, support, and/or join in their efforts.

While this study focuses on one university and its partnership projects with HSI community colleges in one state, it provides evidence-based insights gained from leveraging and developing partnership capital in a rural, mid-western, higher education context over a 20-year period. This study not only identifies strategic considerations and promising practices that could prove useful for other institutions with similar characteristics, but also it illuminates and elevates the capital of community colleges and the profoundly important role they can/do play in systemic improvement of CLD student access and success (particularly in remote regions). Furthermore, it points to the need for universities writ large to better understand, respect, and appreciate the realities and contributions of community colleges as viable partners in higher education.

REFERENCES

Amey, M. J., Eddy, P. L., & Campbell, T. G. (2010). Crossing boundaries creating community college partnerships to promote educational transitions. *Community College Review, 37*(4), 333–347.

Amey, M. J., Eddy, P. L., & Ozaki, C. C. (2007). Demands for partnership and collaboration in higher education: A model. *New Directions for Community Colleges, 139,* 5–14.

Armistead, C., Pettigrew, P., & Aves, S. (2007). Exploring leadership in multi-sectoral partnerships. *Leadership, 3*(2), 211–230.

Association of American Colleges & Universities (AAC&U). (2016). *In Texas, a collaborative approach to the two-year to four-year transition.* Author. http://www.aacu.org/campus-model/texas-collaborative-approach-two-year-four-year-transition

Bailey, T., Jeong, D. W., & Cho, S. (2010). *Student progression through developmental course sequences in community college.* Community College Research Center, Teachers College, Columbia University.

Baxter, B. (2008). The power of partnership. *Community College Journal, 79*(2), 10–13.

Carter, P. L., Welner, K. G., & Ladson-Billings, G. (2013). *Closing the opportunity gap: What America must do to give all children an even chance.* Oxford University Press.

Cohen, A. M., Brawer, F. B., & Kisker, C. B. (2014). *The American community college* (6th ed.). Jossey Bass.

Contreras, F. (2011). Strengthening the bridge to higher education for academically promising underrepresented students. *Journal of Advanced Academics, 22*(3), 500–526.

Crisp, G., & Nuñez, A. M. (2014). Understanding the racial transfer gap: Modeling underrepresented minority and nonminority students' pathways from two- to four-year institutions. *The Review of Higher Education, 37*(3), 291–320.

Farrell, P. L., & Seifert, K. A. (2007). Lessons learned from a dual-enrollment partnership. *New Directions for Community Colleges, 139,* 69–77.

Gist, C., Bianco, M., & Lynn, M. (2018). Examining grow your own programs across the teacher development continuum: Mining research on teachers of color and nontraditional educator pipelines. *Journal of Teacher Education,* 1–13.

Gonzales, L. D., & Terosky, A. L. (2016). Colleagueship in different types of post-secondary institutions: A lever for faculty vitality. *Studies in Higher Education,* 1–14.

Hatch, D. (2017). The structure of student engagement in community college student success programs: A quantitative activity systems analysis. *AERA Open, 3*(4), 1–14.

Hagedorn, L. S., Purnamasari, A. V. (2012). A realistic look at stem and the role of community colleges. *Community College Review,* 40(2), 145–164.

Hatch, D. K., Garcia, C. E., & Sáenz, V. B. (2016). Latino men in two-year public colleges: State-level enrollment changes and equity trends over the last decade.

Faculty Publications in Educational Administration, 43. http://digitalcommons.unl .edu/cehsedadfacpub/43

Herrera, S. G., Morales, A., Holmes, M., & Herrera-Terry, D. (2011). From remediation to acceleration: Recruiting, retaining, and graduating future CLD educators. *Journal of College Student Retention, 13*(2), 229–250.

Hillman, N. W. (2016). Geography of college opportunity the case of education deserts. *American Educational Research Journal, 53*(4), 987–1021.

Hoffman, E., Starobin, S. S., Laanan, F. S., & Rivera, M. (2010). Role of community colleges in stem education: thoughts on implications for policy, practice, and future research. *Journal of Women and Minorities in Science and Engineering, 16*(1), 85–96.

Holmes, M., Fanning, C., Morales, A., & Herrera, S. (2012). Contextualizing the path to academic success: culturally and linguistically diverse students gaining voice and agency in higher education. In Y. Kanno & L. Harklau (Eds.), *Linguistic minority students go to college: Preparation, access, and persistence* (pp. 201–219). Routledge.

Jain, D., Herrera, A., Bernal, S., & Solórzano, D. (2011). Critical race theory and the transfer function: Introducing a transfer receptive culture. *Community College Journal of Research and Practice, 35*(3), 252–266.

Johnson, J. D., Starobin, S. S., & Laanan, F. S. (2016). Predictors of Latina/o community college student vocational choice in stem. *Community College Journal of Research and Practice, 40*(12), 983–1000.

Kanno, Y., & Harklau, L. (2012). Introduction. In Y. Kanno & L. Harklau (Eds.), *Linguistic minority students go to college: Preparation, access, and persistence* (pp. 1–16). Routledge.

Kefalas, M., & Carr, P. (2001). *Hollowing out the middle: The rural brain drain and what it means for America.* Beacon Press.

Kezar, A. J., & Lester, J. (2009). *Organizing higher education for collaboration: A guide for campus leaders.* Jossey-Bass.

Kift, S., Nelson, K., & Clark, J. (2010). Transition pedagogy: A third generation approach to FYE—A case study of policy and practice for the higher education sector. *The International Journal of the First Year in Higher Education, 1*(1), 1–20.

Kisker, C. B. (2007). Creating and sustaining community college—university transfer partnerships. *Community College Review, 34*, 282–301.

Kisker, C. B. (2016). An inventory of civic programs and practices. *New Directions for Community Colleges, 2016*(173), 13–21.

Knackendoffel, A., Dettmer, P., & Thurston (2017). *Collaboration, consultation, and teamwork for students with special needs.* Pearson.

Kuh, G. D. (2008). *High-impact educational practices: What they are, who has access to them, and why they matter.* Association of American Colleges and Universities.

Kuh, G. D., & Kinzie, J. (2018). What really makes a "high-impact" practice high impact? Inside Higher Ed. http://www.insidehighered.com/views/2018/05/01/kuh -and-kinzie-respond-essay-questioning-high-impact-practices-opinion

Lebrón, J. L., & Lester, J. (2017). No longer junior colleges: Integrating institutional diversity into graduate higher education programs. *Journal for the Study of Postsecondary and Tertiary Education, 2,* 147–162.

Lohfink, G., Morales, A., Shroyer, G., & Yahnke, S. (2011). Building a distance-delivered teacher education program for rural CLD teacher candidates and the lessons learned. *The Rural Educator, 33*(1), 25–36.

Ma, J., & Baum, S. (2016). Trends in Community Colleges: Enrollment, Prices, Student Debt, and Completion. *College Board Research Brief.* https://research .collegeboard.org/pdf/trends-community-colleges-research-brief.pdf

Monaghan, D. B., & Attewell, P. (2015). The community college route to the bachelor's degree. *Educational Evaluation and Policy Analysis 37*(1), 70–91.

Morales, A. (2019). Understanding and valuing rural dexterity: Experiential funds of knowledge, science education, and rural kids. *Great Plains Research, 29*(Spring), 33–40. [Special Issue: Framing an Education Research Agenda of/for the Great Plains].

Morales, A. (2011). Factors that foster Latina, English, language learner, non-traditional student resilience in higher education and their persistence in teacher education. Unpublished dissertation, Kansas State University.

Morales, A. R., & Shroyer, M. G. (2016). Personal agency inspired by hardship: Bilingual Latinas as liberatory educators. *The International Journal of Multicultural Education, 18*(3), 1–21.

National Student Clearinghouse Research Center (NSCRC). (Spring 2017). Contribution of two-year institutions to four-year completions (Snapshot Report). National Student Clearinghouse Research Center. https://nscresearchcenter.org/ snapshotreport-twoyearcontributionfouryearcompletions26/

Phelps, L. A., & Prevost, A. (2012). Community college–research university collaboration: Emerging student research and transfer partnerships. *New Directions for Community Colleges, 157,* 97–110.

Rooks, D. (2018). The unintended consequences of cohorts: How social relationships can influence the retention of rural teachers recruited by cohort-based alternative pathway programs. *Journal of Research in Rural Education, 33*(9), 1–22.

Schmitt-Wilson, S., Downey, J., & Beck, A. E. (2018). Rural educational attainment: The importance of Context. *Journal of Research in Rural Education, 33*(1), 1–14.

Shroyer, G., Morales, A., Yahnke, S., & Bietau, L. (2013). Researching PDS initiatives to promote social justice across the educational system. In K. Zenkov, D. Corrigan, & R. Beebe (Eds.), *Professional development schools and social justice: Schools and universities partnering to make a difference* (pp. 243–260). Lexington Books.

Shroyer, G., Yahnke, S., Morales, A. Dunn, C., Lohfink, G., & Espinoza, P. (2009). Barriers and bridges to success: Factors for retention of nontraditional Mexican American students in teacher education. *Enrollment Management Journal, 3*(3), 40–73.

Soria, K. M. (2015). *Welcoming blue-collar scholars into the ivory tower: Developing class-conscious strategies for student success.* University of South Carolina, National Resource Center for The First-Year Experience and Students in Transition.

Starobin, S. S., Smith, D. J., & Laanan, F. S. (2016). Deconstructing the transfer student capital: Intersect between cultural and social capital among female transfer students in stem fields. *Community College Journal of Research and Practice, 40*(12), 1040–1057.

State Department of Education. (2020). KSDE Data Central Report. Retrieved from https://datacentral.ksde.org/report_gen.aspx

Vidotto, J. (2014). *The influences of leaders and organizational cultures in sustaining multi-institutional community college partnerships*. Unpublished doctoral dissertation, West Carolina University.

Wilcox, P., Wyn, S., & Fyvie-Gauld, M. (2006). "It was nothing to do with the university, it was just the people": The role of social support in the first-year experience of higher education. *Studies in Higher Education, 30*(6), 707–722.

Zamani, E. M. (2010). Institutional responses to barriers to the transfer process. *New Directions for Community Colleges, 114*, 15–24.

Zeidenberg, M. (2012). *Valuable learning or "spinning their wheels"? Understanding excess credits earned by community college associate degree completers.* Community College Research Center, Teachers College, Columbia University.

Chapter 17

Increasing the Latinx Teacher Pipeline

Disrupting Cultural and Linguistic Mismatches While Creating Models of Success

Charlotte R. Hancock, John A. Williams,
III, and Greg A. Wiggan

A monumental growth in immigration from Latinx countries in the 21st century has undeniably led to the increase of culturally and linguistically diverse students in public schools (Baker, 2019, 2021; Camarota, 2011; National Center for Education Statistics [NCES], 2019, 2021b). However, amidst these changes, the teaching force remains majority White (79%) and female (76%) (NCES, 2021a) and there are major shortages in the fields of English learners (ELs) and bilingual education (Sutcher et al., 2016). There are three times as many Spanish-speaking bilingual students in comparison to Latinx teachers (Mahnken, 2018) even though Latinx students instructed by a Latinx teacher show higher academic achievement (Weisman & Hansen, 2008). Thus, to provide salient recommendations that will aid in these critical issues, this chapter explores the following research questions: (1) What are the causes and consequences of the Latinx teacher shortage (2) What are possible solutions for increasing Latinx representation in the teaching force in general, and particularly in bilingual education and EL services? In exploring these research questions, the authors use critical race theory (CRT) and LatCrit (Latino/a critical race theory) to investigate extant literature and recent data regarding the topic.

BACKGROUND

The U.S. has witnessed an influx in immigration unequaled to previous eras, with the first decade of the century 2000–2010 being characterized as a record-setter (Camarota, 2011). From 2014 to 2018, there was an increase in over 100,000 naturalizations in the U.S., with 756,800 approved cases in 2018 alone (U.S. Citizenship & Immigration Services, 2018). Over 13 million lawful, permanent residents lived in the U.S. in 2019, with 30% from Mexican origin (Baker, 2019). It is estimated that there were 11.4 million undocumented immigrants residing in the U.S. in 2018, an increase of almost three million since 2000 (Baker, 2021). Of those 11.4 million, 48% of this population originated from Mexico with an additional 20% arriving from the Spanish-speaking countries of El Salvador, Guatemala, Honduras, Colombia, and Venezuela (Baker, 2021). In parallel with the influx of Latinx immigration, the number of Latinx and linguistically diverse students has risen. In public schools, Latinx students accounted for over 25% of the student population, an increase of 10% since 2000, and it is projected that these students will account for nearly 30% of the total student population by 2027 (NCES, 2019a). In 2018, there were nearly five million students identified as ELs, an increase of over one million students since 2000, with approximately 75% of those students speaking Spanish in the home (NCES, 2021b).

Coupled with this increase of Spanish-speaking ELs, there are reported national teacher shortages in EL services and bilingual education (Sutcher et al., 2016). Wiggan, Smith, and Watson-Vandiver (2020) found that the national teacher shortage is connected to the cycles of the economy, and they highlighted the growing need for more Latinx teachers. Carrier and Cohen (2005) also proposed exploring how the large number of Latinx individuals in the U.S. could help alleviate the crisis in the teacher shortage. Amidst these recommendations, the teacher workforce remains mostly White (79%), female (76%), and with minimal Latinx representation (9%) (NCES, 2021a). If provided with the appropriate learning environment, the large number of linguistically diverse students could provide remedy to the bilingual teacher shortage. Current EL learning environments prove to be insufficient as other populations consistently have higher scores on state-mandated accountability measures (NCES, 2020a, 2020b). Thus, ensuring that linguistically diverse students are surrounded by an environment that helps alleviate the opportunity gap is a necessity. This chapter provides tangible solutions and specific policy reforms to address these critical issues.

CRITICAL RACE THEORY AND LATCRIT THEORY

Critical race theory (CRT) is an analytical tool, lens, or framework to examine the effect of race and racism in society (DeCuir & Dixson, 2004). While CRT is visible in extant literature in the early 20th century (Du Bois, 1903), scholars in the latter part of the century tendered the first official demarcation of this theory in the field of critical legal studies (Bell, 1995), which then resulted in this theory transferring towards the field of education (Crenshaw, 1995; Ladson-Billings & Tate, 1995). CRT contains five tenets: (1) race and racism are ingrained within the fabric of society, especially in the U.S. (Ladson-Billings & Tate, 1995); (2) Whiteness is a signature classification and status that is protected as a physical, literal, and virtual property (Harris, 1995); (3) the promotion of nondominant groups only occurs through a color-blind "neutral" ideology that primarily benefits Whiteness by the way of interest convergence (Delgado & Stefancic, 2001); (4) traditional or ahistorical examinations of society must occur through an interdisciplinary lens that is rooted in a social justice praxis (Tate, 1997); and (5) the dominant narrative is only refuted through the incorporation of the lived experience which is only captured through the promotion of counternarratives (Solórzano & Yosso, 2002). The transitioning of these tenets was the result of scholars, reflecting and analyzing the damaging impact of race and racism on the very lives of Black people in the U.S. and throughout the world.

LatCrit Theory

While scholars utilized CRT lens to interrogate how education, as both a function and institution in society, serves as an accelerant of racism towards Black students, LatCrit as a theory attempts to widen the CRT lens beyond the binary examination of Black and White as it relates to race and racism (Solórzano & Yosso, 2001). LatCrit when applied to education centralizes the lived experiences of Latinx people, and acknowledges that in education, the institution itself operates often to marginalize and oppress the Latinx community while promising to liberate and empower the same oppressed community (Solórzano & Bernal, 2001). Ideally, LatCrit attempts to tether theory with practice in the form of teaching that harnesses the transformative assets enmeshed within the community and promote counternarratives to dismantle the complex and deficit dominant discourse that restricts equitable educational opportunities in and around the Latinx community (Valdes & Bender, 2021). A critical element within LatCrit is centering the lived experiences of the Latinx community as counternarratives to the racialized dominant discourse that persists in educational spaces. Additionally, scholars and practitioners employing this framework are challenged to interrogate how inequities can be resolved by promoting a social justice praxis, through activism, that forms collaborations between stakeholders, without enabling or disabling marginalized groups and communities. The usage of LatCrit to examine education and higher education is extensive (Alemán, 2009; Pérez Huber, 2010; Yosso, 2000), however, there is a shortage in the literature that examines the recruitment and retention of Latinx teachers with LatCrit (Lavadenz & Colón-Muñiz, 2017). The following sections lean on LatCrit to better understand the shortage and consequence of a having a scarcity of Latinx teachers in the profession and glean what specific measures can be implemented to increase the number of highly effective Latinx teachers to support the emerging bilingual learner population.

WHERE DID ALL THE LATINX TEACHERS GO?

In the parlance of LatCrit, the shortage of Latinx teachers in the current teacher workforce can be viewed as an outcome of well-crafted policies (federal, state, and local) and practices that operated to sustain a monolingual and primarily White teacher workforce (Dometrieus & Siegelman, 1988; Ingersoll et al., 2021; Winstead & Wang, 2017). For almost a century, Jim Crow policies and practices disallowed students of color (Black and Latinx) and White students to be educated in the same school facilities. Latinx students were excluded because of race/ethnicity but also due to the myth that their lack of fluency in English equaled a learning deficit (Acuna, 1988; Strum, 2010). The inequitable conditions and practices against Latinx students, ironically, gave cause for Latinx college students to take up the career of teaching in these segregated schools to eliminate such conditions (San Miguel, 1999; Winstead & Wang, 2017). However, the removal of Latinx teachers came about because of three major reasons; the elimination of schools in predominantly Latinx or Black communities (Fiel, 2013; Valencia, 1980); the discriminatory hiring practices of human resource personnel in largely White schools and school districts (Boser, 2011; Darling-Hammond, 1984; Young et al., 2002); and the reluctance of universities and teacher education programs to actively recruit and retain Latinx students to replenish the novice teacher population through culturally responsive methods (Diaz-Rico & Smith, 1994; Garza, 2019; NCES, 2021a). While each of these reasons alone could stifle the growth of the Latinx teacher workforce, collectively, these reasons showcase from a LatCrit lens, the systemic and institutional forms of oppression based on race/ethnicity and language.

As Latinx students were forced to integrate into predominantly White schools through busing it created a cascading effect. For most White families who were opposed to desegregation, rather than sending their student(s) to predominately Latinx schools in the same district they either chose to send their children to private schools or they relocated to still segregated school districts (Fiel, 2013). The commitment by many White families to remain segregated stripped many predominantly Latinx schools of their ability to remain open, because of the low student enrollment. Besides low enrollment, individual states began closing schools due to the terrible physical conditions of the school (as the result of inequitable funding per Jim Crow policies) or shutting down schools completely because of poor academic performance (Fiel, 2013; Sunderman et al., 2017). Latinx teachers who attempted to secure employment in "integrated" schools were either denied employment, required to pass "newly formed" credentialing tests, or refused employment even after completing the credentialing process for less qualified White applicants (Boser, 2011). Per LatCrit, in understanding the counternarrative, Latinx teachers did not just disappear, rather, like Black teachers, they were forcibly removed from the teaching profession because of individual actions and institutional policies that were committed to upholding racism in education.

The conditions that debilitated the Latinx teacher workforce are only heightened by the limited effort by teacher education programs to purposefully attract Latinx students to become teachers. For many Latinx students, who are typically first-generation college goers, attending college can be an intimidating experience, socially, academically, culturally, and financially. These aspects are supported by research (Shapiro & Partelow, 2018; Turner et al., 2017), however, there are few teacher education programs that offer programs that target Latinx students with the necessary support to alleviate such obstacles while promoting the rationale of current Latinx teachers for why they enter and remain in the profession. Research highlights that for Latinx teachers, the ability to be a change agent and facilitate knowledge acquisition through community building are critical reasons they enter and remain in the profession (Ocasio, 2014; Turner et al., 2017; Weisman & Hansen, 2008). From a LatCrit framework, the failure to account for the lived experience of the Latinx teachers and their rationale for teaching underscores the ahistorical approach teacher education programs utilize when seeking to attract Latinx students to their campuses. The role of racism has not only diminished the presence of Latinx teachers in the teacher workforce, but it is also hindering teacher education program's ability to attract a new generation of Latinx teachers to support the cultural wealth within the growing preK–12 Latinx and bilingual learner population.

SOLUTIONS

Understanding the past will aid in providing solutions for the future to increase Latinx representation in the teaching force in general, and particularly in bilingual education and EL services. A teaching force that is predominantly White, female, and monolingual did not occur by chance but rather has its roots in a historical evolution in the teaching force that worked towards such a result (Goldstein, 2014). In conjunction with the historical evolution of the teaching force is the problematic schooling experience that surrounds multilingual learners.

In the perspective of CRT and LatCrit, Latinx students are not being provided with essential learning opportunities within US schools. As Solórzano and Yosso (2001) explore in their first tenet the intersection of other forms of subordination, it is critical to explore how immigration and language could be providing for additional forms of racism against Latinx students in schools. It is hard to ignore the negative media surrounding immigrants from Latinx countries as well as the dominant ideology that runs rampant in US society of a monolingual push towards the proficiency of standard, academic English as a way to maintain superiority over others. Hence, recognizing through the lens of LatCrit the intersection of these different forms of subordination may be key in analyzing why there are not more teachers applying to work in the fields of ESL, bilingual education, and world language education. Through the perspective of LatCrit, the major focus on monolingualism in the US schools and the lack of support for the development of multilingualism in educational policy creates students that leave schools without the skill of multilingualism that is important in filling those vacant positions. It is essential to remove the current deficit framing lens of linguistically diverse students and create policies that support multilingualism in schools to begin shifting the current state of teacher shortages in the fields of ESL, bilingual education, and world languages. Through the lens of LatCrit, a critical group of individuals that should be supported are the current Latinx students who are enrolled in US schools and who could enter the future teaching workforce if supported in appropriate ways.

A solution that could alleviate the current teacher shortage in the fields of multilingualism would be educational policies and programs that seek to maintain the rich linguistic repertoires that Latinx students bring with them to the school setting rather than attempting to assimilate them into a monolingual setting that removes their home language. Utilizing dual language (DL) programs that aim to not only maintain their home language, but also aim to create bilingual and biliterate students as an end result is critical. If Latinx students speak their language in their homes but are not also provided additional opportunities in school to develop this language through a wide array of literacy skills, as is the case with the learning of English in schools, then Latinx students may leave schools feeling possibly not fully prepared to become teachers in realms that require a firm command of two languages. Schools and teachers have a duty to applaud students for their linguistic capital and work towards providing an environment that allows students to further develop their multilingualism to ensure Latinx students leave the schools feeling empowered for their language skills.

Extensive research exists surrounding DL programs and the successful outcomes this program model has on linguistically diverse students (Collier & Thomas, 2009; Lindholm-Leary, 2001; Steele et al., 2017; Thomas & Collier, 2012). A DL program is where the medium of instruction is in both English and an additional language and is considered an *additive* program by simultaneously supporting the development of two languages (Thomas & Collier, 2012). Current services for ELs, however, are more *subtractive* in nature, meaning that students are learning English while subtracting their home language (Thomas & Collier, 2012). Unlike subtractive programs, DL programs have the potential to close the opportunity gap that currently exists. Students, including students labeled as ELs, that are within DL programs outperform their counterparts not in DL programs on standardized academic assessments (Collier & Thomas, 2009; Thomas & Collier, 2012). Additionally, students who participate in DL programs may have a firmer cultural identity, more positive attitudes towards bilingualism, higher self-esteem, better attendance in schools, and less discipline referrals (Thomas & Collier, 2012). Further, students labeled as EL who are in DL programs where the language of instruction (i.e., Spanish) matches their home language demonstrate the best results in exiting the EL status (Steele et al., 2017). Collier and Thomas (2012) concluded that a DL program model that instructed students 90% of the time in the language other than English in the earlier years of the program (referred to as a 90:10 program) and that integrated students from homes that were both native English speakers and native speakers of the other language of instruction (referred to as a two-way program) was able to close the second language gap for EL students in the shortest amount of time. Yet Hancock and Sancyzk (2019) found that a two-way 90:10 DL program was not the most common program type in five large urban districts with high numbers of Latinx students. Through the perspective of LatCrit, this raises concerns surrounding the lack of these program models despite extant research that demonstrates the benefits.

Schools should be opening doors of opportunity to Latinx students, not closing them as would be a critique through the lens of LatCrit. In addition to providing Latinx ELs with supportive learning environments, additional means are necessary to increase Latinx individuals into the teacher pipeline.

Providing specific grants that are geared towards Latinx students that could cover the cost of college if they agree to go into the field of teaching, such as the Teacher Education Assistance for College and Higher Education (TEACH) grant, would be a way to encourage and support this critical group of students into entering the teaching force. Thus, two ways that could aid in increasing Latinx individuals into the teaching force could be providing learning environments beginning in kindergarten that maintain and develop their home language in conjunction with providing a pathway to the field of education through specialized grants.

CONCLUDING THOUGHTS AND RECOMMENDATIONS FOR THE FUTURE

In the purview of LatCrit, there are specific steps that practitioners can take to support Latinx students, thereby aiding in the efforts to increase the number of Latinx individuals in the teaching force. It is recommended that educators and district and school leaders seek ways to implement a DL program in their own school contexts. One way to accomplish this is by discussing with key stakeholders the benefits of DL programs. Strategic planning will be important before the implementation of the program, including considerations regarding program type, staffing, and resources. Future considerations of implementing a pathway for DL students into the teacher pipeline by the way of scholarships or grants should also be part of initial conversations. Further, honor students for being multilingual and create a classroom and school culture that embraces and strives for multilingualism. School leaders and educators can create learning environments that promote high levels of success for Latinx ELs, which in turn could alleviate the current teacher shortages. The aim of this chapter was to provide concrete recommendations that would aid in these efforts.

REFERENCES

Acuna, R. (1988). *Occupied America: A history of Chicanos* (2nd ed.). Harper & Row.
Alemán Jr, E. (2009). LatCrit educational leadership and advocacy: Struggling over whiteness as property in Texas school finance. *Equity & Excellence in Education, 42*(2), 183–201.
Baker, B. (2019). *Estimates of the lawful permanent resident population in the United States and the Subpopulation Eligible to Naturalize: 2015–2019*. Retrieved January 16, 2021, from https://www.dhs.gov/sites/default/files/publications/immigration -statistics/Pop_Estimate/LPR/lpr_population_estimates_2015_-_2019.pdf.pdf

Baker, B. (2021). *Estimates of the unauthorized immigrant population residing in the United States: January 2015–January 2018*. Retrieved June 16, 2021, from https://www.dhs.gov/sites/default/files/publications/immigration-statistics/Pop_Estimate/UnauthImmigrant/unauthorized_immigrant_population_estimates_2015_-_2018.pdf

Bell, D. A. (1995). *Who's afraid of critical race theory*. U. Ill. L. Rev., 893.

Boser, U. (2011). *Teacher diversity matters: A state-by-state analysis of teachers of color*. Center for American Progress.

Camarota, S. (2011, October 5). *A record-setting decade of immigration: 2000–2010*. Center for Immigration Studies. Retrieved April 9, 2020, from https://cis.org/Report/RecordSetting-Decade-Immigration-20002010

Carrier, K., & Cohen, J. (2005). Hispanic individuals in their communities: An untapped resource for increasing the bilingual teacher population. *Journal of Hispanic Higher Education, 4*(1), 51–63. https://doi.org/10.1177/1538192704271485

Collier, V. P., & Thomas, W. P. (2009). *Educating English learners for a transformed world*. Dual Language Education of New Mexico Fuente Press.

Crenshaw, K. W. (1995). Mapping the margins: Intersectionality, identity politics, and violence against women of color. In K. Crenshaw, N. Gotanda, G. Peller, & K. Thomas (Eds.), *Critical race theory: The key writings that formed the movement* (pp. 357–383). The New Press.

Darling-Hammond, L. (1984). *Beyond the commission reports. The coming crisis in teaching*. The Rand Corporation.

DeCuir, J. T., & Dixson, A. D. (2004). "So, when it comes out, they aren't that surprised that it is there": Using critical race theory as a tool of analysis of race and racism in education. *Educational Researcher, 33*(5), 26–31.

Delgado, R., & Stefancic, J. (2001). *Critical race theory: An introduction*. New York University Press.

Diaz-Rico, L. T., & Smith, J. (1994). Recruiting and retaining bilingual teachers: A cooperative school community-university model. *The Journal of Educational Issues of Language Minority Students, 14*(4), 255–268.

Dometrius, N. C, & Sigelman, L. (1988). The cost of quality: Teacher testing and racial-ethnic representativeness in public education. *Social Science Quarterly, 69*(1), 70–82.

Du Bois, W. E. B. (2015). *The souls of Black folk*. Yale University Press.

Fiel, J. E. (2013). Decomposing school resegregation: Social closure, racial imbalance, and racial isolation. *American Sociological Review, 78*(5), 828–848.

Garza, R. (2019). Paving the way for Latinx teachers: Recruitment and preparation to promote educator diversity. *New America*. newamerica.org/education-policy/reports/paving-way-latinx-teachers/

Goldstein, D. (2014). *The teacher wars*. Anchor Books.

Hancock, C.R., & Sancyzk, A. (2019). Cultural and linguistic responsiveness: Empowering Spanish-speaking English learners through dual language. *Urban Education Research and Policy Annuals, 6*(2), 62–76.

Harris, C. I. (1995). Whiteness as property. In K. Crenshaw, N. Gotanda, G. Peller, & K. Thomas (Eds.), *Critical race theory: The key writings that formed the movement* (pp. 357–383). The New Press.

Ingersoll, R., May, H., Collins, G., & Fletcher, T. (2021). Trends in the recruitment, employment and retention of teachers from under-represented racial-ethnic Groups, 1987 to 2016. In T. Bristol (Ed.), *The American education research association handbook of research on teachers of color.*

Ladson-Billings, G., & Tate, W. (1995). Toward a critical race theory of education. *Teachers College Record, 97,* 47–68.

Lavadenz, M., & Colón-Muñiz, A. (2017). The preparation of Latino/a teachers: A LatCrit analysis of the role of university centers and Latino/a teacher development. In *Learning from emergent bilingual Latinx Learners in K–12* (pp. 79–101). Routledge.

Lindholm-Leary, K. (2001). *Dual language education.* Multilingual Matters.

Mahnken, K. (2018). There are three times as many Latino students as teachers in America. In *The 74.* Retrieved June 6, 2021, from https://www.the74million.org /there-are-three-times-as-many-latino-students-as-teachers-in-america-two-new -reports-show-why-thats-bad-for-both/

National Center for Education Statistics. (2019). *Status and trends in the education of racial and ethnic groups: Elementary and secondary enrollment.* Retrieved June 6, 2021, from https://nces.ed.gov/programs/raceindicators/indicator_rbb.asp

National Center for Education Statistics. (2020a). *Mathematics performance.* Retrieved June 6, 2021, from https://nces.ed.gov/programs/coe/indicator_cnc.asp

National Center for Education Statistics. (2020b). *Reading performance.* Retrieved June 6, 2021, from https://nces.ed.gov/programs/coe/indicator_cnb.asp

National Center for Education Statistics. (2021a). *Characteristics of public-school teachers.* Retrieved June 16, 2021, from https://nces.ed.gov/programs/coe/indicator /clr

National Center for Education Statistics. (2021b). *The condition of education: English language learners in public schools.* Retrieved June 6, 2021, from https:// nces.ed.gov/programs/coe/indicator_cgf.asp

Ocasio, K. M. (2014). Pathways to teaching: Exploring the Latino/a teacher pipeline (Order No. 3633469). Available from ProQuest Dissertations & Theses Full Text: The Humanities and Social Sciences Collection. (1611960808). http://proxy .lib.csus.edu/login?url=http://search.proquest.com.proxy.lib.csus.edu/docview /1611960808?accountid=10358

Pérez Huber, L. (2010). Using Latina/o critical race theory (LatCrit) and racist nativism to explore intersectionality in the educational experiences of undocumented Chicana college students. *Educational Foundations, 24,* 77–96.

San Miguel, G. (1999). The schooling of Mexicanos in the southwest, 1848–1891. *The elusive quest for equality, 150,* 31–51.

Shapiro, S., & Partelow, L. (2018). *How to fix the large and growing Latinx teacher-student gap.* Center for American Progress. https://files.eric.ed.gov/fulltext /ED586238.pdf

Solórzano, D. G., & Bernal, D. D. (2001). Examining transformational resistance through a critical race and LatCrit theory framework: Chicana and Chicano students in an urban context. *Urban Education, 36*(3), 308–342.

Solórzano, D., & Yosso, T. (2001). Critical race and LatCrit theory and method: Counter-storytelling. *International Journal of Qualitative Studies in Education, 14*(4), 471–495. https://doi.org/10.1080/09518390110063365

Solórzano, D. G., & Yosso, T. J. (2002). Critical race methodology: Counter-storytelling as an analytical framework for education research. *Qualitative Inquiry, 8*(1), 23–44.

Steele, J., Slater, R., Zamarro, G., Miller, T., Li, J., Burkhauser, S., & Bacon, M. (2017). Effects of dual-language immersion programs on student achievement: Evidence from lottery data. *American Educational Research Journal, 54*(1suppl), 282S–306S. https://doi.org/10.3102/0002831216634463

Strum, P. (2010). Separate [not equal to] equal: Mexican Americans before *Brown v. Board. Poverty & Race, 19*(5), 1–268.

Sunderman, G.L., Coghlan, E., & Mintrop, R. (2017). School closure as a strategy to remedy low performance. National Education Policy Center. http://nepc.colorado.edu/publication/closures

Sutcher, L., Darling-Hammond, L., & Carver-Thomas, D. (2016, September 15). *A coming crisis in teaching? Teacher supply, demand, and shortages in the U.S.* Learning Policy Institute. Retrieved June 6, 2021, from https://learningpolicyinstitute.org/product/coming-crisis-teaching-brief

Tate, W. F. (1997). Critical race theory and education: History, theory and implications. In M. W. Apple (Ed.), *Review of research in education* (vol. 22, pp. 191–243). American Educational Research Association.

Thomas, W. P., & Collier, V. P. (2012). *Dual language education for a transformed world.* Dual Language Education of New Mexico Fuente Press.

Turner, C. S., Cosmé, P. X., Dinehart, L., Martí, R., McDonald, D., Ramirez, M., & Zamora, J. (2017). Hispanic-serving institution scholars and administrators on improving Latina/Latino/Latinx/Hispanic teacher pipelines: Critical junctures along career pathways. *Association of Mexican American Educators Journal, 11*(3), 251–275.

U.S. Citizenship & Immigration Services. (2018). *2018 USCIS statistical annual report.* Retrieved June 6, 2021, from https://www.uscis.gov/sites/default/files/USCIS/statistics/2018_USCIS_Statistical_Annual_Report_Final_-_OPQ_5.28.19_EXA.pdf

Valdes, F., & Bender, S. W. (2021). *LatCrit: From critical legal theory to academic activism.* NYU Press.

Valencia, R. R. (1980). The school closure issue and the Chicano community. *The Urban Review, 12*(1), 5–21.

Weisman, E., & Hansen, L. (2008). Student teaching in urban and suburban schools: Perspectives of Latino preservice teachers. *Urban Education, 43*(6), 653–670. https://doi.org/10.1177/00420 8590731183 4

Wiggan, G., Smith, D., & Watson-Vandiver, M. (2020). The national teacher shortage, urban education and the cognitive sociology of labor. *The Urban Review.* https://doi.org/10.1007/s11256-020-00565-z

Winstead, L., & Wang, C. (2017). From ELLs to bilingual teachers: Spanish-English speaking Latino teachers' experiences of language shame & loss. *Multicultural Education, 24*, 16–25.

Yosso, T. J. (2000). *A critical race and LatCrit approach to media literacy: Chicana/o resistance to visual microaggressions.* University of California.

Young, I. P., & Fox, J. A. (2002). Asian, Hispanic, and Native American job candidates: Prescreened or screened within the selection process. *Educational Administration Quarterly, 38*(4), 530–554.

Chapter 18

Teacher Mindset

A Case Study of Embracing Multiculturalism and Multilingualism as Strategies for Effective and Just Teaching

Jeanne Carey Ingle

English Language Learners (ELLs) are the fastest growing population in US public schools, increasing by 60% over the last 10 years (Quintero and Hansen 2017). US ELLs rarely reach academic parity with their English-speaking peers (NAEP, 2018). In Canada, by contrast, nearly 30% of all public-school students (over 50% of the students in the Toronto public schools) are ELLs. Regardless of age or income, within three years of arriving in Canada's public schools ELL children do as well in reading and math as native English speakers and graduate at the same rate as native English speakers (Cardoza, 2019).

What are teachers in Toronto doing? How are they teaching ELLs and what are the programs and strategies used? With a researcher's skill set and a practitioner's eye, the author set out to answer these questions.

During the late spring and early fall of 2019, the author observed and interviewed classroom teachers, principals, and ELL staff in the Toronto District School Board (TDSB). What emerged was a teaching approach and mindset so deeply ingrained in teachers and administrators as to be considered second-nature. Multiculturalism and multilingualism were not trendy ideas or district-mandated pedagogy—they were part of a culture and mindset actively embodied by teachers. This chapter will share an exploration of the multicultural mindset of TDSB teachers and administrators and the educational strategies and practices that emerge from this mindset.

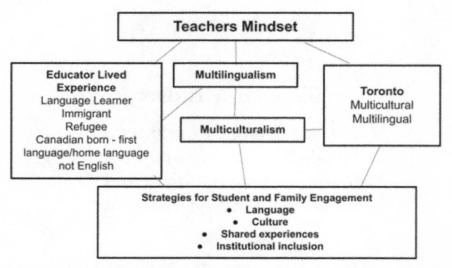

Fig. 18.1. Teacher mindset is deeply influenced by multiple factors which in turn influence their pedagogical strategies for student and family engagement. Courtesy of the author.

TEACHER MINDSET: MULTICULTURALISM/ MULTILINGUALISM AND THE EDUCATOR'S LIVED EXPERIENCES

Teacher attitudes and beliefs are a major influence on the learning of students (Kim, 2021). Mindset, according to Dweck (2006), refers to individuals' self-perception or self-theory: how teachers view themselves affects how they view their students. Gagné et al.'s (2017) adaptation of the KARDS model (Kumaravadivelu, 2012) reveals teacher beliefs, identities and values as a crucial component in ELL education. In the current study, teachers' beliefs, identities, and values centered on their commitment to multiculturalism and multilingualism, strongly influenced by both educators' own experiences as well as the uniquely multicultural nature of Toronto. The educators interviewed shared attitudes and beliefs that reflect this growth mindset but also a deeper aspect which includes cultural and linguistic anchors. In this chapter, the term *teacher mindset* is used, as it reflects a deeper commitment and belief in their own agency to influence children's lives.

TEACHER MINDSET: LIVED EXPERIENCE AND MULTILINGUALISM

How a teacher views themself both as an educator and as a member of the larger society influences their approach to their work. Bacon's (2020) work on teacher monolingual ideologies clearly demonstrated that teachers' view of language acquisition and multilingualism influences their approach to teaching. The teachers and administrators of the TDSB presented a philosophy of teaching and a mindset of multiculturalism and multilingualism so deeply ingrained as to be considered commonplace. All but two of the teachers who participated in this study were ELLs. The rest of the participants were representative of the students they worked with, some were refugees, other immigrants and some Canadian-born but learned English only after they began attending public school. It became apparent in conversations that a teacher's own experience with language, as well as the experience of being both a language learner and a newcomer or child of immigrants, had a profound impact on their sense of themselves as teachers. Significantly teachers' recognition of their own value as language learners emerged as an educational strategy. The comments below demonstrate that this strategy of connection and understanding was used both to relate to students and to develop rapport with families.

> I remember my mom coming [to school] and you know, as a silly girl, just being a little embarrassed, because she doesn't speak the language. But now, realizing years later, now I'm in a position of doing an interview with a parent and I took myself back and thought how nervous my mom must have been . . . she was scared. Because she [my mother] said "I was so worried that anything I said may have been used against you." So now, her conversation, I replay it, when I see that parent who doesn't speak the language. (Helen, ELL Teacher)

> I would say less using my first language but more incorporating the fact that I'm not—I wasn't born in Canada. The students that were not born in Canada can make connections as well and feel comfortable and enjoy the fact that even if English is not their first language, you can still move forward and keep moving along. I like to build the connections to my history with their own. (Martin, STEM teacher)

> I could relate to the kids that came to Canada. When I was in grade 8 . . . I remember that feeling of walking into a classroom and being introduced to [the] class and not knowing what's going on. So, I can really relate to that . . . when I tell them that story, they can't believe it. they're a little bit taken back. They're like, "Oh, you came here when you were 13?" (Anna, Math/LEAP teacher)

Let's say a child is of Chinese background, they're celebrating the Moon Festival . . . I also celebrate Moon Festival. When I share my experience, my traditions, and my celebration with them, then right away, you can see their eyes twinkle, like, "Oh, my teacher also celebrates the same thing." So right away, there's an instant connection. And I think that sharing our experiences with what the child or the children are experiencing, making that personal connection is very important . . . you're increasing the comfort level for them, they know that this is a safe environment. (Mai, Primary School Teacher)

Teachers and administrators spoke of a generalized culture of intentional and focused work that recognized and included the broad cultural diversity of the students as well as the staff. It was clear too in the comments of teachers and principals that there was an organizational commitment and a culture of valuing both the languages that the children of the TDSB speak, as well as the cultures they bring to their classrooms. As Bacon writes, "Whether intentional or not, language work is always ideological" (2020).

So, to really understand how students acquire language, and what you do as a teacher to help them acquire that language is really fundamental. That as well as the other aspect is knowing—you know, cultures, and how they perceive education, their attitude towards education. (Josefina, administrator)

I think that's a major part of it having them feel that you're allowed to celebrate your own culture, you're allowed to do what you're doing in your other country here—it's not that now that you're in Canada, you need to do this and this and this. (Anna, Math/LEAP teacher)

Teacher Mindset: Teachers as Multilingual

Semi-structured interview protocols were used in this study and unexpected data emerged regarding the participants' language ability. Early in these interviews the educators began to discuss the importance of their own multilingualism as a way of understanding their own and the TDSB system's commitment to multiculturalism. Further conversations and observations revealed the importance of recognizing and exploring the cultural and linguistic backgrounds of the educators.

The teachers and administrators of the TDSB who participated in this study were overwhelmingly multilingual. Their comfort and pride in speaking multiple languages was shared early in interviews and was often cited as a reason that they both understood and could engage their students and their students' families at a deeper level. Research on multilingual teachers has shown that this skill base and/or the experience of acquiring English as a second, third, or later language better equips educators to work with ELLs

(Weekly, 2019). Further, Matsumoto's 2018 study argued that teachers who are non-native English speakers work harder to address cultural miscommunications and actively seek to bridge cultural gaps. The participants of this study clearly saw their role and responsibility as polyglots to use their language skills not to simply translate but also to welcome newcomers and alleviate cultural barriers.

The 11 teachers and administrators who participated in this study spoke over 15 different languages. The chart above lists the languages spoken by the participants of this study. While many of the study participants had immigrated to Canada as children, all the teachers and administrators had gone to public school in Canada and had studied French. Thus, either through public school education, their home language(s), or the acquisition of multiple languages while living in refugee camps, each of the educators was multilingual. This language ability became a teaching tool for these educators:

> I use it for parent teacher interviews when—even though we have interpreters, like Mandarin-speaking interpreters, Vietnamese and Cantonese interpreters, and quite a few others. But sometimes parents are comfortable just talking to me, rather than having [an] interpreter. (Mai, Primary Teacher)

> I think that there's the comfort level when you speak their first language with them so that they can understand a little bit more in terms of what I do with their child, both at school, also giving them a suggestion as to what they can do at home. (Madija, Writing/LEAP Teacher)

Table 18.1. Participant Language Skills

Languages Spoken	Teachers	Administrators	ELL/Special Education Teachers
English	X	X	X
French	X	X	X
Arabic	X	X	X
Urdu	X		
Greek		X	X
Macedonian		X	X
Hungarian		X	
Farsi	X		
Italian	X		
Portuguese	X		
Spanish	X		
Mandarin	X		
Cantonese	X		
Vietnamese	X		
Other (regional languages)	X	X	X

The teachers' and administrators' experience as ELLs had a significant influence on their teaching. They discussed not only how they used their language but ability but also, and with pride, their own language acquisition:

> I spoke my mom's native language, and father's, which was Greek. And so, it was interesting because they called it the "hyphenated child," because you came from two different worlds so your reality at home was very different than what you were exposed to in the school system. I speak English, Greek, Macedonian, Slovakian, and Bulgarian. (Helen, ELL Teacher)

> Okay, so let me take it back to my origins. I am an ELL learner. My first language was not English. I was born in Vietnam, and I left Vietnam in 1979, came to Canada in 1980. My mother too is Chow Chil, which is a Chinese dialect— and I am also fluent in Cantonese—and now English. (Mai, Primary Teacher)

> So, it helps also with the families, right? When the EL teachers have their own culture or close to their [the students'] culture they tend to trust them a little more: the establishment, the school, recommendations we might make. You know, suggestions about you know, how they can do better in, at school. (Anna, Math/LEAP teacher)

> I try not to, but sometimes if it means the kid will only understand it, if I speak it in the language that they know, so I do use [Farsi, Arabic or Urdu]. (Madija, Writing/LEAP Teacher)

Teacher Mindset: Toronto

The perception of Toronto as a multicultural city was at the heart of many of the teachers' conversations around language and culture. This aspect also presented in the study participants as a responsibility to maintain and to personify. As Kate, a primary teacher, explained, "It's just who we are, we're Toronto, we're a multicultural city." This attitude toward ELLs is not always the norm in schools and it is clear from earlier research (see Kim's 2021 meta-analysis of teacher attitudes and beliefs toward ELLs) that teachers often have strong biases toward students who most closely resemble the dominant culture. However, since the culture in Toronto is so diverse, teacher attitudes clearly demonstrated a pride in the variety of cultures represented both in the school system and in the city.

> . . . because the city is such a multicultural city and there are so many immigrants or newcomers to Toronto, that there are a lot of programs that encourage newcomers to get integrated into society and use their language more than anything else. (Josefina, Primary School Administrator)

I also think, just in terms of the Toronto culture, that we do a very, very good job, in teaching the fact that part of being Canadian and being part of the Toronto community is also celebrating whatever background or whatever culture you have. So, it's not like you're Canadian, and you need to follow this. You're Canadian, AND wherever other culture you celebrate. (Jane, Primary Teacher)

AREAS FOR FUTURE STUDY

In 2019, Canada resettled 30,000 refugees and over 300,000 immigrants. Forty-five percent of those immigrants and refugees settled in Ontario (El-Assal, 2020), with the great majority settling in the Toronto area. The Toronto school system was well placed to provide a model for how to provide opportunities and access effectively and comprehensively for the youngest immigrants into the educational and social fabric of the country.

The educators who participated in this study, shared a system of attitudes and supports that meshed the resources of a multicultural city with a large district and a linguistically and culturally skilled workforce. The inclusive and targeted programs for ELLs coupled with the skill of their teachers, allowed these children the space, support and educational normalization to easily become part of a classroom that was both culturally welcoming and academically ready to meet their needs.

This study took place in the spring and fall of 2019 prior to the COVID-19 pandemic. This factor is important to note as this study explored the unique culture of the teachers and staff of the TDSB prior to school building closures in the spring of 2020 and the move to remote and hybrid teaching in fall 2020 that continued throughout in winter and spring 2021. The teaching and learning experience of ELLs and their educators has changed. Children spent months immersed in their home language without the community and educational supports that have been critical to their transition to a classroom and their acquisition of English. Thus, the work of this study, to truly understand how teachers can best educate the English learners in their classroom, also demands that this study acknowledge and then explore the effects of the COVID-19 pandemic on the learning experience of ELLs in Toronto. This is the subject of a future study, and the author wishes to recognize the changes to education which must emerge from the pandemic experience.

CONCLUSIONS

While no school system or even teacher is without flaws, the purpose of this study was to look at a success story and to learn from it. This study began with multiple reports in the news media of the success of ELLs in the TDSB. As a long-time educator, the researcher set out to find strategies and programs to bring back to pre-service and in-service teachers. The expectation was to return with books, videos and pedagogy that would enhance practice and develop syllabi but much more was found. Among the study participants and within the schools was a system and community of professionals who believed deeply in their work and who valued the children it was their charge to educate.

A review of the data led to the following key takeaways for educators:

1. Build a multilingual/multicultural workforce. The teachers of this study had origin stories and life experiences that mirrored those of their students. They had learned another (often more than one) language, served as translators for their parents, lived in refugee camps, had gaps in their education and had established homes and careers in a new country as ELs. This skill base framed their teaching.
2. View language ability and immigrant experiences as assets. The educators who participated in this study were proud of their cultures but most clearly—and this served as a powerful model for their students—they were extremely proud of their own intelligence, skill and life experience.
3. Student engagement must be coupled with family engagement and based on cultural and linguistic connections are powerful teaching tools. Two clear views of ELL families emerged from my conversations with these educators: parents are partners; and parents may need help. There was often a sense from the teachers and administrators that an important part of their job was to help parents navigate their children's education.

REFERENCES

Ardasheva, Y., & Tretter, T. R. (2013). Contributions of individual differences and contextual variables to reading achievement of English language learners: An empirical investigation using hierarchical linear modeling. *TESOL Quarterly, 47*(2), 323–351. doi: 10.1002/tesq.72

Bacon, C. K. (2020). "It's not really my job": A mixed methods framework for language ideologies, monolingualism, and teaching emergent bilingual learners. *Journal of Teacher Education, 71*(2), 172–187. doi:10.1177/0022487118783188

Budiman, A. (2020, September 22). *Key findings about U.S. Immigrants.* Pew Research Center. https://www.pewresearch.org/fact-tank/2020/08/20/key-findings-about-u-s-immigrants/

Cardoza, K. (2019, February 20). In Canada's public schools, immigrant students are thriving. Education Week. https://www.edweek.org/ew/articles/2018/02/28/in-canadas-public-schools-immigrant-students-are.html

Cerna, L. (2019). Refugee education: Integration models and practices in OECD countries. *OECD Education Working Papers*, No. 203, OECD Publishing, Paris. https://doi.org/10.1787/a3251a00-en

Colegrove, K. S.-S., & Adair, J. K. (2014). Countering deficit thinking: Agency, capabilities and the early learning experiences of children of Latina/o immigrants. *Contemporary Issues in Early Childhood, 15*(2), 122–135. doi: 10.2304/ciec.2014.15.2.122

Coughlan, S. (2017, August 2). How Canada became an education superpower. BBC News. https://www.bbc.com/news/business-40708421

Domise, A. (2019, June 5). The rise of an uncaring Canada. Macleans.ca. https://www.macleans.ca/news/canada/the-rise-of-an-uncaring-canada/

Dweck, C. S. (2006). *Mindset: The new psychology of success.* Random House.

El-Assal, K. (2020, February 10). Canada broke another record by welcoming 341,000 immigrants in 2019. CIC News. https://www.cicnews.com/2020/02/canada-broke-another-record-by-welcoming-341000-immigrants-in-2019-0213697.html#gs.spkc3t

Erion, J. R. (2006). Parent tutoring: A meta-analysis. *Education and Treatment of Children, 29*(1), 79–106.

Gagné, A., Schmidt, C & Markus, P. (2017). Teaching about refugees: Developing culturally responsive educators in contexts of politicised transnationalism. *Intercultural Education, 28(*5), 429–446. https://doi.org/10.1080/14675986.2017.1336409

Hill, N. E., & Tyson, D. F. (2009). Parental involvement in middle school: A meta-analytic assessment of the strategies that promote achievement. *Developmental Psychology, 45*(3), 740–763.

Hoover-Dempsey, K., Walker, J., Sandler, H., Whetsel, D., Green, C., Wilkins, A., & Closson, K. (2005). Why do parents become involved? Research findings and implications. *The Elementary School Journal, 106*(2), 105–130. doi:10.1086/499194

Jeynes, W. H. (2003). A meta-analysis: The effects of parent involvement on minority children's academic achievement. *Education and Urban Society, 35*, 202–218.

Jeynes, W. H. (2005). A meta-analysis of the relation of parental involvement to urban elementary school student academic achievement. *Urban Education, 40*(3), 237–269.

Jeynes, W. H. (2007). The relationship between parental involvement and urban secondary school student academic achievement: A meta-analysis. *Urban Education, 42*, 92–109.

Jeynes, W. H. (2012). A meta-analysis of the efficacy of different types of parental involvement programs for urban students. *Urban Education, 47*(4), 706–742.

Kim, S. L. (2021). A review of the literature on teachers' beliefs about English language learners. *International Journal of Educational Research Open, 2.* https://doi-org.libserv-prd.bridgew.edu/10.1016/j.ijedro.2021.100040

Kovinthan, T. (2016). Learning and teaching with loss: Meeting the needs of refugee children through narrative inquiry. *Diaspora, Indigenous, and Minority Education, 10*(3), 141–155. doi: 10.1080/15595692.2015.1137282

Kumaravadivelu, B. (2012). *Language teacher education for a global society.* Routledge.

Leu, D. J., Forzani, E., Rhoads, C., Maykel, C., Kennedy, C., & Timbrell, N. (2014). The new literacies of online research and comprehension: Rethinking the reading achievement gap. *Reading Research Quarterly, 50*(1), 37–59. doi: 10.1002/rrq.85

Matsumoto Y. (2018). Teachers' identities as "non-native" speakers: Do they matter in *English as a lingua Franca* interactions? In B. Yazan and N. Rudolph (Eds.), *Criticality, teacher identity, and (in)equity in English language teaching. Educational linguistics* (p. 35). Springer, Cham. https://doi.org/10.1007/978-3-319-72920-6_4

Mellom, P. J., Straubhaar, R., Balderas, C., Ariail, M., & Portes, P. R. (2018). "They come with nothing": How professional development in a culturally responsive pedagogy shapes teacher attitudes towards Latino/a English language learners. *Teaching and Teacher Education, 71*, 98–107. https://doi-org.libserv-prd.bridgew.edu/10.1016/j.tate.2017.12.013

Miller, J. (2011). Jan Stewart. Supporting refugee children: Strategies for educators. *Canadian Ethnic Studies Journal, 43*(3), 252+. https://link.gale.com/apps/doc/A328419181/LitRC?u=mlin_b_massblc&sid=LitRC&xid=60f1aa46

Minkel, J. (2020, December 2). Bridging the chasm between teachers and parents (opinion). Education Week. https://www.edweek.org/tm/articles/2018/10/24/bridging-the-chasm-between-teachers-and-parents.html?cmp=eml-enl-tu-news1-rm&M=58650809&U=2046187&UUID=f7789490d3a9456aa633216790f218ea&print=1

National Center for Education Statistics. (2018, April 10). *2017 NAEP mathematics and reading assessments: Highlighted results at grades 4 and 8 for the nation, states, and districts.* National Center for Education Statistics (NCES) Home Page, a part of the U.S. Department of Education. https://nces.ed.gov/pubsearch/pubsinfo.asp?pubid=2018037

National Immigration Forum. (2020, November 5). *Fact sheet: U.S. refugee resettlement.* National Immigration Forum. https://immigrationforum.org/article/fact-sheet-u-s-refugee-resettlement/#:~:text=For%20FY%202020%2C%20the%20administration,11%2C814%20people%20in%20FY%202020.

Patall, E. A., Cooper, H., & Robinson, J. C. (2008). Parent involvement in homework: A research synthesis. *Review of Educational Research, 78*(4), 1039–1101.

PBS NewsHour. (2018, April 10). New York.

Pomerantz, E. M., Wang, Q., & Ng, F. F. (2005a). Mothers' affect in the homework context: The importance of staying positive. *Developmental Psychology, 41*, 414–427.

Pomerantz, E. M., Ng, F. F., & Wang, Q. (2006). Mothers' mastery-oriented involvement in children's homework: Implications for the well-being of children with negative perceptions of competence. *Journal of Educational Psychology, 98*(1), 99–111.

Quintero, D. & Hansen, M. (2017). English learners and the growing need for qualified teachers. https://www.brookings.edu/blog/brown-center-chalkboard/2017/06/02/english-learners-and-the-growing-need-for-qualified-teachers/1/4

Richardson, E., Education Development Trust (United Kingdom), & United Nations Educational, S. and C. O. (UNESCO) (France), I. I. for E. P. (IIEP). (2018). Teachers of refugees: A review of the literature. *Education Development Trust.*

Senechal, M. & Young, L. (2008). The effect of family literacy interventions on children's acquisition of reading from kindergarten to grade 3: A meta-analytical review. *Review of Educational Research, 78*(4), 880–907.

Stewart, J. (2011). *Supporting refugee children: Strategies for educators.* University of Toronto Press, Higher Education Division.

Takeuchi, M. (2015). The situated multiliteracies approach to classroom participation: English language learners' participation in classroom mathematics practices. *Journal of Language, Identity & Education, 14*(3), 159–178. doi: 10.1080/15348458.2015.1041341

Toronto District School Board. (2021). Toronto District School Board. https://www.tdsb.on.ca/

Toronto District School Board. (2021). *English as a second language/English literacy development.* Toronto District School Board. https://www.tdsb.on.ca/High-School/Your-School-Day/English-as-a-Second-Language

United Nations High Commissioner for Refugees. (2020, June 18). *Figures at a glance.* UNHCR. https://www.unhcr.org/en-us/figures-at-a-glance.html#:~:text=How%20many%20refugees%20are%20there,under%20the%20age%20of%2018

United Nations High Commissioner for Refugees. (2021). *Refugee statistics—United Nations refugee agency.* UNHCR Canada. (2021, January 26). https://www.unhcr.ca/in-canada/refugee-statistics/#:~:text=Between%20November%202015%20and%20April,Immigration%2C%20Refugees%20and%20Citizenship%20Canada

Wang, M. & Sheikh-Khalil, S. (2014). Does parental involvement matter for student achievement and mental health in high school? *Child Development, 85*(2), 610–625.

Vance, N. (2021). *Culture and language.* Salem Press Encyclopedia.

Weekly, R. (2019). "English is a mishmash of everything": Examining the language attitudes and teaching beliefs of British Asian multilingual teachers. *Critical Inquiry in Language Studies, 16*(3), 178–204.

Wilder, S. (2014). Effects of parental involvement on academic achievement: A meta-synthesis. *Educational Review, 66*(3), 377–397.

Williams, A. (2011). A call for change: Narrowing the achievement gap between White and minority students. *The Clearing House: A Journal of Educational Strategies, Issues and Ideas, 84*(2), 65–71. doi: 10.1080/00098655.2010.511308

Whitley, J., Klan, A., & D'Agostino, B. (2020). Narratives of funding related to inclusive education: Canadian news media from 2014 to 2019. *International Journal of Inclusive Education.* DOI: 10.1080/13603116.2020.1821446

Yılmaz, F. (2016). Multiculturalism and multicultural education: A case study of teacher candidates' perceptions. *Cogent Education, 3*(1). DOI: 10.1080/2331186X.2016.1172394

Chapter 19

Re-imagining Science Education for English Language Learners Through Integrated STEM and Multicultural Education

Paulo A. Oemig

ABSTRACT

This chapter is grounded in two studies: (1) a two-semester long fieldwork with ENLACE students enrolled in-person classes pre-COVID-19 pandemic, (2) the other study involves five students (three high school and two middle school students) enrolled in online learning during the pandemic. The research questions bridge two modalities of learning; Face-to-Face (F2F) and online (synchronous and asynchronous): What kind of science classroom (F2F and online) learning environment supports science-literate identities for English Language Learners (ELLs)? What sorts of integration exist among STEM subjects and has the potential to increase critical literacy? And what does multicultural education mean for the pre- and post-pandemic science classroom? Focus group and individual interviews of Latinx[1] secondary level students and classroom observations were conducted to describe how science is taught and to capture students' perceptions of these classes. An integrated STEM approach to teaching science whereby Common Core State Standards and the integration of multicultural education may advance the scientific discourse and science-literate identity of ELLs.

INTRODUCTION

Undoubtedly, we are living in challenging times. More than ever before, public education is being heavily scrutinized. The effects of the COVID-19 pandemic are stretching the limit of what public education can offer. We still press on, educating at home, remotely, but usually, with a blanket curriculum. The English Language Learners, often marginalized, are now at even more risk of not benefiting from a complete education. This period in history presents an opportunity to continue challenging injustices and advocating for educational equity.

All subjects taught in K–12 must address multicultural principles. Science is NOT a neutral subject. This chapter examines the academic engagement and perceptions of a group (N=30) of high school students and their science-literate practices in a pre-pandemic world. These students were participating in an ENgaging LAtino Communities in Education (ENLACE) program whose purpose was to increase Latinx high school graduation rates and assist them with college entrance requirements. The students were enrolled in different science classes to fulfill the science requirements for graduation. In addition, five Latinx students, ranging from grades seventh through eighth grades, were interviewed while participating in online learning during the coronavirus pandemic. This chapter is driven by three questions: (1) What kind of science classroom learning environment supports science-literate identities for ENLACE students? (2) What sorts of integration exist among STEM subjects and carries the potential to increase critical literacy? and (3) What does multicultural education mean for the science classroom today?

The literacy practices of scientists, such as questioning all things, interpreting data, evaluating claims based on evidence, and considering actions' consequences, among others, can help students become critical thinkers. Integrating multicultural education (MCE) into STEM is challenging: First, multicultural education is not a pedagogy nor a curriculum; it is a holistic educational process toward transforming schooling in order to serve all students and their communities, regardless of race, gender, culture, nationality, or sexual orientation (Gay, 2010). Second, multicultural education often takes the form of culturally responsive pedagogy (Au, 1993) in the classroom, but it is misunderstood as just good teaching for many educators (Au, 2009). That is, good teaching being good teaching irrespective of the students' needs and diversity in the classroom. Thirdly, science has traditionally been understood as culturally devoid of values; however, there is no value-free production of knowledge (Espinoza, 2012). Yet, students' access alone to literacy practices in STEM does not explain how students might learn to understand what integrated STEM is, use STEM for personal and social transformation, or engage in public debate. Integrating MCE into STEM challenges the sociopolitical context of how and why students are taught to extend their understanding of the world, thus confronting the STEM pipeline view that promotes economic growth at the cost of minority and marginalized groups.

Background

The problem investigated concerned how ENLACE students viewed themselves as scientists as a result of engaging in the practices of the science classroom. The study also examined the role of the science learning environment (e.g., type of instruction: teacher-centered, student-centered) in facilitating the learning for the ENLACE students. Developing a sense of self as someone who is good at doing science partly depends on experiencing inquiry-based instruction. Accomplishing this is complex, as students must take courses where different disciplinary literacies are expected (Shanahan & Shanahan, 2008, 2012). For English learners and Latinx students who share a group membership not typically represented in STEM fields nor science textbooks (Grant & Sleeter, 2009; Spring, 2007), developing a science-literate identity is more challenging. Thirty high school ENLACE students participated in this study during the 2016–2017 school year. Many of them had been or were, at the time of the study, in an English as a Second Language program (for detailed demographics, ACCESS scores, and study construct, see Oemig & Baptiste, 2018). Five Latinx students, two in middle school (7th and 8th grade) and three in ninth grade participated in a case study during the 2020–2021 school year. Both studies were conducted in the Southwest, in the same school district.

Despite educational progress in the last two decades, Latinx students are at the highest risk of high school dropout and less likely than any other subgroup to possess a college degree (The Education Trust, 2018). Results from the National Assessment of Educational Progress (NAEP) show that most adolescents lack advanced science literacy skills needed for knowledge production and innovation. Hispanic, Black, and American Indian students continue to underperform in science compared to their White peers (National Center for Education Statistics [NCES], 2019). Not surprisingly, most STEM workers in the U.S. are White (69%), and compared with their share in the overall workforce, Whites and Asians are over-represented; Blacks and Hispanics are under-represented in the STEM workforce (Funk & Parker, 2018).

Theoretical Framework and the Science-Literate Identity Construct

This study is complemented by social practice, which aligns with a socio-cultural framework. Social practice serves to recognize identity formation as the interplay between structures and agency (Wortham, 2006). Students can be described according to certain characteristics or behaviors, but as Wortham points out, "all social identification happens in practice" (p. 30), where signs of identity assume meaning via contextualization. Social practice understands that cultural production is the result of how cultural meanings are produced amid practices. Identity is developed in practice, and meanings are context-dependent, emerging from local practice and histories of practice like literacy. That is, learning becomes situated as language assumes a particular discourse in a particular situation (Gee, 2004, 2015).

Sociocultural orientations are poised to focus on "the description of the 'ways of knowing' unique to particular social, cultural, and educational groups" (Alexander & Fox, 2013, p. 17). It is this sociocultural perspective that provides the most appropriate springboard for examining the needs of culturally and linguistically diverse learners. Practices contextualize a notion of identity, which permits understanding it as a "process of coming to *be,* of forging identities in activity" (Lave & Wenger, 1991, p. 3). Appropriating a set of practices for situations determines and is part of an

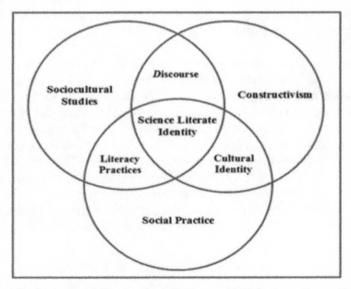

Fig. 19.1. The dynamics within the theoretical construct of science-literate identities.
Oemig, 2016, p. 14

identity make-up. At the intersection of the theoretical assumptions rests the construct of science-literate identities. See Figure 19.1.

Sociocultural studies recognize the cultural make-up of individuals and their relationships to histories and communities. As such, a sociocultural analysis does not focus on deficits in terms of knowledge but rather on differences due to cultural practices. Constructivism attends to cognitive and mental representations in processing information, and, in science education, inquiry has been the mean through which to facilitate the construction of knowledge. Gee's (2015) notion of discourse as part of an "identity kit" connects language to social roles and cultural contexts.

The Next Generation Science Standards (NGSS, 2013) recognizes that language intensive practices are implicated in science learning. When understood as a discipline of inquiry and scientific practices, science in the classroom can strengthen literacy in the discipline (Pearson, Moje, & Greenleaf, 2010). To access knowledge for making an inquiry, science literacy is needed. Developing a sense of self as someone who is good at practicing science will partly depend on experiencing inquiry-based instruction and science and engineering practices. Science-literate identity (SLI) refers to literacy practices associated with science *and* its multiple forms of linguistic expressions and representations. Science-literate identity, then, is the authoring or enactment of oneself that reflects such literacy practices, ways of knowing, doing, thinking, and acting (Gee, 2015).

INTEGRATION OF MULTICULTURAL EDUCATION (MCE) INTO INTEGRATED STEM

The integrative framework proposed here incorporates James Banks' (2016) five dimensions of multicultural education—content integration, knowledge construction process, prejudice reduction, equity pedagogy, and empowering school culture and social structure. The notion of integrating common concepts among science, technology, engineering, and mathematics (iSTEM) within K–12 has risen as a possibility with the CCSS, particularly with the NGSS focusing on practices, cross-cutting concepts, and disciplinary core ideas (NGSS, 2013; National Research Council [NRC], 2012, 2014). Encouraged by Banks' dimensions—a learning progression in which multicultural education can be incorporated into STEM—integrating multicultural education into integrated STEM (iMCEiiSTEM) can be envisioned. The significance of this construct is essential as it challenges the idea that STEM fields are neutral and objective disciplines, recognizes the influence of a "hidden curriculum" (Apple, 2019) in education, and is attuned to the needs of ELLs and Latinx students.

Integrating STEM fields in the teaching of science and engineering suggests positive outcomes such as meaningful learning, student-centered,
increased engagement, and requiring higher thinking skills (Stohlmann,
Moore & Roehrig, 2012). Integrated STEM education, along with the
three-dimensionality of science learning (Science and engineering practices,
disciplinary core ideas, and cross-cutting concepts), has the potential to
contribute to the development of "civic scientific literacy" (Miller, 2016).
The National Academy of Engineering and the Board on Science Education
(NRC, 2014) have proposed a framework for STEM integration, comprised
of four features: (1) goals (STEM literacy, 21st-century competencies, workforce readiness, and engagement in STEM); (2) outcomes (development of
a STEM identity and ability to transfer understanding across STEM disciplines); (3) nature and scope of integration (type of connections, disciplinary emphasis, and duration, size, and complexity of the initiative); and (4)
implementation (instructional design, educator supports, and adjustments to
the learning environment).

FINDINGS

Although six themes emerged in the in-person learning ENLACE study
(teacher-student interaction, bookwork and tests, purpose of writing and
reading, being good at science, utility of science, and reading habits) and
four themes (teacher-student interaction, purpose of learning online, sports/
extracurricular activities, engagement/socialization) emerged in the case
study of the online learning among the five middle and high school Latinx
students; for this chapter, the focus is on the common theme between the two
groups: teacher-student interaction. Participants placed the greatest value on
the degree they perceive they were understood by their teachers and how
they felt the teachers listened to them. For the Latinx students enrolled in
online learning during the pandemic, this aspect was even more pronounced.
Students felt they did not have many opportunities to engage in "classroom"
discussions with teachers and peers.

When asked about what would make the science classes they are taking or
have taken more engaging, a common response among 27 of the 30 ENLACE
students was related to doing "more labs," "more hands-on," and "experi-
ments." Another typical response students had was related to the importance
of the type of "relationship" with the teacher. Students felt more engaged in
science when they perceived their teachers respected them for their experiences and knowledge. For example, Danny[2] (11th-grade ENLACE student)
said, "interacting with the teacher instead of giving us a lecture" while
thinking about what would make a science class more meaningful. Another

ENLACE student, Anna (10th grader), stated, "science has never been important to me, so it's all about the teacher to me, because if they make it exciting for me, I pay more attention." Bang, et al. (2017) propose that equitable opportunities are reachable when relationships are fostered—"by attending closely to what students actually say and do in science, teachers can expand the relationships that are possible among themselves, their students, and science" (Bang et al., 2017, p. 33).

Among the online learning Latinx students, there was a sense of disconnect with learning in general and difficulty in staying engaged. When asked what could make their online science classes better, Brian (7th grader) stated, "All my classes are boring; in Mrs. L class, all she does is have us read and answer questions through Amplify [online learning platform]; same exact app over and over again, never a change." Another student, Robert (8th grader), stated, "Mrs. K tries to make it a real classroom; she is in the classroom and does the breakout rooms, but it's not the same; don't feel like participating because I don't know many of the students. . . . I gave up except for algebra and language arts because they count for high school [credit]." For the three high school students, Lenny, Laura, and Mike, learning during the pandemic was even more of a disconnect. The three students were new as ninth graders and did not know many of their peers. Laura stated, "I don't feel the [science] teacher knows me or cares about what's going on in my life . . . how am I supposed to learn from PowerPoint and tons of lectures." Lenny pointed to the importance of doing stuff, "I like to learn by doing, like a coach that helps me do better, and the coach gets to know you . . ." Mike mentioned the importance of small talk in getting to know the teacher and the teacher the students, "We do a lot of breakout rooms like Mr. G gives us a question and we solve it in small groups, but then we get to talk about other stuff too. . . . Mr. G talks about other stuff too." Teacher-student relationships are fundamental for creating student engagement, positive mindsets, and framing meaning making with students' identities in mind (Short & Hirsh, 2020, p. 21).

APPROACHES TO ADVANCING SCIENTIFIC DISCOURSE AND SCIENCE-LITERATE IDENTITY

In all the discussions and classroom observations with ENLACE students and interviews with the online learning Latinx students, two features are important: (1) teacher-student interaction, and (2) active discourse anchored in real-world examples. Having opportunities to engage in science practices ("by doing") approaches the instantiations of scientific communities of practice. The NGSS stresses that "science education should reflect the interconnected nature of science as it is practiced and experienced in the real world"

(2013, Appendix A). Research points to the benefits of recognizing students' backgrounds and contextualizing science instruction in real-world examples by promoting meaningful learning (Achieve, NGSS, Next Generation Storylines, & STEM Teaching Tools, 2016; González, Moll & Amanti, 2009; Lee & Buxton, 2010).

In framing science learning through three dimensions: science and engineering practices, cross-cutting concepts, and core ideas, the NGSS refines the meaning of "inquiry-based learning" by identifying science and engineering practices within a coherent progression of disciplinary core ideas. The *Framework for K–12 Science Education* (NRC, 2012; hereafter called "Framework") proposes integrating these three dimensions to reflect the work of scientists and engineers better and create meaningful learning opportunities.

> . . . K–12 science and engineering education should focus on a limited number of disciplinary core ideas and crosscutting concepts, be designed so that students continually build on and revise their knowledge and abilities over multiple years, and support the *integration* [emphasis added] of such knowledge and abilities with the practices needed to engage in scientific inquiry and engineering design. . . . To support students' meaningful learning in science and engineering, all three dimensions need to be integrated into standards, curriculum, instruction, and assessment. (NRC, 2012, p. 2)

STEM integration may contribute to fostering students' early science-literate identities. Researchers have found that integrating engineering learning modules and technology into STEM positively influences elementary students' content knowledge (Godwin, Cribbs & Kayumova, 2020). While alluding to extensive disciplinary literacy research, Alberts (2010) contends that integrating science inquiry skills and literacy "through collaborative and critical discourse" (Alberts, 2012, p. 405) can help in increasing competence and affinity. The Framework (NRC, 2012) further develops this statement by the incorporation of science and engineering practices; these practices "can actually serve as productive entry points for students from diverse communities . . . particularly second-language learners" (NRC, 2012, p. 283). Ultimately, STEM integration should lead to a more equitable "STEM literate society" (Simpson & Bouhafa, 2020).

An all-encompassing approach to reaching all students, which incorporates the features, including some MCE dimensions, is OpenSciEd. As an open educational resource (OER) licensed by Creative Commons Attribution, OpenSciEd provides science educational units and training for teachers facilitated by 10 state education agencies. OpenSciEd incorporates the three dimensions of science and engineering learning, Universal Design for

Learning (UDL) (CAST, 2018), and the science storyline model (Novak & Reiser, 2016; Reiser, Novak, & McGill, 2017); all these combined allow a shift from "learning about" to "figuring out." In flipping the script, students take charge of co-constructing meaning with peers and teachers. All units have an anchoring phenomenon, a 'hook' to catch the attention of all students and anchor the flow of the questioning and investigations to come. The OpenSciEd approach is based on student-driven questioning, science talks, and student-generated data to make sense of the anchoring phenomena.

In the pre-COVID-pandemic high school science classrooms observed, the dominant discursive practices were manifested through exchanges between teacher and students and, much less frequent, among students. The instructional delivery often took the form of the teacher initiating (I) a topic by asking a question, a student responding (R), the teacher evaluating (E) the answer and/or offering (F), and usually followed by another question by the teacher. This Initiation-Response-Evaluation/Feedback (IRE/F) sequence is representative of many instructional situations, and it is among the least effective interactional arrangements in the classroom (Cazden, 2001); this teacher-initiated sequence aligns with the "pedagogy of telling" (Tovani & Moje, 2017). The OpenSciEd approach recognizes the language students bring to the classroom. McNeill (Short & Hirsh, 2020, p. 27) suggests that frontloading students with vocabulary and science ideas does not contribute to engagement. This shift places emphasis on phenomena and activity before concepts.

IMPLICATIONS FOR EDUCATORS AND CONCLUSION

Most students observed in the science classrooms and interviewed remembered doing labs as a highlight in these courses. However, when asked about the purpose of the labs, they were hard- pressed to recall. As any dedicated science educator would argue, completing labs is important; we also know they are time-consuming. Prep time, safety considerations, transition times between classes, cleaning up, and resources are among some of the factors that enter the equation of offering labs. The coherence of the labs or activities to ensure meaningful investigations must be accounted for. Learning science by making sense of phenomena through interconnected navigation of a unit will embed investigations risen from students' curiosity.

Latinx students and English language learners would benefit from a STEM education that takes into account: An integrated model of STEM, including engineering; fosters scientific inquiry through science and engineering practices; considers multiple forms of expression and representation to communicate science, rising from the nature of science and the diversity of students; favors collaborative opportunities for students to engage in the language of science; educators establish caring, and positive relationships with their students; where every attempt is made to connect students with STEM practitioners who reflect the diversity of educators' classrooms; engages multicultural education principles, and offers a coherent phenomenon-based approach to teaching science.

Understanding the factors at play within the science classroom concerning language learners' engagement and perception, influences the development of their science-literate identities. This chapter has attempted to show, through two different studies, with similar student populations, and at two different points in time (pre- and during pandemic), the relevance of teacher-student relationships and of having a coherent set of integrated investigations in building Latinx students' self-esteem and confidence in STEM.

NOTES

1. This term is used as all-encompassing to refer to Latin American immigrants and their descendants. The only exception is when we refer to ENgaging LAtino Communities in Education (ENLACE) to specify ENLACE students who participated in this study.

2. Pseudonyms are used for students' names to protect their identity.

REFERENCES

Achieve, NGSS, Next Generation Storylines, & STEM Teaching Tools. (2016). *Using phenomena in NGSS—Designed lessons and units.* http://stemteachingtools.org/assets/landscapes/STT42_Using_Phenomena_in_NGSS.pdf

Alberts, B. (2010). Prioritizing science education. *Science, 328*, 405.

Alexander, P. A., & Fox, E. (2013). A historical perspective on reading research and practice, redux. In D. E. Alvermann, N. J. Unrau, & R. B. Ruddell (Eds.), *Theoretical models and processes of reading* (6th ed., pp. 3–46). International Reading Association.

Apple, M. W. (2019). *Ideology and curriculum* (4th ed.). Routledge.

Au, K. H. (1993). *Literacy instruction in multicultural settings.* Harcourt Brace Jovanovich.

Au, K. H. (2009). Isn't culturally responsive instruction just good teaching? *Social Education, 73*(4), 179–183.

Bang, M., Brown, B., Calabrese Barton, A., Roserbery, A., & Warren, B. (2017). Toward a more equitable learning in science: Expanding relationships among students, teachers, and science practices. In C. V. Schwarz, C. Passmore, & B. J. Reiser (Eds.), *Helping students make sense of the world using next generation science and engineering practices* (pp. 33–58). NSTA Press.

Banks, J. A. (2016). Multicultural education: Characteristics and goals. In J. A. Banks & C. A. M. G. Banks (Eds.), *Multicultural education: Issues and perspectives* (9th ed., pp. 2–23). Wiley.

Cazden, C. B. (2001). *Classroom discourse: The language of teaching and learning*. Heinemann.

Center for Applied Special Technology [CAST]. (2018). *Universal design for learning guidelines version 2.2*. http://udlguidelines.cast.org

Education Trust. (2018). *The state of higher education equity*. https://edtrust.org/the-state-of-higher-education

Espinoza, F. (2012). *The nature of science: Integrating historical, philosophical, and sociological perspectives*. Rowman & Littlefield.

Funk, C., & Parker, K. (2018). Diversity in the STEM workforce varies widely across jobs. Pew Research Center. https://www.pewresearch.org/social-trends/2018/01/09/diversity-in-the-stem-workforce-varies-widely-across-jobs/

Gay, G. (2010). *Culturally responsive teaching: Theory, research, and practice* (2nd ed.). Teachers College Press.

Gee, J. P. (2004). *Situated language and learning: A critique of traditional schooling*. Routledge.

Gee, J. P. (2015). *Social linguistics and literacies: Ideology in discourses* (5th ed.). Routledge.

Godwin, A., Cribbs., J., & Kayumova, S. (2020). Perspectives of identity as an analytic framework in STEM education. In C. C. Johnson, M. J. Mohr-Schroeder, T. J. Moore, & L. D. English (Eds.), *Handbook of research on STEM education* (pp. 267–277). Routledge.

González, N., Moll, L. C., & Amanti, C. (2009). *Funds of knowledge: Theorizing practices in households, communities, and classrooms*. Routledge.

Grant, C. A., & Sleeter, C. A. (2009). *Turning on learning: Five approaches for multicultural teaching plans for race, class, gender, and disability* (5th ed.). Wiley.

Lave, J., & Wenger, E. (1991). *Situated learning: Legitimate peripheral participation*. Cambridge University Press.

Lee, O., & Buxton, C. A. (2010). *Diversity and equity in science education: Research, policy, and practice*. Teachers College Press.

Miller, J. D. (2016). *Civic scientific literacy in the United States in 2016: A report prepared for the National Aeronautics and Space Administration by the University of Michigan*. https://science.nasa.gov/science-pink/s3fs-public/atoms/files/NASA%20CSL%20in%202016%20Report_0_0.pdf

National Center for Education Statistics. (2019). *The condition of education 2019*. https://nces.ed.gov/pubsearch/pubsinfo.asp?pubid=2019144

National Governors Association Center for Best Practices (NGA Center) & Council of Chief State School Officers (CCSSO). (2010). *Common Core State Standards*. National Governors Association Center for Best Practices, Council of Chief State School Officers.

National Research Council. (2012). *A framework for K–12 science education: Practices, crosscutting concepts, and core ideas*. National Academies Press.

National Research Council. (2014). *STEM integration in K–12 education: Status, prospects, and an agenda for research.* National Academies Press.

Next Generation Science Standards (NGSS Lead States). (2013). *Next generation science standards: For states, by states.* National Academies Press.

Novak, M., & Reiser, B. J. (2016). *Developing coherent storylines for NGSS lessons.* Presentation prepared for the NSTA Area Conference, Portland on Nov. 10. https://www.academia.edu/42018699/Developing_Coherent_Storylines_for_NGSS_Lessons

Oemig, P. A. (2016). Mapping classroom experiences through the eyes of ENLACE students: The development of science-literate identities. (Publication No. 10582978) [Doctoral dissertation, New Mexico State University]. ProQuest Dissertations and Theses Global.

Oemig, P. A., & Baptiste, H. P. (2018). Investigating the development of science-literate identities through a multicultural perspective. *Multicultural Perspectives, 20*(2), 81–91.

Pearson, D. P., Moje, E., & Greenleaf, C. (2010). Literacy and science: Each in the service of the other. *Science, 328*(5977), 459–463.

Reiser, B. J., Novak, M., & McGill, T. A. (2017). *Coherence from the students' perspective: Why the framework for K-12 science requires more than simply "combining" three dimensions of science learning.* Paper prepared for the Board on Science Education Workshop "Instructional Materials for the Next Generation Science Standards," 6/27/2017. https://sites.nationalacademies.org/cs/groups/ dbassesite/documents/webpage/dbasse_180270.pdf

Shanahan, T., & Shanahan, C. (2008). Teaching disciplinary literacy to adolescents: Rethinking content area literacy. *Harvard Educational Review, 78*(1), 40–59.

Shanahan, T., & Shanahan, C. (2012). What is disciplinary literacy and why does it matter? *Topics in Language Disorders, 32*(1), 7–18.

Short, J., & Hirsh, S. (2020). *The elements: Transforming teaching through curriculum-based professional learning.* Carnegie Corporation of New York. https://www.carnegie.org/topics/topic-articles/professional-learning-educators/elements-transforming-teaching-through-curriculum-based-professional-learning/

Simpson, A., & Bouhafa, Y. (2020). Youths' and adults' identity in STEM: A systematic literature review. *Journal for STEM Education Research, 3*, 167–194.

Spring, J. H. (2007). *Deculturalization and the struggle for equality: A brief history of the education of dominated cultures in the United States* (5th ed.). McGraw-Hill.

Stohlmann M., Moore T. J., & Roehrig G. H. (2012). Considerations for teaching integrated STEM education. *Journal of Pre-College Engineering Education Research, 2*(1), 28–34.

Tovani, C., & Moje, E. B. (2017). *No more telling as teaching: Less lecture, more engaged learning.* Heinemann.

Wortham, S. E. F. (2006). *Learning identity: The joint emergence of social identification and academic learning.* Cambridge University Press.

Chapter 20

Dual Language Education

A Model of Academic, Cultural, and Social Equity for English Language Learners

Tammy Oberg De La Garza and Erin Mackinney

In the field of English Language Learner (ELL) education, there is a wide variety of instructional pedagogies from which to choose. Yet, decisions about which ELL approach to take are often based on tradition, staffing limitations, and misinformation. Understanding the goals and outcomes of each model is critical before an educator can make an informed choice about the most socially just approach to teaching ELLs.

This chapter will provide an overview of English language instructional pedagogies in the nation, exploring the underlying goals of each, and critically examining the equity issues that exist in one specific additive model of ELL education—dual language education. Equity considerations must be made at school and district levels regarding programming equity and staff preparation/development. Within these considerations are explicit and implicit messages about language status and multicultural education.

Research demonstrates that subtractive methods strip diverse populations of their native language, familial value systems, cultural appreciation, and self-esteem; while additive approaches strengthen each aspect and result in higher levels of academic achievement (Alvear, 2019; Baker, Basaraba, & Polanco, 2016; Met & Lorenz, 1997; Valenzuela, 1999). On a methodological spectrum from subtractive to additive methods are: Sheltered English Instruction, Structured English Immersion, English as a Second Language (ESL) Pull-out, ESL Push-in, bilingual early-exit, bilingual late-exit and

English Language Instruction Program Model Continuum

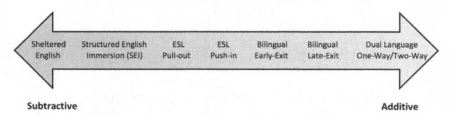

Fig. 20.1. English Language Instruction Program Model Continuum. Oberg De La Garza & Mackinney, 2018.

One-Way/Two-Way Dual Language Education (Lindholm-Leary & Genesse, 2010; Oberg De La Garza & Mackinney, 2018).

SUBTRACTIVE MODELS

At the most subtractive end of the instructional spectrum, sheltered English instruction and structured English immersion (SEI) programs both aim to expose children to English as quickly as possible (Adams & Jones, 2006; Johnson et al., 2018). Rather than explicitly teaching English, students engage in English content with a focus on comprehending the information. Sheltered English instruction teachers rely entirely on English, using gestures and visuals to aid understanding, while structured English immersion teachers can frugally use a student's native language to clarify students' misunderstandings (Cruze et al., 2019; López & McEneaney, 2012). One infamous example of this subtractive instructional approach is Arizona Proposition 203. Beginning in the 2001–2002 school year, students were only allowed to receive instruction in English, resulting in fewer than 11% of ELL's meeting state goals and failing to close achievement gaps (Garcia et al., 2012).

Another subtractive approach that is failing to close achievement gaps are ESL models, which combine students from different language backgrounds in the same class. Mainstreaming students into English proficiency and the American culture is the goal of this English-only model, deteriorating students' esteem towards their home culture and value system (Eshraqi, 2021). In ESL pull-out models, children are removed from their mainstream classrooms for a specific portion of each day to receive ESL instruction, while the ESL push-in model provides a classroom instructional aide to provide interpretation when needed.

English Language Learners in English-only programs such as SEI and ESL rarely attain the same level of academic achievement as their native English-speaking peers. They subsist in the lowest levels of academic achievement and drop out of school at the highest rate in the nation (Chang et al., 2007; Sugarman, 2019; Thomas & Collier, 2002). These subtractive, language education models leave ELLs behind and are the least socially just approach to educating diverse student bodies.

Additive Models

Models that do not subtract from students' funds of knowledge (language, culture, value system, etc.), and instead contribute to a child's bank of experience and knowledge, are additive programs. Such transitional bilingual programs incorporate students' native language into content, emphasizing the retention of language and culture, while expanding students' English repertoire. Early-exit models aim for a 1- to 3-year transition to mainstream classrooms, while late-exit models place a larger importance on developing and extending students' native linguistic skills and typically feature a 5- to 7-year transition.

Both types of bilingual programs demonstrate higher academic achievement than English-only programs, but there is a growing body of research on one program that offers even greater benefits academically, socially, and culturally for ELLs, and that is dual language (DL) education (Flores et al., 2021; Lindholm-Leary & Borsato, 2006; McKay, 2011; Thomas & Collier, 2002, 2012). The DL model is built upon longitudinal research that demonstrates students who are literarily fluent in their native language attain higher English achievement levels than their peers in English-only education programs (August & Shanahan, 2006; Collier & Thomas, 1997). Simply put, literacy in a child's native language is an advantage to learning to speak, read, and write in English.

Ideally, DL classes are made up of an equal percentage of English speakers and non-native English speakers. In the primary grades, 50% to 90% of the students' day is conducted in the minority (or partner) language. Thomas and Collier (2012) note that "the rationale for [ELLs and native, English speakers] initially receiving large amounts of curricular time in the minority language is that society provides a great deal of access to academic English outside of school, and much less for the minority language" (p. 14). Lessons in the intermediate grades progresses to a 50% balance, expanding academic mastery in both languages and continuing through the high school experience.

Socially Equitable Dual Language Instruction

When considering which educational model to employ with ELLs, considerations around social justice should dictate the decision-making process. The most equitable model should enable ELLs to close the academic gap with English-only peers and empower them to recognize the value of their home language, culture, and experiences, all while equipping them with the tools to successfully attain academic and social capital in the classroom and the world.

Academic Performance

Unlike other models for ELLs, one of the goals of DL education is to help students achieve high levels of proficiency in two languages—English and their heritage language, which for most ELLs and simultaneous bilinguals is Spanish. Students in DL education engage in 5 to 12 years of native and English language instruction to foster academic language fluency in both languages.

Taking a closer look at literacy and academic achievement in DL models, research demonstrates that ELLs participating in DL models for more than 6 years outperform their ELL peers in every other model of ELL instruction (Gándara & Slater, 2019). In fact, by the sixth year in the program, dual language students achieve greater linguistic and academic success than their monolingual English peers. The following figure portrays longitudinal

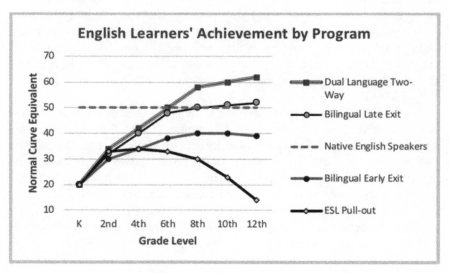

Fig. 20.2. English Learners' English Reading Achievement by Program. Thomas & Collier, 2012.

data from Thomas and Collier's 2012 noteworthy findings, highlighting the English reading achievement benefits of DL over any other model of English language instruction.

The significance of this increase in academic achievement is important at the school reform level (Lindholm-Leary & Borsato, 2006). Schools that adopt this approach to teaching ELLs have overall improved scores as well as increased connections to parents and the community (Slater, 2018).

Social Currency/Community Cohesion

Learning in a system that values the ELL's heritage language and culture has far-reaching benefits. Receiving instruction in their home language affirms students' funds of knowledge or collections of knowledge acquired from families, traditions, and daily routines. Students gain a greater understanding and appreciation of their language, family, and community. Rather than receiving the unspoken message of "leave everything you know and love at the door," ELL students in DL classrooms are recognized as rich contributors to the collective body of knowledge.

These students make up the fabric of school, reducing the implicit bias ELLs may feel in more subtractive programs that academics is for "others." While integrating into the American culture, ELLs in DL programs take pride in their skills and themselves, resulting in less behavior problems, higher attendance, school performance and graduation rates (Anberg-Espinosa, 2008; Ramírez, Yuen, & Ramey, 1991; Slater, 2018; Thomas & Collier, 2012). The DL paradigm increases academic achievement and self-esteem of students, promotes a welcome environment for minority-speaking parents, and strengthens schools and communities.

Social Justice Considerations

For any DL program to be sustainable, there must be a thorough understanding of the model and support for DL at every level of the school—from superintendent to principal to faculty to office staff. Without this layering of support, the program itself and/or the potential benefits are subject to deterioration.

Programming Equity

There are several administrative considerations that need to be weighed through the social justice lens when planning for or refining a dual language program: school selection, space and resource equity, assessment accountability, parent/community partnership, language distribution, and equity in access (Lindholm-Leary, 2018).

- School Selection—the process of selecting the school site and the students for the DL program is challenging, as there are generally more students that desire DL programming than programs. "Decisions about where to locate DL and whether DL will be whole school, or 'strand' can have a major impact (sometimes unintended) on neighborhood and school demographics. It can also exacerbate transportation issues" (Gándara & Slater, 2019, p. 3). School selection should be based on district needs and accessibility of marginalized populations, including transportation availability in lower SES communities.
- Space and Resource Equity—in schools with DL and non-DL programming, DL classrooms should be allocated the space for teaching and learning that is allocated to non-DL classrooms. Spaces include instructional areas, wall space, storage, and a classroom library. Furthermore, there are sufficient resources to develop and/or purchase, including books, curriculum and assessments in both languages, and instructional technology. Resources should reflect the experience of the language minority students (Palmer et al., 2019).
- Assessment Accountability—there must be assessment in both languages to authentically measure the growth in both languages (not just English). Assessments in the partner language need to be recognized as valid for school, district, and state purposes such as academic achievement and graduation.
- Parent/Community Partnership—the community must have a voice in the decision-making process; whether Spanish is the partner language, which language distribution model to select, and who has access to programming. Parent voice should represent the wide range of cultural, linguistic, and socio-economic groups in the community.
- Language Distribution—programs that have a 90/10 distribution of Spanish to English in the early grades is a more socially just approach than the 50/50 model. The latter does not sufficiently expand the native language of ELLs, while the former has been associated with larger gains across programs and populations. There should also be time or acknowledgment for everyday student language use through translanguaging (Palmer et al., 2019)
- Equity in Access—The DL program should serve equal numbers of native English and native Spanish students. "The ideal [two-way DL] model is a balance of 50% English and 50% partner language speakers. The effort to enroll and appease parents of English speakers by allowing programs to become unbalanced, or the practice of tipping the enrollment balance toward speakers of the partner (e.g., Spanish) language significantly impacts the power of the two-way model" (Gándara & Slater, 2019, p. 3). The language minority students should be the first

priority of any two-way DL program, in order to prevent the overemphasis on demands placed by advantaged majority students (native English-speakers) and their parents (Cervantes-Soon, 2018).

Staffing and Professional Development

Although it is critical that lead teachers of ELLs are knowledgeable and highly skilled in teaching a second language and credentialed, not every educator in DL programming has to be bilingual. Many DL classrooms feature one teacher who exclusively teaches in English (i.e., in the morning), and a team-teacher who teaches in Spanish (or the target language in the afternoon). All teachers should have targeted, extensive preparation for teaching DL settings and sufficient guided experience in the DL classroom

Savvy principals recognize that the responsibility for teaching ELLs rests on every teacher, so it is critical that the entire staff engages in ongoing professional development addressing culturally responsive topics such as English language acquisition, cross-linguistic awareness, assessment, differentiated instruction, and teaching language through content. It is important to note that ELLs are overidentified as having special needs due to language differences, so teachers should also be skilled in the proper assessment and identification of ELLs with disabilities, instructional services, and resources available (Liu & Barrera, 2013).

CONCLUSION

The goals of the teaching and learning of ELLs have evolved from assimilation to a dual mastery of language, culture, and literacy. English Language Learners in DL classrooms have the opportunity to not only close the achievement gap between ELLs and English-only speakers, but to outperform them. This learning approach offers a brighter future for ELLs who will emerge bilingual, biliterate, bicultural, and socially conscious. Both native English speakers and ELLs benefit from the explicit and implicit messages about language status and multicultural education. Through community need, visionary leadership, and trained educators and staff, dual language education is a collective effort that bridges home, school, and community. It is a socially just educational model in need of replication.

REFERENCES

Adams, M., & Jones, K. M. (2006). Unmasking the myths of structured English immersion: Why we still need bilingual educators, native language instruction and incorporation of home culture. *Radical Teacher, 75*, 16–21.

Alvear, S. A. (2019). The additive advantage and bilingual programs in a large urban school district. *American Educational Research Journal, 56*(2), 477–513.

Anberg-Espinosa, M. (2008). *Experiences and perspectives of African American students and their parents in a two-way Spanish immersion program* (Doctoral Dissertations, 155). https://repository.usfca.edu/diss/155

August, D., & Shanahan, T. (Eds.). (2006). *Executive summary. Developing literacy in second-language learners: Report of the national literacy panel on language-minority children and youth.* Lawrence Erlbaum.

Baker, D. L., Basaraba, D. L., & Polanco, P. (2016). Connecting the present to the past: Furthering the research on bilingual education and bilingualism. *Review of Research in Education, 40*(1), 821–883.

Cervantes-Soon, C. (2018, December 7–8). Race, social justice, and power equity. [Paper presentation]. UCLA Forum on Equity and DL Education, Los Angeles, CA.

Chang, F., Crawford, G., Early, D., Bryant, D., Howes, C., Burchinal, M., . . . Pinata, R. (2007). Spanish-speaking children's social and language development in pre-kindergarten classrooms. *Early Education and Development, 18*, 243–269.

Collier, R., & Thomas, W. P. (1997). School effectiveness for language minority students. *Resource Collection Series #9.* National Clearinghouse for Bilingual Education.

Cruze, A., Cota, M., López, F. (2019). A decade after institutionalization: Educators' perspectives of structured English immersion. *Language Policy, 18*(3), 431–453.

Eshraqi, M. (2021). The effect of ESL learning on self-esteem, self-efficacy, confidence, stress, and anxiety. *Applied Linguistics Research Journal, 3*, 223–230.

Flores, N., Tseng, A., & Subtirelu, N. (2021). *Bilingualism for all?: Raciolinguistic perspectives on dual language education in the United States.* Multilingual Matters.

Gándara, P., & Slater, R. (2019). Confronting the equity issues in dual language immersion programs: A summary of the 2018 UCLA forum on equity and DL education. *UCLA Civil Rights Project/Provecto Derechos Civiles.* https://www.civilrightsproject.ucla.edu/research/k-12-education/language-minority-students/summary-report-confronting-the-equity-issues-in-dual-language-immersion-programs/Spencer-Equity-Report-final-for-attendees-w.0.pdf

Garcia, E., Lawton, K., & Diniz De Figueriedo, E. (2012). The education of English language learners in Arizona: A history of underachievement. *Teachers College Record, 114*(9), 1–18.

Johnson, D., Stephens, C., Nelson, J., & Johnson, E. (2018). Violating Lau: Sheltered English instruction programs and equal educational opportunity. *Journal of Education Policy, 33*(4), 488–509.

Lindholm-Leary, K. J., & Borsato, G. (2006). Academic achievement. In F. Genesee, K. Lindholm-Leary, W. Saunders, & D. Christian (Eds.), *Educating English* language learners: A synthesis of research evidence (pp. 176–222). Cambridge University Press.

Lindholm-Leary, K. J., & Genesee, F. (2010). Alternative educational programs for English learners. In California Department of Education (Eds.), *Improving education for English learners: Research-based approaches*. CDE Press.

Lindholm-Leary, K. (2018, December 7–8). Dual language program planning and equity [Paper presentation]. UCLA Forum on Equity and DL Education, Los Angeles, CA.

Liu, K., & Barrera, M. (2013). Providing leadership to meet the needs of ELLs with disabilities. *Journal of Special Education Leadership, 26*(1), 31–42.

López, F., & McEneaney, E. (2012). State implementation of language acquisition policies and reading achievement among Hispanic students. *Educational Policy, 26*(3), 418–464.

McKay Wilson, D. (2011). Dual language programs on the rise: "Enrichment" model puts content learning front and center for ELL students. *Harvard Education Letter, 27*(2).

Met, M., & Lorenz, E. (1997). Lessons from U.S. immersion programs: Two decades of experience. In R. Johnson & M. Swain (Eds.), *Immersion education: International perspectives* (pp. 243–264). Cambridge University Press.

Oberg De La Garza, T., & Mackinney, E. (2018). Teaching English in the United States: Looking back and moving towards a brighter future. *Studies in English Language Teaching, 6*(2), 86–96.

Palmer, D., Cervantes-Soon, C., Dorner, L., & Heiman, D. (2019). Bilingualism, biliteracy, biculturalism, and critical consciousness for all: Proposing a fourth fundamental goal for two-way dual language education. *Theory into Practice, 58*(2), 121–133.

Ramírez, J. D., Yuen, S. D., & Ramey, D. R. (1991). *Final report: Longitudinal study of structured English immersion strategy, early-exit and late-exit transitional bilingual education programs for language-minority children*. United States Department of Education.

Slater, R. (2018, December 7–8). Overview of the field of dual language instruction [Paper presentation]. UCLA Forum on Equity and DL Education, Los Angeles, CA.

Sugarman, J. (2019). *The unintended consequences for English learners of using the four-year graduation rate for school accountability*. Migration Policy Institute.

Thomas, W. P., & Collier, V. P. (2002). *A national study of school effectiveness for language minority students' long-term academic achievement*. Center for Research and Education, Diversity and Excellence.

Thomas, W. P., & Collier, V. P. (2012). *Dual language education for a transformed world*. Fuente.

Valenzuela, A. (1999). *Subtractive schooling: US-Mexican youth and the politics of caring*. State of University of New York Press.

Chapter 21

Using Cultural and Political Vignettes in the Professional Development of Teachers of English Language Learners

Jacqueline Darvin

What are cultural and political vignettes (CPVs) designed for teachers of English Language Learners (ELLs)?

- A new student from India comes to your high school and on her first day in the cafeteria, she begins eating rice with her hands. Several of the children make fun of her (Nieto, 1999, p. 74). You are her English as a new language (ENL) teacher and are in the lunchroom when this happens. What do you do?
- You have been hired as the new ENL teacher at a middle school in Queens. As part of your position, you must "push in" to several content area teachers' classes to assist the students that need of ENL services. One of the science teachers with whom you work clearly does not want you coming into his/her class and even prevents you from working with your students at times. Last week, during your regularly scheduled time with the students in that class, they went on a field trip, and the teacher did not even inform you about it. What would you do?
- You are an untenured ENL teacher teaching eighth grade. You observe that because ELLs are mainstreamed into English-only instruction in seventh grade, in anticipation of the 8th grade ELA state test, there are many referrals into special education for your students. What can you do to further investigate your observation that ELLs at your school are being over-referred to special education? How might you inform your

colleagues and administrators of the information you uncovered in a professional and politically sensitive manner?

- There are several foreign-born students in your fourth period biology class. As ELLs, you know that it is important for them to be given many opportunities to practice speaking English, but when they try and participate in discussions, the native speakers of English make fun of their accents and tease them. How would you deal with this issue?

- A new student from Japan named Yuichi enters your 7th grade class. You are on the playground at recess and overhear a group of children making fun of Yuichi's name. The next day, Yuichi's father comes to school and asks to talk briefly with you. During your conversation, Yuichi's father requests that you and the rest of the class please call him Tom from this point forward. You know that names are very important to people's identities and that Yuichi is at an age when his identity and sense of self are being crafted. What would you do?

The preceding scenarios about ELLs are examples of what the author has termed cultural and political vignettes (CPVs). "CPVs are cultural and/or political situations, real or imaginary, which are presented to learners so that they can practice the decision-making skills that they need to be successful in today's diverse classrooms and communities" (Darvin, 2015, p. 3). Although most secondary teachers know the content that they teach and have command of classroom management, far fewer feel confident facilitating conversations around culturally and politically controversial and sensitive issues in ways that honor their diverse students' voices and lead to critical, transformative thinking and, more importantly, action (Darvin, 2015, p. 2). These skills and abilities have become increasingly important for ENL teachers and the educational leaders who supervise them, as classrooms in the United States have become progressively diverse and political climates have become exceedingly contentious.

The CPVs are geared specifically toward teachers and administrators of secondary ELLs and are designed to sensitize them to the issues surrounding the teaching of ENL students and provide ways for them to consider these complex, multifaceted issues from social change and social justice perspectives. They invite both pre-service and in-service teachers to dialogue around controversial and sensitive issues related to ELLs that they need to respond to and evaluate critically. The CPVs presented and discussed in this chapter can be used by ENL teachers, content area teachers who work with ELLs, teacher educators, professors, school administrators, ENL Coordinators, and other professional development providers and community activists as part of pre-reading, during-reading and/or post-reading and writing professional development activities, all aimed at creating more inclusive and effective learning environments for ELLs.

These CPVs are specifically designed to enhance both secondary-level, classroom content area teachers' and ENL teachers' understandings of ENL students' unique cultural and political issues and can be used as springboards for creating more successful classrooms, curricular materials, instructional strategies, and community resources for ELLs. The focus of this chapter is on how can be used to increase secondary teachers' sensitivity to and knowledge about ELLs and how these CPVs can further enable them to view ELLs' challenges from multiple perspectives and act accordingly in their practice. It is the author's intention to explore topics such as cultural relevance, multiculturalism, microaggressions, linguistic diversity and discrimination using CPVs that can be responded to by teachers in writing and as part of situated performances. Sample role-plays of CPVs involving secondary teachers of ELLs are presented, as are tips for how CPV activities can move from initial conversations to real changes in practice that will foster social justice and positively impact schools and communities.

CPVS AS A PEDAGOGICAL MODEL: STAGES ONE THROUGH THREE

The pedagogical model of implementing CPVs is designed as a four-stage model that begins with stage one, which involves the teachers being presented with CPVs in writing and them responding to them in writing, sharing their responses verbally with others, and discussing their responses from multiple perspectives. The model begins in this way so that teachers can build trust with each other and create a professional learning community (PLC) while discussing sensitive and sometimes controversial issues surrounding ELLs. Once teachers have become more comfortable responding to the cultural and political vignettes, they are ready to begin stage two, creating and exchanging their own CPVs. This process is fascinating in that the kinds of vignettes that teachers create are strongly influenced by their own cultural backgrounds, past experiences as teachers and students, political views, current events, and a myriad of other factors. This second phase of CPVs is termed "Create and Exchange" by the author.

A more advanced way of using cultural and political vignettes in teacher professional development comes with Stage Three, when teachers become comfortable enough to role-play the proposed situations in real time. This third technique is employed later, when teachers have already created and exchanged CPVs several times and feel somewhat comfortable with the process. At stage three, teachers are selected to play roles in the vignettes (i.e.,

ELL student, ENL teacher, parent, principal, school board member, etc.) and try and respond to the vignette as it actually unfolds. When using this technique, it is important to emphasize to the teachers in the audience, who are watching the situated performances, that this is an extremely difficult activity and that the whole point of the exercise is to allow them to "make mistakes" in a safe and controlled environment. The other teachers are there to support the actors in the performances, not to point out all the things the actors do wrong or to criticize.

Situated performances of CPVs are especially useful for demonstrating to teachers how much of communication is nonverbal. By watching CPVs being acted out in physical ways, they observe that the gestures, postures, intonations, and various other nonverbal characteristics of a particular teacher are just as important, if not more so, than the words that he/she says. Kohl asserts that "language is an everyday, every minute matter and nuances of inflection, tone, modulation, and vocabulary are constantly in play in the interaction of students and teachers. There is an unarticulated linguistic sensibility that determines the nature and quality of interaction in the classroom" (p. 147). Perhaps the linguistic sensibility to which Kohl refers need not be unarticulated, if we provide greater opportunities for teachers to observe, analyze, and discuss nonverbal aspects of communication. Then, it makes sense that they will be better prepared to recognize the "nature and quality of interactions" in their diverse classrooms and schools and respond accordingly.

Situated performances also provide excellent opportunities to demonstrate and discuss microaggressions that occur in schools, since part of becoming a more culturally responsive teacher involves effectively recognizing and responding to microaggressions in daily interactions with students, colleagues, administrators, and parents. The following CPV could be used as a springboard for the study of microaggressions, as they pertain to ELLs:

- Imagine a situation in which students are giving oral presentations in front of a class. One of the students is an English Language Learner (ELL) and is very nervous about speaking in front of her peers. She begins her presentation tentatively and is having difficulty being heard or understood by her classmates because of her soft voice and thick accent. From somewhere in the back, an unidentified male student yells, "Honey—We can't understand a damn thing you're saying." The other students all laugh as the ELL student turns red with embarrassment. What should the teacher do? (Darvin, 2018, p. 3)

In this CPV, the teacher of the ELL student is placed in a difficult situation that warrants further exploration. Having teachers that can identify microaggressions, facilitate thoughtful dialogue around them, and address them appropriately both within their lessons and beyond will serve to improve the nature of individual exchanges with students, colleagues, and parents, as well as the overall social justice climate of the classrooms and school.

Microaggressions are defined as "brief and commonplace daily verbal, behavioral, or environmental indignities, whether intentional or unintentional, that communicate hostile, derogatory, or negative racial slights and insults toward people of color" (Sue et al., 2007, p. 271). The definition and study of microaggression (Nadal et al., 2014; Solorzano et al., 2000; Boysen and Vogel, 2009; Sue et al., 2009) has been further expanded to include other forms besides those against people of color, including those that specifically target Latinx Americans (Nadal et al., 2014) and those microaggressions related to gender, sexual orientation, and disability (Sue et al., 2007). CPV situated performances provide excellent opportunities to provide professional development to ENL and content area teachers about microaggressions and to enable them to practice handling situations involving microaggressions so that when they occur in their classrooms and schools, they have already rehearsed appropriate responses and are prepared to manage them in a sensitive and professional manner.

STAGE FOUR OF CPV IMPLEMENTATION: "READ AND REVISIT" EXAMPLES

The author terms the fourth stage of CPVs "Read and Revisit." This is done by pairing a CPV with one or more texts that relate to the issue(s) depicted in the vignette. One way to do this is as an exercise to see if teachers' views have changed over time, as a result of reading and discussing pivotal texts. For example, teachers could be given the following CPV:

• You are teaching in a high school where the population in predominantly African American. Most of your students speak Black vernacular English in their homes and communities. You want to help them to acquire written and spoken standard English because you know that this is the dialect that they will need to use to be successful in college and to attain good careers as adults. When and how would you teach standard English to these students?

The responses are collected, and the teachers are told that they will be revisited later. Several readings can then be completed by the teachers that deal with issues of language variation and nonstandard dialects in the classroom, including chapters from *The Skin That We Speak* (Delpit & Kilgour-Dowdy, 2002). All the authors in this edited volume discuss the pivotal role that language plays in a person's identity, the impact that negative judgments about a person's home language can have on their self-esteem and willingness to participate in formal education, code-switching, issues pertaining to variations in students' dialects, and ways that teachers can effectively support the learning of Standard English without rejecting students' home languages/dialects and fostering language biases.

After reading a text such as *The Skin That We Speak* as a book club or PLC anchor text, teachers can be asked to reflect upon their own experiences with language and identity and to discuss the various chapters and their implications for classroom practice. After reading and discussion, the preceding CPV can be redistributed to the teachers, along with their original responses, made before reading the text. They can then be asked to respond to the CPV a second time and to answer the following questions:

- Did your response to the CPV change after reading the text or remain the same? If it changed, please explain why, citing activities and/or readings when applicable. If it remained unchanged, please explain why, citing activities and/or readings when applicable.

This CPV Read and Revisit exercise enables teachers to "operationalize" the theories they read about in the text and make direct connections between the text and how it might influence their behavior as teachers in the future.

A second way to pair texts with CPVs is more of a short-term exercise in which teachers respond to a CPV, read a short text at home, such as an article or singe book chapter, and then respond to the CPV again during the next PLC meeting. An example of this strategy could employ the following CPV on articulating one's views on social justice teaching:

- You are unhappy with your current teaching position at a high school and decide to interview for a new position. At the interview, one of the administrators asks you what your beliefs are concerning teaching for social justice and to give one example of how you would implement your beliefs in your classroom. How would you respond?

One appropriate text that could be paired with this short-term Read and Revisit CPV is Chapter 4, titled "Teaching for Social Justice," in *Walking the Road: Race, Diversity and Social Justice in Teacher Education* (Cochran-Smith, 2004). In this chapter, Cochran-Smith presents Six Principles of Pedagogy for social justice. The principles encourage building on students' prior knowledge and interests (Principle 2), collaborating with individuals, families, and communities (Principle 4) and making equity, power, and activism explicit parts of the curriculum (Principle 6). The chapter also emphasizes that "teaching for social justice is difficult and uncertain work" (Cochran-Smith, 2004, p. 82) and "as much a matter of developing a particular kind of pedagogy as it is learning to theorize pedagogy and participate in a community of professionals also engaged in this work" (Cochran-Smith, 2004, p. 82).

After reading this chapter or another text that is similarly themed, teachers could be asked to respond to the social justice CPV a second time and then partner with a colleague to discuss what changes (if any) they both made to their responses and why. These discussions between partners might give birth to a whole group discussion regarding the teachers' feelings of being unprepared for complex questions on interviews and not being provided with authentic opportunities in which to "rehearse" putting difficult ideological questions (such as the one presented in the CPV) into succinct answers that would be well received. Perhaps this Read and Revisit discussion might also lead to a dialogue about how theories about social justice are operationalized in different classrooms settings at different grade levels and how teachers can move from beliefs to actions in ways that make sense in the context of their schools and communities. Regardless of the directions in which these conversations go, they ultimately will enable teachers to engage in discussions around issues that might be far more difficult to discuss without the CPV to function as both a catalyst and something to come back to if conversations stray off topic or become contentious.

TEACHERS OF ELLS USING CPVS WITH THEIR OWN STUDENTS

Once teachers of ELLs have been exposed to professional development using CPVs as a pedagogical model, they can begin to use CPVs with their own students to help facilitate conversations around sensitive topics and create student learning communities (SLCs) around issues of equity and social justice. Teachers can choose to implement the entire four-stage model of CPV implementation in their classrooms or simply create one or more CPV units or lessons that they believe fit well with their curriculum and objectives. For example, Rachell, a Spanish teacher in New York recently created a CPV unit for her secondary students on "Colorism, Racism, and Afro Latinidad in Dominican Culture." She wrote in her unit rationale:

> Last year and now, our students are engaged in e-learning or attending school in person as the world around them shines light on the systemic racism and violence affecting their communities. The Coronavirus pandemic magnified the pervasive inequalities that non-White Americans, especially Black, Hispanic,

and Native American people face in the United States. Our students watch and listen to news on their cell phones or TV, like the situation where a woman called the police on a black man birdwatching in Central Park, and sadly enough, this has become a "normal" ordeal. Our students also observe and absorb a plethora of social occurrences related to critical topics such as race, gender, sexuality, social class and beyond. Our students have questions, opinions, and beautiful minds in need of nourishment. Our students need a critical approach to their education. And here I am, a second-year Spanish teacher, committed to doing more. I've always believed that teaching a subject goes beyond teaching that subject. To me, teaching Spanish means connecting Spanish to the world around, taking Spanish on many road trips out of the classroom. The undeniable need for conversations on race, gender and culture in schools is not exempt in any subject, and when I began to ponder on how I could incorporate cultural and political vignettes for the first time into a lesson or unit, I immediately thought about connecting my own immigrant experiences to a relevant topic in the adolescent experience. The truth of the matter is that as soon as I began to think about an important issue for my Latinx students related to the social climate we are in, I began to reflect on my Dominican upbringing and sat with uncomfortable truths of my culture and many racial microaggressions I grew up with. I remembered being told to not date a black boy because I would "dañar la raza" (trans: damage the race), being told my natural hair needed straightening and receiving compliments for my light skin color. I even remember my father sharing offensive jokes about Haitians with his friends, and my classmates criticizing our French teacher's Spanish because of his Haitian heritage. Racism and colorism in the D.R. and Dominican-Americans is a reality, which feeds the normalized anti-Haitian sentiment and anti-blackness ideology.

Two teachers of Chinese, Yuki and Zizhen, also in New York, created a CPV unit for 9th grade students on "Conflicts Due to Cultural Differences." They wrote the following CPV:

Early on in the outbreak of COVID-19, the Chinese students began to wear masks to school, but the American students believe that wearing a mask means that you are sick and should stay home. However, Chinese students believe that masks are necessary not just for people who may be sick; they are also a way to prevent the spread of the virus. Also, some of American students have told the Chinese students that the coronavirus is a "Chinese Virus." When the Chinese students heard the American students say this, they became angry. What do you think of this situation? What might you say or do?

In their CPV unit, the teachers went on to say the following in their rationale:

One of the main goals of our CPV unit is helping students respect and embrace all cultures both inside and outside the classroom. This is not an easy task since the world is complex and diverse. Additionally, there are many factors that influence how a learner perceives other cultures besides his or her encounters in the microcosmic classroom environment. Normally, students portray in-group and out-group behaviors, and most are comfortable interacting with those from a similar background. In most cases, this leads to misunderstandings and conflicts, when students get divided based on cultural backgrounds. Teaching this CPV lesson on how to address conflicts caused by cultural differences will help students develop different viewpoints and learn that all cultures are to be cherished and appreciated.

Most conflicts that arise between members of different culture are due to the fact that none understands why the other behaves differently. In addition, students have different stereotypes regarding minority cultures and will associate them with negative attributes such as low socioeconomic background, among others. This makes students from minority cultures believe that they are inferior, making them shy away from participating in class, and this leads to poor performance. In other cases, they start hating their language and culture and imitate ways of the superior culture.

Another way in which this unit will help students is by encouraging them to love and embrace their own cultures. For example, during the COVID-19 Pandemic, many American students did not wear masks to school, yet Chinese students wore masks as a preventive measure. Chinese students were ridiculed by American students, and they might have stopped wearing masks. This happens when minority students feel pressured to dispose of their norms and cultures. Through this unit, students will learn to investigate the unique facets of their culture, and this will help them appreciate it and love it more. This means that even when pressured by other students, they will not easily abandon their own cultural norms. The unit will also benefit students by showing how to solve different issues that may arise due to cultural differences.

CONCLUSION

As demonstrated in this chapter, using cultural and political vignettes in the professional development of teachers of ELLs to explore social justice perspectives can have positive impacts on teachers, as well as on their students. Teachers of ELLs can take what they learn in a PLC that employs CPVs as a pedagogical strategy and use this knowledge to create engaging lessons, units, and student learning communities (SLCs) using CPVs. In closing, using the words of cultural anthropologist Margaret Mead, "Never doubt that a small group of thoughtful, concerned citizens can change world. Indeed, it is the only thing that ever has."

REFERENCES

Boysen, G. A., & Vogel, D. L. (2009). Bias in the classroom: Types, frequencies, and responses. *Teaching of Psychology, 36*(1), 12–17.

Cochran-Smith, M. (2004). *Walking the road: Race, diversity, and social justice in teacher education.* Teachers College Press.

Darvin, J. (2015). *Teaching the tough issues: Problem-solving from multiple perspectives in middle and high school humanities classes.* Teachers College Press.

Darvin, J. (2018). Becoming a more culturally responsive teacher by identifying and reducing micro-aggressions in classrooms and school communities. *Journal for Multicultural Education, 12*(1), 2–9.

Delpit, L., & Kilgour-Dowdy, J. (Eds.). (2008). *The skin that we speak: Thoughts on language and culture in the classroom* (2nd ed.). The New Press.

Kohl, H. (2002). Topsy-turvies: Teacher talk and student talk. In L. Delpit & J. Kilgour-Dowdy (Eds.), *The skin that we speak: Thoughts on language and culture in the classroom* (pp. 145–161). The New Press.

Nieto, S. (1999). *The light in their eyes: Creating multicultural learning communities.* Teachers College Press.

Nadal, K. L., Mazzula, S. L., Rivera, D. P., & Fujii-Doe, W. (2014). Microaggressions and Latina/o Americans: An analysis of nativity, gender, and ethnicity. *Journal of Latina/o Psychology, 2*(2), 67–78.

Solorzano, D., Ceja, M., & Yosso, T. (2000). Critical race theory, racial microaggressions, and campus racial climate: The experiences of African American college students. *Journal of Negro Education, 69*(1/2), 60–73.

Sue, D. W. (2015), *Race talk and the conspiracy of silence: Understanding and facilitating difficult dialogues on race.* Wiley.

Sue, D. W., Lin, A. I., Torino, G. C., Capodilupo, C. M., & Rivera, D. P. (2009). Racial microaggressions and difficult dialogues on race in the classroom. *Cultural Diversity and Ethnic Minority Psychology, 15*(2), 183–190.

Sue, D. W., Capodilupo, C. M., Torino, G. C., Bucceri, J. M., Holder, A. M. B., Nadal, K. L., & Esquilin, M. (2007). Racial microaggressions in everyday life: Implications for clinical practice. *American Psychologist, 62*(4), 271–286.

Index

excluded from, 48; teacher support, varied experiences with, 48. *See also* challenges in U.S. public schools, African English learners; transition into U.S. public schools, African English learners

Afro-Latinx, 149; influence on music industry and culture, 150; students, 149, 150

Aisha's experience, 45; helpful teachers, 45; interaction with teachers, 45

Ajayi (2011), 16

Alemán, 2009: 32, 174; LatCrit in education and higher education, 174

Allegorical tale, 11; "The Woodcrafter's City" (Traw, 2002), 11

Allen, Andrea, 109

American Indian children, 232; Holly Hunts, 232

American Indian ELLs, 52; academic English skills improvement, 58; anecdotal evidence of self-esteem and cultural pride, 58; building literacy skills, 60; decrease in number, 54; English as-a-second language (ESL) certificate, 60; Montana, 54, 55, 60; professional development support, 60; standardized test scores, 58; U.S. Federal Native American Language Policy, 58

American Indian English, 57; impact on education and employment, 57

American students, 225; mask-wearing, 225

Amey, Marilyn, 156; partnership model (2010), 156, 158; research on educational collaborations and community college partnerships (2007), 158

anthropology, 235; culture and linguistics focus, 235; Katie Richards, 235

anti-Blackness ideology, 224

anti-Haitian sentiment, 224

Antiracist Black Language Pedagogy, xviii; framing ideas, 94, 95

apartheid, 21; impact on Black South African students, 22, 25; laws and language policy, 21, 22; socioeconomic challenges, 25

apathy, 68; reframing apathy as withdrawal, 68; withdrawal due to lack of engagement, 68

applications of translanguaging, 139. *See also* English language arts classes and translanguaging; math classes and translanguaging

Arizona, 124; Arizona Department of Education (2013), 127, 128; Arizona English Language Learner Assessment (AZELLA), 127; ELL Identification, Assessment, and Exiting Protocol, 126; Home Language Survey, 126, 127; Identification, Assessments, Exiting Protocol, and Monitoring, 125, 126

art class, Eleena's experience, 47; cultural background incorporation, 47; teacher interest in African art, 47

articulation agreements, 155

assessment accountability, 211; Dual Language Programming, 211

assessment, xvii; cultural expressions, 107; culturally and linguistically diverse (CLD) students, 11–13; dynamic assessment, 102, 103, 106; equitable assessment, 103, 104; formative assessment, 69, 104; inequitable learning environments, 107; performance-based assessment, 105; perspectives in assessment, 106; summative assessment, 13, 14, 128; traffic light assessment tool (Black et al., 2004), 13; translanguaging assessment practices, 102. *See also* authentic assessment; English Learners (EL) assessment; high stakes testing and assessment; standardized tests and assessment asset-based approach, 68; culturally relevant pedagogy, 68; culturally responsive teaching, 68; culturally sustaining pedagogy, 68; California English Learner Roadmap, 68

assets, pedagogies recognizing, 120; attitudes towards language, 92; biases, 92, 93; hypercorrection, 94, 96; negative attitudes, 92; teacher attitudes, 92

authentic and strategic relationships around a common vision, 163; deep relationships, 163; gatekeepers, 163; like-minded project personnel, 163; trust building, 163

authentic assessment, xvii, 11–13, 103–105; benefits for English Learners, 103–105; characteristics, 104, 105

authentic communication, 83; call and response approach, 83; co-taught classroom, 83; sustainable co-teaching, 83; student facilitators, 83

autonomy, 8, 23, 79, 150

awards, 102; Academic Achievement Award, Amber Riehman, 236; Leader in Biliteracy Award, Amber Riehman, 236

bachelor's degree, 155, 235

Baetens-Beardsmore, 2008, 7; bilingual students' benefits, 7

Basic Interpersonal Communication Skills (BICS), 59; Cognitive Academic Language Proficiency (CALP), 59; Cummins (2008), 59; Indian English dialect (Leap, 1993), 59

Beech (2011), 120

Bell, xvii; Bell (1980), 31; Bell (1992), 31; Bell (1995), Critical Race Theory in critical legal studies, 173; Bell (2016), xvii, 110, 138; Bell (2016), social justice education, 110

BESITOS Program, 160; Bicultural Education Students Interacting to Obtain Success, 160; development and features, 160; related projects (e.g., Project Synergy, Chrysalis, AccessUS), 160

bicultural students, 112; cultural traditions, 113; experiences living in different countries, 113

Biddle & Berliner (2002), 6; democratic process and student leadership, 6

bilingual and dual language programs, 236; Kip Téllez, 236

bilingual classroom, 6; equity and social change, 1, 2, 6; intercultural approach, 1; linguistic mediation strategies, 1; social interaction and academic performance, 3, 4, 8; language proficiency, 3, 8; mediation activities and strategies, 5, 7; multicultural understanding, 6, 7; social interaction, 4, 8

bilingual education, xviii; African American students, xviii, 89, 90, 94; Antiracist Black Language Pedagogy, xviii, 90, 94; Anti-Black Linguistic Racism, xviii, 89, 90, 94; dual language education programs (Kim et al., 2015), 130; Ebonics, 89, 90; maintenance bilingual education (Téllez, 2018), 130; Paulo Oemig, 235; Singapore, 23; transitional bilingual education, 130; White Mainstream English (WME), 90. *See also* dual language education programs (Kim et al., 2015)

bilingual program, xviii; equitable school culture, 110, 111; Japanese high school, 110; social justice principles, 110, 112; teacher expectations, 92, 112

bilingual-bicultural education, 233; Dr. Amanda L. G. Montes, 233

bilingualism, 118; Emergent bilinguals
(EBs), 129; emerging, 118; flexible,
118; traditional views, 119
Black language, 89; origins, 95;
perceptions, 92–93; social settings,
95; stereotypes, 93
Blackman & Fairey (2007), 31, 33
boarding schools, Indian, 55; abuses, 55,
56; language oppression, 56
Boser (2011), 174; discriminatory hiring
practices in schools, 174
boundaries, socially constructed, 118
Bourdieu (1986), 136; habitus and
capital, 136
Broad (2001), 16
Buchanan (2017), 135; teaching as a
political act, 135
building classroom relationships, 77;
environment, aesthetically inclusive
spaces, 79; environment, displaying
native languages, 79; knowing
students, connecting with families
and communities, 80; knowing
students, introductory videos, 80

Cadierno & Eskildsen (2015), 4; usage-
based language learning, 4
Caldera, Altheria, 230
Calderon-Berumen, Freyca, 101, 230
California, 66; Amber Riehman at El
Cajon Valley High School, 236;
California Department of Education
(2017), 66; California Department
of Education (2021), 128; Katie
Richards at El Cajon Valley High
School, 235; Katie Richards at
University of California, Los
Angeles, 236; ELPAC (English
Language Proficiency Assessments
for California), 126, 128; ELL
Identification, Assessment, and
Exiting Protocol, 126; home
language survey, 125–127;
identification, assessments, exiting
protocol, and monitoring, 126;

University of California, Los
Angeles, 231
Canada, 110; immigrants and
refugees, 187, 189
Carjuzaa & Ruff, 51, 53, 54
Carjuzaa, Jioanna, 51, 229
CAST, 203; Universal Design for
Learning (UDL) (2018), 202, 203
Castillo (2021), 130; translanguaging
controversy, 130
Cazden, 2001, 203; Initiation-Response-
Evaluation/Feedback (IRE/F)
sequence, 203
CEFR (Common European Framework
of Reference), 1; language activities,
1; mediation tasks and strategies, 6
census, 136
Center for Intercultural Multilingual
Advocacy (CIMA), 160
challenges in U.S. public schools,
African English learners, 41, 42,
48; cultural and linguistic barriers,
42; Eurocentric curriculum, 42,
43; misrepresentation and lack of
reference, 43
challenges, 2; student-centered, 73;
systematic barriers, 67; teacher-
centered, 67; time constraints, 68
charter schools, 147, 150
classroom discussions, 83; opportunities
for reflection, 83, 200; student
feedback, 83
classroom environment, 3, 8, 80, 112
classroom management, 218
classroom settings, 4; effectiveness of
mediation, 8; empowerment and
autonomy of students, 8
Cochran-Smith, 222; Teaching for
Social Justice, 222; Six Principles of
Pedagogy, 222
code meshing, 118
code-switching, 222
Cohen, Brawer, & Kisker (2014), 157
College of Education, 160; Linda P.
Thurston at Kansas State University,

236; Greg Wiggan at University of North Carolina, Charlotte, 236; Kevin Roxas at Western Washington University, 236
Collier & Thomas (2009), 177; dual language program outcomes for linguistically diverse students, 177
colonial language, 19; social, political, and economic disadvantages, 19
colonialism, 19; effects on Indigenous languages, 19, 20; language policies, 19
color blindness, 31
colorism, 223
Common Core State Standards (CCSS), 195
communication: clear and consistent communication, 164; cross-institutional professional development, 164; nonverbal, 220; regular check-ins, 164
communicative dimension, 6; cultural mediation, 6; intercultural communication, 6; mediator role and responsibilities, 7
communities, engagement with, 118
community cohesion, 211; dual language education, 211
community college-university transfer partnerships, 158; creation and sustainability (Kisker, 2016), 158
community cultural wealth theory (Yosso, 2005), 145, 148
community languages, lived experiences, 119
community: involvement, 151; leaders, 151–152; understanding, 147–148
complex linguistic repertoire, 119
composite counter-stories, 32
conceptual mediation, 6; group work and leadership, 6; soft skills, 6; transversality, 6
concluding thoughts and recommendations for the future, 178; DL (Dual Language) program

implementation, 178; increasing Latinx individuals in teaching force, 178; Latinx students, support for, 178; pathway for DL students into teacher pipeline, 178; school culture, promoting multilingualism, 178; strategic planning for DL program implementation, 178
Condition of Education 2020 report, 51, 53
conflict resolution, 6; intercultural mediation, 6
conflicts, 4; cultural differences, 224, 225
connection between home and school, 12; culturally responsive pedagogy, 12
content area teachers, 217–219, 221
content objectives, 104
contributors, 229; Amber Riehman, 236; Greg Wiggan, 236; John A. Williams, 237; Katie Richards, 235; Kevin Roxas, 236; Kip Téllez, 236; Landon Wilson, 237; Linda P. Thurston, 236
core practices, 77; critiques, 78; goals of linguistically and culturally sustaining MLL students, 78; orchestrating a full class discussion, 78
Coronavirus pandemic. *See* COVID-19 pandemic
Corrientes, translanguaging, 102
Council of Europe, 1; 2001, initial concept of linguistic mediation, 1, 4; 2020, expanded concept of linguistic mediation, 5, 6
counterstories, 149, 151
counter-storytelling: 30, 32
COVID-19 pandemic, 189, 196; effect on ELLs, 196; remote and hybrid teaching, 196
Creative Commons Attribution, 202; OpenSciEd, 202
Crenshaw (1991), 31, 32
Criterion Referenced Test (CRT), 55

238

Index

La Lotería, 151

language, xvii; bilingualism, 26, 118; development and theory, 118; gaps, alternation as a coping strategy, 119; language demands, explicit attention, 120; performance, contextualizing, 118; proficiency scores, 118; sociopolitical constructions, 234

language acquisition and multilingualism, 183; influence on teaching approach, 184; teachers' experiences, 184; teachers' multilingual skills, 184

language and identity, 89; Ebonics, 89; Black language (BL), 89; linguistic racism, 89; sociopolitical grounds, 89

Language and Leadership department, 231; Tammy Oberg De La Garza, 231

language arts, 139; Landon Wilson, 237

language expectations, 92

language ideologies, 90; socially constructed hierarchies, 136, 137

language loss and oppression, 56

language objectives, 60; separating from content objectives, 103

language of instruction, 20; impact on learning, 21, 117

language policy, 26; colonialism effects, 26; Ashley Karlsson, 233; STEM success, 26

language proficiency, 8; bilingual context, 7, 8

language status, 26; dual language education, 26, 207, 213

language teaching community, 130; linguistic resources discussions, 130

language use in praxis, 116; asset-based language, 116; deficit-oriented labels, 117; multilingual learners, 116; Villegas & Garcia (2021), 117

Larsen-Freeman (2012), 118

LatCrit Theory, 173; application in education, 173; centralizing Latinx experiences, 173; counternarratives

and lived experiences, 173; examination beyond Black and White binary, 173; intersection of race, ethnicity, and language, 173

Latinx epistemology, 148

Latinx student achievement, 232; María L. Gabriel, 232

Latinx students, xix; online learning during the pandemic, xix; teacher-student interaction, xix

Latinx teacher shortage, 171; background, 172; bilingual education, 171; causes and consequences, 172; critical race theory (CRT), 171; LatCrit (Latino/a critical race theory), 171; solutions, 172; teaching force, 172

Lavadenz & Colón-Muñiz (2017), 174; Latinx teacher recruitment and retention, 174

Lawrence (1993), 32

Lazar & Schmidt (2018), 119

Leader in Biliteracy Award, 236; Amber Riehman, 236

leadership, 6; classroom roles, 6; language teaching, 6

Leap (1993), 57, 59

Lee & Buxton (2010), 202; recognizing students' backgrounds in science instruction, 202

Lee & Jeong (2020), 4; social learning for children learning a new language, 4

lessons learned, 109, 156, 160, 162, 166

Leung & Valdés (2019), 118

Li (2018), 136; idiolects and language use, 136

Li & Ho (2018), 136; Welsh revitalization programs and translanguaging, 136

Liddicoat et al. (2003), 4; intercultural language learning, 4

Limited English Proficient, 101; Texas education code, 101

multiculturalism and multilingualism, 183; commitment in educators' attitudes and beliefs, 183; TDSB (Toronto District School Board) culture and mindset, 183; teacher mindset and agency, 183
multidisciplinary, 118
multilingual education, 21; South Africa, 21–22; Singapore, 21–22
multilingual learners (MLLs), 77; asset-based phrases, 116; core practices for educators, 78; culturally sustaining pedagogy, 36; educational settings, 36; emerging bilinguals, 116; linguistically sustaining core instructional practices, 78, 79, 84; research-based suggestions for practitioners, 36
multilingual STEM workforce, 25
multilingualism, 19; as an asset, 120; in educational spaces, 121; importance for filling vacant teaching positions, 176; normalization in educational spaces, 189; support in educational policy, 176
multimodal assessment, 104, 105
multinationalism, 118
music, 104, 150

National Center for Education Statistics (NCES), 2018, 51; English Language Learners (ELLs), 109
National Education Assessment Program (NAEP), 55
National Institute of Health (NIH), 161
National Research Council (NRC), 124; integrated STEM framework (2012, 2014), 199; Next Generation Science Standards (NGSS) (2013), 199
National Science Foundation (NSF), 161
national teacher shortages, 172; bilingual education, 172; English learner (EL) services, 172
nation-building, 119

Native American Languages Act (NALA) (1990), 58; language preservation and community pride, 58; student achievement improvement, 58; 25 U.S.C. 2903, 58
native language, 19; additive models, 209; dual language education, 209; subtractive models, 208
navigating curriculum, 44; curriculum, feeling excluded from, 44; teachers, role in helping newcomer students, 44
neoliberal education context, 146; market-based approaches, 146; school choice, 146; anti-teacher union policies, 146; standardized testing, 146
neutrality, 31
Newcomer African high school students, 43; participant selection, 43; homogeneous purposive sample technique, 43; experiences, 43; role of teachers in transitional processes, 43; navigating the new curriculum, 43
New London group, 1996, 118; multiliteracies, 118
new teachers, 44; Aisha's experience with helpful teachers, 45; Eleena's varied experiences with approachability, 45
New York State School District Leader, 231; Jacqueline Darvin, 231
New York, 223; Rachell, Spanish teacher, 223; Yuki and Zizhen, Chinese teachers, 224
Nieto, 52, 217
Nikula (2007), 7; benefits of mediation, 7
No Child Left Behind (NCLB), 15, 116, 127, 229,
non-mainstream languages, 92; Hmong, 92; Mien, 92; Spanish, 92
Nordlund et al. (2015), 113; inclusive practice, 113; multiple voices, 113

About the Editors and Contributors

Dr. Elvira J. Abrica is an assistant professor in educational administration and higher education. Her research interests focus on increasing access to higher education for historically underrepresented groups across post-secondary institutional contexts. Her agenda centralizes students' subjective experiences with race, ethnicity, and immigrant generation and includes research on experiences and outcomes for men of color; student identity exploration and development in science, technology, engineering, and mathematics (STEM) fields; organizational change and student equity in community colleges; and institutional research and assessment.

Andrea Allen is a PhD student and teaching fellow in the Department of Curriculum and Instruction at the University of Houston. She has several years of experience teaching in formal and informal educational settings in Texas and Japan and now focuses on increasing the representation of women of color in the field of art education.

Dr. Miguel Fernández Álvarez is an associate professor in the Department of Linguistics Applied to Science and Technology at the Universidad Politécnica de Madrid. He holds a PhD in English Philology (University of Granada, Spain) and two master's degrees: MA in Education (University of Granada, Spain) and MA in Language Testing (Lancaster University, UK). His areas of interest include bilingual education, second language acquisition, and language testing. He is the author of *A Test Impact Study Under the No Child Left Behind Act: The Case of the ACCESS for ELLs* (2010). He has also authored and coauthored over twenty articles in the field of language acquisition and language testing.

Judith Blakely is academic coordinator at Walden University and serves a vital role in maximizing student achievement by incorporating leadership, advocacy, and collaboration.

Jioanna Carjuzaa earned a PhD in multicultural, social, and bilingual foundations of education from the University of Colorado–Boulder at Montana State University (MSU) she is a professor and serves as the executive director of the Center for Bilingual and Multicultural Education. She teaches courses for undergraduate and graduate students in education, Native American studies, and ESL/EFL methodologies. Jioanna serves as the facilitator for Indian Education for All (IEFA) professional development opportunities and has hosted over 20 IEFA conferences/workshops. She also serves as the faculty advisor for the Society of Indigenous Educators for Native students pursuing teaching careers. She is the author of *Teaching in the Middle and Secondary Schools*, Pearson's leading methodology textbook now in its 11th edition. She provides professional development for Class 7 Indigenous Language and Culture teachers across Montana. She was the recipient of the national 2013 G. Pritchy Smith Multicultural Educator of the Year Award.

Altheria Caldera is presently completing a 9-month fellowship with the Intercultural Development Research Association (IDRA) in San Antonio, Texas. As an education policy fellow, she is advocating for state-level policies that prioritize the needs of students of color in Texas. In August 2021, she will begin a new role as assistant professor of reading and language arts at Howard University. She is a teacher educator and scholar activist who advances educational equity in the areas of linguistic justice, Black girls and school discipline, and anti-racist pedagogies.

Freyca Calderon-Berumen is an assistant professor of elementary and early childhood education at Penn State University, Altoona. As a woman of color in the US, she seeks to explore possibilities for community building for marginalized and under-theorized groups and contributing to the teacher education field by linking theoretical perspectives with everyday experiences and developing culturally relevant and decolonizing understandings. She conducted research seeking ways to transcend traditional educational paradigms through transformative, culturally responsive pedagogies.

Marta Carvajal-Regidor, PhD, teaches English for academic purposes at the University of Kansas. Her research and teaching interests include language ideologies and language practices and how to better support students' linguistic rights through pedagogy and curriculum.

Dr. Tamara Collins-Parks teaches credential and masters level courses for the department of Dual Language and English Learner Education at San Diego State University where she is the graduate adviser. Her work is published in *Literacy Ideology, Teachers' Beliefs, Language Policy and Parent*

Voice and she coauthored *Teaching Literacy Across the Content Areas: Effective Strategies That Reach All K–12 Students* (2016).

Dianisha Lanette Croft is a Christian, wife, and mother. She is currently seeking a PhD in Language and Literacy at Cardinal Stritch University in Wisconsin. Her research interests include Black language, identity, and code switching, culturally sustaining pedagogy, the Black doctoral experience, and the Black Minds Matter Movement.

Jacqueline Darvin, PhD, is a deputy chair, program director, and professor of secondary literacy education at Queens College of the City University of New York (CUNY). She is currently pursuing another advanced degree in Educational Leadership and credentials as a New York State School District Leader. Before becoming a professor at Queens College, Dr. Darvin taught middle and high school English for twelve years. In 2015, she published a book with Teachers College Press titled *Teaching the Tough Issues: Problem-Solving From Multiple Perspectives in Middle and High School Humanities Classes*. She was the recipient of the Long Island Educator of the Month Award, featured in a cover story of *New York Teacher*, the official publication of the New York State United Teachers' Union, and a recipient of the Queens College Presidential Award for Innovative Teaching. Her presentations include both national and international conferences on topics related to literacy teaching and learning.

Rachael Dektor is a PhD student at University of California, Santa Cruz. As a former elementary school teacher, she has experience working in Central and Southern California schools. Rachael's research interests include California teachers and their experiences working with the growing population of Indigenous language speakers from Mexico.

Tammy Oberg De La Garza is a full professor at Roosevelt University in Chicago. She is the director of the Dual Language Teacher Leadership graduate program, and the chair of the Language & Leadership Department. Her research interests include Latino literacy and advocacy for academic equity.

Uchenna Emenaha is an assistant professor at the University of Texas at San Antonio. Her research interests include use culturally responsive teaching to support students STEM identify development, reflective teaching practices, and scientific argumentation.

María L. Gabriel, PhD, has worked as a PK–12 public educator in Colorado since 1997. She has devoted her career to increasing access and opportunity for culturally, linguistically, and racially diverse students through direct student support, culturally sustaining family engagement, community-based educational research, and equity leadership. She has served on local and national boards focused on gender and racial equity, multicultural education, and community outreach. Her research interests and local, national, and international presentation topics are related to multicultural education, educational equity, Latinx student achievement, and student voice. Her work has been published in journals such as *Cuaderno de Investigación en la Educación, Educational Leadership,* and the *Journal of Latinos and Education.* She loves to run, travel, take pictures, and write. Her joy in life is spending quality time with her two teenage daughters and her Yorkie pup named Bear.

Charlotte R. Hancock is a doctoral candidate of curriculum and instruction, with a specific focus on Urban Literacy/TESL, at the University in North Carolina at Charlotte. Her research focuses on language education policy, culturally and linguistically diverse students, and on best and effective practices for world language and dual language programs.

Holly Hunts earned her doctorate in consumer economics from Cornell University. She worked as an extension specialist at the University of Illinois for several years before coming to Montana State University in 1996. With an academic background in secondary education and human development/family studies the health and well-being of children are a common theme in her research activities. Much of Holly's research involves working with Native communities in Montana and across the country to address complex "wicked problems." Academic English language acquisition for American Indian children is a profoundly wicked problem where past solutions (i.e., forced attendance at boarding schools to learn English) not only failed to produce academic literacy it spawned many more "wicked problems." Her research passion is to collaboratively discover practical solutions to real-life problems that do not cause more problems.

Dr. Jeanne Carey Ingle is an associate professor of elementary and early childhood education. She teaches courses in English learner education, equity in education and educational technology. Her research includes PK–12 teaching during the COVID-19 pandemic, teaching in a multilingual classroom, English learner access to STEM education and using immersive technologies to prepare pre-service teachers. She is the co-chair for the honors program for elementary and early childhood education and is the coordinator for the Adrian Tinsley Program Undergraduate Research Grant. Dr. Ingle was recently awarded the Bridgewater State University 2020/2021 Honors

Outstanding Faculty Award. Dr. Ingle received her BA from Boston College and her PhD in education from the University of Connecticut.

Ashley Karlsson is an education systems specialist with the SE-Metro Regional Center of Excellence in Rochester, MN. She has an MA in English as a Second Language from Hamline University and a PhD in Education Policy and Leadership from the University of Minnesota. Her current work involves supporting local schools and districts with comprehensive assessment and continuous improvement related to language programming. Additional interests include language policy, linguistically sustaining pedagogies, translanguaging, and teacher development.

Dr. Brenee King is the assistant director for the Office of Undergraduate Research and Creative Inquiry (OURCI) at Kansas State University and the Project Administrator for the Kansas Louis Stokes Alliance for Minority Participation (KS-LSAMP). In both roles she has the privilege of working with first-generation and historically excluded students to help them accomplish their academic goals. Dr. King has developed and implemented several initiatives that focus on student recruitment and retention efforts with a focus on community college students. She is also involved in work focused on leadership development for early career underrepresented faculty. Dr. King holds a doctorate in biomedical science from the University of New Mexico and a BS in chemistry from University of California, Santa Barbara.

Erin Mackinney is associate professor of bilingual/ESL education at Roosevelt University in Chicago. She is a faculty member in the Dual Language Teacher Leadership graduate program. Her research interests include dual language pedagogy, and language development and maintenance.

Dr. Beth Montelone is a professor of biology and the Senior Associate Vice President for Research, who directs the Office of Research Development. In this role, she supports and facilitates the research efforts of K-State's faculty, staff, and students, by helping to coordinate multi-investigator research collaborations, professional development activities for new and continuing researchers, and university-wide research initiatives.

Dr. Amanda L. G. Montes is an assistant professor in the bilingual-bicultural education program at Northeastern Illinois University in Chicago, Illinois. She holds a PhD in applied linguistics from Arizona State University. Her areas of interest include examining bilingual educators from culturally and linguistically diverse backgrounds, language attitudes, culturally responsive teaching, liberatory pedagogy, and arts integration in bilingual education settings. She has worked in the field of bilingual education for over 18 years in a variety of settings including elementary education, higher education, and with bilingual educators providing professional development and technical assistance to school districts.

Dr. Amanda R. Morales currently is an associate professor of multicultural & multilingual education in the Department of Teaching, Learning, and Teacher Education at the University of Nebraska–Lincoln. Dr. Morales's research addresses issues of social justice, equity, and access for minoritized students across the PK–16 education continuum. More specifically, her current work focuses on teacher diversification pathways, teacher preparation for working with (im)migrant, multilingual, and minoritized students, as well as the experiences of Black, Indigenous, and People of Color (BIPoC) pre-service and in-service teachers in predominately White institutions.

Leah Mortenson, PhD, is a clinical instructor in the School of Education at St. John's University. Her teaching and research focus on engaging teacher candidates with social justice issues related to education and incorporating social justice pedagogy into EAP teaching.

Olivia Murphy, PhD, has her doctorate in literacy education from the University of Maryland, College Park. Her research interests include critical and other social justice literacy practices and literacy teacher education, and she was previously a high school literacy teacher in Brooklyn.

Dr. Brenda Muzeta is an assistant professor in secondary education at Kutztown University. She holds a PhD in teacher education and curriculum studies from the University of Massachusetts, Amherst. She takes a broad interest in issues pertaining to language, culture, identity, social justice, and equity in education. Her research guided by identity, sociocultural, and post-colonial theories, focuses on the sociocultural and sociopolitical contexts in which students from linguistically and culturally diverse backgrounds develop and learn, and how these experiences inform teacher education. With teaching experiences in both U.S. and international contexts, Dr. Muzeta's goal is to highlight the relationship between language, identity and culture by illuminating student voices and experiences. Her research further explores connections and implications of linguistic and cultural diversity in classroom practices. In order to create a more socially just and equitable classroom environment, Dr. Muzeta advocates culturally relevant pedagogies for practicing teachers and pre-service teachers.

Paulo A. Oemig is the director of the New Mexico Space Grant Consortium (NMSGC) and the New Mexico NASA EPSCoR program. Paulo is an Assistant Professor in the College of Health, Education and Social Transformation at New Mexico State University. He teaches courses in research methods, bilingual education, and methods of teaching science. His research areas are integration of STEM education and the development of science-literate identities, particularly among underrepresented and underserved students. Paulo completed an Albert Einstein Distinguished Educator Fellowship with NASA, has five years of experience as a chemist and ten years of experience as a STEM educator. Paulo Oemig completed a bachelor's degree in chemistry, master's degree in anthropology and a PhD in science and bilingual education. Dr. Oemig is a member of the Math and Science Advisory Council of the New Mexico Public Education Department.

Izamar D. Ortíz-González is a graduate student at School Organization and Policy at the University of California, Davis. She calls northern California home as she was raised between San Jose, California, and the Central Valley. She grew up navigating multiple narratives—Eurocentric stories she learned in school by her teachers—and her mother's stories of Mexico. Bridging the gap between these narratives has motivated her career as an educator, organizer, and now scholarship. She taught six years in Sacramento ranging from the K–12. She currently serves as the chair of the Sacramento chapter of the Association of Raza Educators. Her current research interest seeks to center the voices of students, teachers, and communities of color in education policy and school practices.

Kyongson Park is an assistant professor of education at the University of Michigan–Dearborn. She teaches ESL teaching methods, assessments, and literacy, culture and power courses in the TESOL/ESL endorsement programs for undergraduate and graduate students. Her research interest includes teacher education for ELs, interactive online teaching, and inclusive education.

Carol Revelle has been an educator for 24 years and is currently an assistant professor in the Reading Program for Curriculum and Instruction at Texas A&M University–Commerce. Revelle strives to be a productive state literacy leader and an active member of her writing project. Her research emphasis is on equity in literacy instruction. Currently, Revelle is working with secondary teacher candidates to prepare them to be advocates for their students and leaders in their classrooms, schools, and districts.

Katie Richards teaches science and literacy at El Cajon Valley High School in San Diego where she is a team lead in her department. Katie completed her BA at the University of California Los Angeles where she majored in anthropology with a focus on culture and linguistics. She completed her MA in dual language and English learner education with an emphasis in educational leadership at San Diego State University.

Amber Riehman is a 2020–2021 Teach Plus California Policy Fellow who teaches social science at El Cajon Valley High School in San Diego where she also serves as one of the school's English learner (EL) coordinators and union site representatives. Amber has been recognized with an academic achievement award as well as the Leader in Biliteracy Award. Amber completed her MA in critical literacy and social justice from San Diego State University's Department of Dual Language and English Learner Education (DLE), where she was voted outstanding graduate for her cohort.

Kevin Roxas (PhD, Michigan State University) is a professor and department Chair in the Secondary Education Department in the Woodring College of Education at Western Washington University. His research examines three interrelated areas of concern: (a) the often inequitable nature of the social contexts of reception in school and communities for immigrant and refugee students and their families; (b) the dynamic creation of adolescent identity for immigrant and refugee youth in response to systems of oppression and discrimination they face in schools; and (c) how pre-service, in-service teachers, and social service providers can and must critically examine and reconceptualize the ways in which they respond to the needs of immigrant and refugee students in their classrooms and in local communities.

Kip Téllez is professor and former chair of the Education Department at the University of California at Santa Cruz. He began his career teaching English learners in both elementary and secondary schools. His research interests include teacher education, second language education, bilingual and dual language programs, and educational policy. His most recent book is *The Teaching Instinct: Explorations Into What Makes Us Human* (2016).

Dr. Linda P. Thurston is a Professor Emeritus in Special Education, Counseling, & Student Affairs at Kansas State University. Having last served as the associate dean for research and external funding within the College of Education, Linda implemented a range of successful programs for faculty mentoring and development as well as grant-based projects to broaden participation of historically underrepresented populations in science, technology, engineering, and mathematics (STEM) and STEM education.

Greg A. Wiggan is professor of urban education at the University of North Carolina at Charlotte. His research addresses school processes that promote high achievement among urban and minority students. He has published over 100 publications, inclusive of 28 education books, with notable titles such as: *Power, Privilege and Education: Pedagogy, Curiculum and Student Outcomes* (2011); *Teacher Education to Enhance Diversity in STEM* (2020); *Sister Outsider in the Academy* (2020); and *The Healing Power of Education* (2021).

John A. Williams III is an assistant professor of multicultural/urban education at Texas A&M University at College Station. His research focuses on identifying affirmative policies, practices, and personnel dispositions to reduce and eliminate school discipline disparities for Black and Brown children.

Landon Wilson is a US Navy veteran and a 2017 Tillman Scholar. He currently teaches secondary language arts in the southeast.

Printed in the USA
CPSIA information can be obtained
at www.ICGtesting.com
LVHW041945031123
762909LV00004B/38